NEWCASTLE UNITED

NEWCASTLE UNITED

FIFTY YEARS OF HURT

GED CLARKE
FOREWORD BY SIR JOHN HALL

A BITTERSWEET STORY OF NEAR TRIUMPH AND DISASTER

MAINSTREAM
PUBLISHING

EDINBURGH AND LONDON

Reprinted, 2007

First published in Great Britain in 2006 by
MAINSTREAM PUBLISHING COMPANY
(EDINBURGH) LTD
7 Albany Street
Edinburgh EH1 3UG

ISBN 9781845960827

A catalogue record for this book is available
from the British Library

Typeset in Caslon and Gill Sans

Printed in Great Britain by
William Clowes Ltd, Beccles, Suffolk

To Jules and Rachel

ACKNOWLEDGEMENTS

I am deeply indebted to the many people who helped make this book possible, some of them blissfully unaware of their part in the process, i.e. the various TV commissioning editors who rejected this as a documentary idea. Thanks to Bill Campbell at Mainstream for realising that it might make a book and to his colleagues Graeme Blaikie and Paul Murphy, who knew how to make it all fit together.

Biggest thanks has to go to my good friend Simon Malia for helping me over the line in the closing stages with his prodigious news editing skills, but more importantly for sharing the pain more than most over the years. One day, mate, eh?

Of course, it wouldn't have been possible without the many former managers and players of Newcastle United who spared the time to offer their thoughts – eternal respect and gratitude to them all. Special thanks to Paul Tully for helping me to track down the more elusive ones! Thanks to Sharon at NUFC and, of course, to Sir John Hall for writing the foreword. Bowing and scraping is also offered in the direction of Paul Joannou and NUFC.com. Any factual errors in this book must be mine, not theirs.

There are several people to thank for taking, finding or releasing photographs: my mate Russell 'Rusty' Cheyne for his fab pics (you haven't lost it, pal!); Bob Bodman at *The Telegraph*; the *Mirror*'s Conor

Hanna and Kevin (not bad for a Mackem) Maguire; Alistair Machray, Mark Thomas and John Thompson at the *Liverpool Post and Echo*; Ann Dixon at *The Chronicle* for all her help; Les Jones, a Canadian exile who answered my appeal in *The Mag*; and Jack Milburn, jun., who proved as reliable as his dad. Gratitude also to Paul Walker for his photo montage and all-round creativity.

Thanks too to *The Chronicle*'s John Gibson and Alan Oliver, and my pals Chris, Mick, Steve and Richard for their voices of bitter experience. And a special thanks to my uncle Richie for taking me to St James' Park on that first, fateful day, back in 1966, and to my mam and dad for letting him.

Last, but not least, I must thank my wife Jules and daughter Rachel for their incredible patience while I locked myself away for months, immersing myself in all things black and white. Can I come out now?

CONTENTS

Foreword by Sir John Hall   11

Introduction   13

1. Fifty Years and Counting . . .   17

2. Decline and Fall (1955–61)   23

3. Come Back Joe (1962–68)   35

4. Every Cloud Has a Silver Lining (1968–69)   51

5. Supermac, Hereford and Mackems (1970–73)   63

6. Wembley Nightmare, Part 1 (1974)   79

7. Gordon Who? (1975–77)   97

8. Hard Times (1978–82)   115

9. Kevin (1982–84)   129

10. Old Ways (1984–88)   139

11. Revolution (1988–92)   161

12. Kevin 2 (1992–96)   177

13. The Nearly Men (1995–96)   189

14. Wembley Nightmare, Part 2 (1997–98)   209

15. Wembley Nightmare, Part 3 (1998–99)   227

16. Old Father Tyne (1999–2004)   245

17. Fifty Years of Hurt (2004–2005)   261

18. Hope and Expectation 273
Appendix 1: Fifty Years of Glorious Failure 281
Appendix 2: Season-by-Season Record Since 1955 285
Bibliography 287

FOREWORD

Newcastle United FC is a big club with a long history. To be a great club it needs constantly to win silverware at the highest levels of domestic and European soccer. This it has failed to achieve, much to the frustration of everyone at the club, especially its huge following of very loyal fans.

Over the years, many questions have been asked about the club's lack of success, and Ged Clarke raises many interesting theories in his book, which makes fascinating reading. From my point of view, it could be said that there was a lack of financial investment in the club by previous boards up to 1990. However, since that date, the regime change which I instigated has invested over £120 million in St James' Park and in the training centre and youth academy. Countless millions have been given by the new board to every manager they have employed to improve the team, but none of this has achieved the success on the playing field which we all desire.

I myself cannot give you an immediate solution to achieve that elusive success but can only suggest that we continue to look at ourselves in depth and examine every facet of the club. It could be that we need to change the role of the manager to that of a coach, employ a director of football, set up a full department of sports medicine and science with all of the relevant specialists to ensure that the club is at the forefront of soccer technology.

However, there is one certain fact. We cannot give up on the quest for success. Ged Clarke should not have to write another similar book in 50 years' time.

Sir John Hall
President, Newcastle United FC
Wynyard
2006

INTRODUCTION

So what's this book all about then? Well, it might be easier to start by saying what it's *not* about. This book is not intended to be a definitive modern history of Newcastle United – for starters, there are much better historians out there than me (step forward Paul Joannou). Nor can I claim that these are the views of the longest-suffering, most loyal and dedicated supporter – there are far better Newcastle fans than me out there as well (but please don't step forward, we haven't organised security). No, I wrote this book simply because I was getting fed up with being part of the largest band of unrewarded football fans in England (Britain? Europe? The World?), and, by employing elementary mathematics, I'd also clocked the fact that when we didn't win anything in 2005, we'd gone 50 years without winning a domestic trophy.

A version of the title first formed in my head back in 1996 when it seemed that every football supporter in England was singing about the 'thirty years of hurt' they'd suffered by not seeing England win the World Cup or the European Championships. Like most football fans, I too would have liked to have seen England repeat their 1966 success at least once in that time. But like most Newcastle supporters, I couldn't pretend to be 'hurt'. 'Mildly disappointed' summed it up more accurately.

That's because we'd already clocked up over 40 years of *proper* hurt. None of this 14-tournaments-without-a-win lark, we were talking 118 goes at trying to win one of the big three – the League Championship, the FA Cup or the League Cup – and with 118 blanks to show for it. Now *that's* real hurt.

This feeling obviously festered. Spool forward another nine years, Newcastle eventually reach the big five-oh, and it was time to do something about it. Not the team, obviously, who still hadn't changed the habits of half a century; no, it was finally time to write the book.

Now, two things have to be cleared up at this point. First of all, I wasn't there for the first ten years of this story (I'm not *that* old), so for the period 1955–65, thanks are due to the historical accounts of others. And second, Newcastle United actually *have* won a proper trophy in the last 50 years. Yes, in 1969, on a glorious, balmy summer night in Budapest, Bob Moncur and his men lifted the European Inter-Cities Fairs Cup. Some of us are old enough to remember it as well – and we still cling to it like a raft in a turbulent ocean. However, '36 Years of Hurt' didn't sound that catchy, so, in the interests of simplicity and nifty titles, I've used the club's last domestic success as my starting point. (It also means that when we still haven't won a trophy by 2019, I can do a rewrite which starts at 1969, and then not even Bob Moncur can quibble about the title.)

So we're talking domestic prizes here. And I don't count the Texaco Cup, which we bizarrely won twice in one year (bloody daft tournament), just the League, the FA Cup and the League Cup: collectively, English football's Holy Trinity; in isolation, Newcastle United's Holy Grail.

As a journalist and TV producer, I am trained in the art of ringing up people who don't know who I am and who would probably prefer not to. I then ask them to tell me stuff. Using this age-old technique,

INTRODUCTION

I managed to track down and speak to some of the greatest names in the modern history of Newcastle United, many of whom I can say, without embarrassment, are heroes of mine. Thanks to them, the book is not just the ramblings of a bitter and twisted fan (though there's plenty of that as well). Hopefully their memories and opinions will give the book a twin perspective, from inside and out.

I must pay a special tribute to Alf McMichael, one of the club's greatest ever servants, who talked warmly and eloquently to me about his 14 years at St James' Park. Sadly, it was the last interview Alf ever gave; he died shortly after, on the day Alan Shearer beat Jackie Milburn's goal-scoring record. My heartfelt condolences go to his widow Lily and their family.

A special mention must also go to all of those poor souls who, at different times along the way, were there with me. From my Uncle Richie McLaughlin, who took me to my first Newcastle match (see what you started!), and cousin Richard McLaughlin, who, like me, has kept going ever since his first game, to my mates Chris Baines, Simon Malia, Steve O'Brien and Mick Ramsey. These are my fellow sufferers, and their opinions crop up from time to time, representing the views of the ordinary fan. Each of them knows that all the names, places and events in this book are entirely real and that any resemblance to fairy tale or science fiction is purely coincidental. After all, this is 50 years of Newcastle United Football Club we're talking about.

Ged Clarke
Liverpool
2006

I

FIFTY YEARS AND COUNTING ...

When I was young, I was told, 'You'll see, when you're 50.' I am 50, and I haven't seen a thing.

Erik Satie (French composer)

When Alan Shearer limped out of the action at the Stadium of Light on 17 April 2006, it was the end of an era. A fabulous career was over. Over the course of 18 years, he'd rattled in 409 goals, including 30 for England – statistics which made him worthy of the legendary status he will carry for ever. But as the plaudits poured in for the greatest centre-forward of his generation, commentators were quick to pick up on one blemish on Shearer's record: he hadn't won much. In fact, a Premiership winner's medal, won with Blackburn Rovers in 1995, was the only silverware he had to show for the titanic effort he'd put into almost two decades of playing the game he loves. Ten years at Newcastle United, his home-town club, had produced an awful lot of goals, but not a single trophy.

This was hardly Shearer's fault. In his decade in black and white, he'd broken the club's all-time goal-scoring record, held since 1957 by Jackie Milburn, its most famous son. But three of Jackie's goals were scored in two FA Cup finals; he actually played in three, all of which were won by Newcastle United in the 1950s. The third of these, in 1955, was the last time the club won a major domestic trophy.

Since that last success, no fewer than thirty-two clubs have won one of the three major domestic prizes in English football. Clubs like Wimbledon, Luton, Burnley, Ipswich, QPR, Swindon, Stoke, Oxford and – God forbid – Sunderland and Middlesbrough have all picked up silverware. But not Newcastle. The second-best supported team in England, and one of the wealthiest in Europe, hasn't had to spend too much on silver polish over the past half-century.

The cast list of those who've tried and failed to end this state of affairs – either on or off the pitch – reads like a *Who's Who of World Football*: apart from Shearer, there's Ossie Ardiles, Jack Charlton, Kevin Keegan, Ruud Gullit, Peter Beardsley, Chris Waddle, Sir Bobby Robson, Kenny Dalglish, Graeme Souness, Paul 'Gazza' Gascoigne, Malcolm 'Supermac' Macdonald, Les Ferdinand, David Ginola, Faustino Asprilla, Michael Owen – the list goes on and on.

Even 'Old Father Tyne' himself, Sir Bobby Robson, couldn't bring glory to Tyneside. His long and distinguished career is littered with prizes won all over Europe, but he paid the price for failing to bring the Holy Grail to the Geordie faithful. Astonishingly, 'Uncle Bobby' wasn't even born the last time the club won the league title. That was in 1927, the year of the first talking picture and the first solo transatlantic flight.

In the 50th season since our last FA Cup victory, Robson's place at the helm was given to Graeme Souness, another football legend and star of the all-conquering Liverpool team of the 1970s and '80s. In his first season, the club made it to an FA Cup semi-final, kindling dreams that the wait for silverware was about to end, appropriately on the 50th anniversary of the last major triumph. But it was not to be. When the Magpies were humbled 4–1 by Manchester United, it was official: we'd gone half a century without a domestic trophy. Newcastle United had never won in colour.

* * *

The fact that a club of such stature and tradition, to say nothing of financial resources, has gone so long with nothing to show for their labours is one of the enduring mysteries of the modern game. Surely the law of averages dictates that we should have won maybe a League Cup? Everybody else seems to have done it. But while Swindon, Stoke City, Oxford United and others have all enjoyed their 90 minutes of glory, Newcastle have run up a list of near misses and disastrous failures in all competitions.

Down the years, fingers have been pointed at dodgy directors, moronic managers and pathetic players, but they account for only a part of the story. If they'd all been dodgy, moronic and pathetic, Newcastle would have gone out of business. We wouldn't have reached four Wembley finals or managed two Premiership runners-up spots. There wouldn't have been ten seasons playing in European competition, including the memorable European Inter-Cities Fairs Cup triumph of 1969.

We've actually had some dynamic directors, magnificent managers and perfect players, but that's what makes it even more infuriating and mystifying. Sir John Hall – a dynamic director – launched a boardroom revolution that shook the club from its slumbers in the early 1990s, rebuilding it and firing it into the upper reaches of the European game. But he went off to well-deserved retirement without a trophy to show for all his vision. Joe Harvey – a magnificent manager – won the Fairs Cup, but he also led us to FA Cup final humiliation at the hands of Liverpool in 1974. Alan Shearer – our perfect player – could have signed for Manchester United and retired with a cabinet full of medals, but he chose to come home, and despite scoring 206 goals, he won nothing. Add to that the Kevin Keegan years, when as both player and manager he brought unparalleled excitement, passion and swashbuckling football – but no prizes – to St James' Park, and the mystery just deepens.

Some say simply that the club is cursed. The stadium is built on the site where, in times gone by, hangings used to take place (hence

'Gallow-gate'), so the restless souls of the evil dead are clearly haunting the place. Legends also abound that former player Hughie Gallagher and/or ex-boss Duggie Livingstone (according to your favoured myth) cursed the club after the way it treated them. Certainly managers like Joe Harvey, Kevin Keegan and Ruud Gullit all made comments about a 'jinx' or a 'curse', Gullit even calling in spiritual consultants at one point.

Many more prosaic theories have also been put forward over the years: a lack of leadership, direction, ambition, common sense or stability in the club. Some say Newcastle's unique position as the biggest city in England with just one professional football team makes it an impossible environment for success. It's claimed that this has produced an interfering and hyper-critical local media, or a lack of patience from an over-demanding public.

But this argument won't wash. As journalist John Gibson, a lifelong supporter who's covered the Magpies for 40 years, told me, 'It's a good excuse, isn't it? They say we're not patient enough. Well, we've waited since 1955, and we're getting *very* impatient. As a reporter, my job is to represent the fans, and they have a right to look for success from Newcastle United. If 50,000 of them turn up every week, which they do, then Newcastle have an obligation to win something for those fans. The fact that they haven't won a domestic trophy in 50 years is a terrible indictment.'

Our desperation to break the cycle of trophyless seasons has led to some sensational signings and even more spectacular welcome parties. After decades of under-investment, the modern Newcastle United has thrown money at the problem, resulting in some famous faces wearing the shirt.

When Michael Owen walked out onto the pitch at St James' Park after signing a four-year contract on 31 August 2005, he must have wondered what he'd let himself in for. There to greet him were 15,000 screaming, cheering, flag-waving Geordies, delirious to see him in black and white. Nothing unusual in that, you'd think, except that this riotous reception took place on a Wednesday morning, not a Saturday afternoon.

For 50 years, these fanatical supporters had been searching for a saviour – someone to make them winners once again. Here was another hero prepared to sign up to the cause.

At 25, Owen was already a goal-scoring legend with Liverpool and England, although he was deemed surplus to requirements at Real Madrid. Now, for the princely sum of £16 million, he was the new Geordie icon, and when he was introduced to the fans, they embraced him like people in an occupied country embrace a liberating army. The 15,000 people who greeted his arrival that day were just the advance welcome party. The 52,000 who regularly fill St James' Park and the hundreds of thousands more who make up the wider Newcastle United family immediately conferred honorary Geordie status on the former European Footballer of the Year, praying he'd be the one to break the spell.

But Owen's first season was plagued by injury – and after another disaster at the World Cup, so was his second – yet more evidence for those who subscribe to the curse theory. And as the team spluttered below midtable, it was Souness's turn to curse – and to pay the price: he was sacked in February 2006. While the injuries were a significant factor in the case for the defence, Souness also faced criticism for his man management, his signings and tactics. An overwhelming majority verdict of 'guilty' was passed by the 52,000-strong jury, and our fifth manager in nine years was on his way.

But once he was gone, the accusers turned their anger on the boardroom and, principally, chairman Freddy Shepherd. In the past, he'd been derided in the press for sacking a string of managers before their seasons had even warmed up. Now, he was being advised to 'get it right or go' – a view which had much support on the terraces. Yet Shepherd could argue that he'd always kept his side of the bargain – funding a catalogue of big-name signings. In fact, in the 13 years between Shepherd's arrival in the boardroom as part of the John Hall revolution and the Owen signing, it's believed the club spent £236 million on incoming transfers, hardly the sign of a board not interested in chasing success.

Shepherd called the day he signed Owen his proudest since he helped break the world transfer record to bring Alan Shearer to Newcastle. But as one cynical observer remarked, 'Chairmen are supposed to be proud of titles or cup runs . . . not simply spending money on England centre-forwards.'

Shepherd's strength is also his weakness – he's a fan. At crucial times when the cool, calm and collected approach is required, he's emotionally back on the terraces and his knee jerks with everyone else's. I'd hate his job. Shepherd himself says, 'We can be accused of many things but never of not having a shot. We've got the best ground and the best supporters, all we need is the best team – it's simple.' But if that's the case, Freddy, why are we still waiting for the elusive silverware?

After Souness, Shepherd knew another knee-jerk reaction was out of the question. He was bought time to deliberate, thanks to caretaker manager Glenn Roeder, who performed minor miracles to lift United to a top-seven finish in 2005–06, and with it, a back-door entry into the UEFA Cup. It was some audition. Shepherd was convinced, and when the season ended, he gave Roeder the job full time.

Ironically, Glenn was born in 1955, the year in which our trophy famine began. Now his goal is to end it – something his 17 predecessors couldn't manage. If he is going to win one of English football's glittering prizes for the longest-suffering fans in the land, he'll do well to study the club's weird and wonderful history. He might just discover where others went wrong and in doing so find out what to do right. Whether he's successful or not, he will be prepared. As a former player and captain, he'll know that Newcastle United is a giant roller-coaster of a club, quite unlike any other in the game. Welcome to the hottest seat in football, Glenn – enjoy the ride, and may you be the man who finally ends our 50 years of hurt.

2

DECLINE AND FALL (1955–61)

'They are the chosen, the darlings. They walk in company with the gods.'

Sports writer Bob Ferrier on Newcastle's
cup teams of the 1950s

Ten to five. Saturday, 7 May 1955. The last time one of the major domestic trophies in English football was handed over to a Newcastle United captain. If you'd mentioned to anyone at the game that this club wouldn't win the cup or the league in the next half-century, you'd have been laughed out of London.

This was the first club to get to ten FA Cup finals, the first to win six FA Cups in the twentieth century and the club with the most wins at Wembley. No one else came close to Newcastle's five victories at that time. On top of that, their star striker Jackie Milburn had just scored the fastest-ever cup-final goal.

Milburn and his colleagues Bobby Mitchell and Bobby Cowell had also joined an elite band of players who'd won three FA Cup-winner's medals. And here they were, climbing up to the royal box to be presented with that illustrious third, the deafening cheers of thousands of Geordies ringing in their ears. Just ahead of them was skipper Jimmy Scoular – a tough-tackling, rock-hard son of a Scottish miner. Scoular was awesome. He'd replaced a legend in the best way possible – by becoming one himself.

Scoular had been bought from Portsmouth in 1953 to fill the boots of Joe Harvey – the first, and up till then the only, man to lift the FA Cup in successive seasons in the twentieth century. Harvey had collected the trophy from the King in 1951 and from Winston Churchill in 1952. Scoular was about to collect the cup from the young Queen Elizabeth II.

In time-honoured fashion, the United captain wiped his hands on his shorts before shaking hands with the Queen, accepted the trophy, and then turned and raised it to the delirious Geordie hordes who'd made the long journey.

Now freeze the frame.

Freeze the frame because an era has just ended and another one is about to start. The era of winning trophies is over; the era of not winning trophies has begun.

Forty-eight years later, I got a phone call. It was one of those breaks that we all dream about. Being a freelance TV producer, I have a pretty good time making programmes about all sorts of things – history, current affairs, the arts, even religion. But the best programmes are always about sport, preferably about football and ideally about Newcastle United. So when I was asked if I'd be interested in making a programme for the BBC about Jackie Milburn's son's pursuit of his dad's life story . . . well, let's just say the words 'Pope' and 'Catholic' figured in the answer.

Jackie's story has been told many times – in print, on film and even on stage. His name, and all that he achieved, has become symbolic of all that was and still is 'great' about Newcastle United. Jackie is the ultimate symbol of the era when the Magpies were among the giants of the game and winning trophies was what we did. In a region where football is a religion, Milburn has been deified. His legend dominates the club. The main stand at St James' Park bears his name. His statue stands outside on the main concourse. But, in some ways, Jackie Milburn is a major part of the problem of why Newcastle can't win a trophy.

For many who have followed, the Milburn legend has been a huge burden. Chairmen, managers and players have all had to live with the fact that anything they've achieved pales into insignificance when compared with 'The Milburn Years'. They are all in the shadow because the name Jackie Milburn is synonymous with success and style, swagger and silverware, three FA Cups and a hatful of adrenalin-rushing goals.

His story is genuine *Roy of the Rovers* stuff. He really *was* given the initials J.E.T., and, yes, he really *did* grow up to run 100 yards in ten seconds. Mind-bogglingly, in this age of millionaire footballers who wouldn't know how to change a plug, he really *did* do a shift down the pit in Ashington then catch the bus to Newcastle to play for the Toon.

His career statistics are fantastic too: 492 games for Newcastle, 238 goals – although 95 of those games and 38 of those goals were scored in wartime so they don't really count, apparently. Still 397 games and 200 goals is fair going by anyone's standards.

So, in 2003 I got to know his son Jack, whose book *Jackie Milburn: A Man of Two Halves* told both sides of his dad's life story – part footballing legend who could do no wrong and part family man who was just an ordinary bloke with the failings and weaknesses that ordinary blokes tend to have.

Jack, jun., is a top bloke, and together with our cameraman Paul Nicholson and our soundman/editor Paul Watson, another exiled Geordie, we set off in search of Jackie Milburn's history. We spent time interviewing living legends: Jackie and Bobby Charlton, Milburn's second cousins, former Newcastle teammate Charlie Crowe, England winger Sir Tom Finney, the then Newcastle manager Sir

Bobby Robson and two more Geordie goal-scoring heroes, Malcolm Macdonald and Alan Shearer.

We were in heaven, and everything these superstars said convinced us that Jackie Milburn probably was too. No one had a bad thing to say about him, and, looking in their eyes, you could see that they all meant every word. The guy clearly was 'a bit special', as football people are fond of saying.

Alan Shearer, who was chasing Milburn's phenomenal Newcastle goal-scoring record at the time, summed up his predecessor: 'You come to Newcastle and the one name that people keep mentioning, over and over again, particularly the older generation, is Jackie Milburn. He's the top man in Newcastle's history and rightly so, because of his record and the goals he scored.'

But what's crucial about Milburn is that three of those goals were scored in cup finals and helped Newcastle lift the FA Cup in 1951 and 1955. With another cup victory sandwiched in between in 1952, his legendary status is secure for all time. While Shearer would eventually overhaul the goals record, he knew he'd never match those three black-and-white FA Cups. In the short time we spent in his company, Alan constantly mentioned his desire to win silverware. He was clearly driven by it, but then, so is everyone who has Newcastle United at heart.

When Shearer finally brought down the curtain on his fanatastic – but trophyless – Newcastle career, he insisted, 'My dream as a kid was to play for Newcastle United and to score goals at St James' Park. It doesn't matter that I didn't win a trophy, because I did it my way, and I lived the dream. Unless you come from the area, you wouldn't understand that mentality. Playing for the club is everything. I broke Jackie's record, and no one can take that away from me. I've never had any regrets.' Proud words, but every Geordie knows that Shearer would have liked nothing more than to lift a cup for his beloved Newcastle.

Like Shearer, I wasn't born when Jackie Milburn was scoring cup-final winning goals. When we were growing up, my mates and I would constantly hear Jackie's name as we went searching for heroes of our own. And when you're young, that's the last thing you want. You actually begin to resent having names from 'the olden days' being pushed down your throat. We wanted our own success. We *still* want our own success. But as time wears on and you begin to appreciate the importance of history and tradition, your attitude to those old names changes. After 50 years in the wilderness, you are drawn to the legends. And it has to be said that 'Wor Jackie' is *the* Newcastle legend. His record of achievement may hang heavy over those who follow, but Newcastle United has two choices: to sink beneath its weight or to use it as inspiration and match it, or even better it, in the future.

Because I wasn't around at the time, all of the information contained in this chapter relies on good old-fashioned research. For me – and I suspect for most of you – it's a bit of a history lesson. But it's interesting history because it's about football.

Let's start with a quiz question. Who wore the No. 9 shirt when Newcastle won the FA Cup in 1955? Most people say Jackie Milburn, but the answer is – Vic Keeble. Vic was an emerging centre-forward who'd actually dislodged Milburn from the team. (Jackie, though, was nothing if not resourceful and won his way back into the side, wearing the No. 8 shirt in the cup final.)

Vic Keeble is one of the few survivors of that famous day. I tracked him down to his native Essex where he now lives in splendid retirement, having worked out his days in football administration with his first club Colchester United and neighbouring Chelmsford City.

A warm and friendly bloke, he was delighted to have a chance to reminisce. So what was the secret of the Newcastle cup sides of the 1950s? Vic told me, 'We had good players – match winners. But the spirit was great. We all got on well. There was a sense of togetherness. Newcastle haven't been that strong at times down the years, and to me those teams didn't have the same togetherness that we had. You can have great players, but you need that team spirit or else you're nothing.'

But while United were the undisputed kings of FA Cup football, their league record in the same period was nothing special. Vic believes that the year *after* the '55 cup win, the team actually played better football and were going particularly well in the league till the cup intervened again – this time in a very different way.

At the end of February, United were third in the league and had drawn Sunderland at home in the FA Cup quarter-finals. The same Sunderland we'd just thrashed 6–1 at Roker Park (hurrah!) and 3–1 at St James' Park (hurrah again!). But football is a bastard with a red-and-white comedy nose sometimes. Sunderland won the cup tie 2–0 (boo!), and United promptly went seven games without a win in the league, eventually finishing a very average eleventh.

This sounds remarkably similar to an experience we would endure some 24 years later. After playing Sunderland on New Year's Day in 1980, we would plummet from the top of Division Two to finish ninth. (Although we did have the consolation of beating the Mackems on that occasion.)

Vic Keeble is still irritated by what happened in 1956: 'We were there or thereabouts in the league and playing well. But when we got knocked out of the cup by Sunderland in the quarter-final, it really knocked us for six. We'd hammered them twice already and really thought we'd beat them easily in the cup, especially as they weren't going well. But our season just fell apart after that.' (Sunderland, of course, lost the semi-final – beaten 3–0 by Birmingham.)

Vic left the following year with a proud record of 67 goals in 120 appearances for United. He joined Second Division West Ham for £10,000 and helped them win promotion the following season. For Newcastle, however, the glory days were fading away.

The break-up of the last great cup-winning side was gradual. The first to go was right-back and unsung hero Bobby Cowell, with the

1955 final proving to be his last game. An injury picked up in the subsequent close-season tour of Germany would end his career.

Within a year, the cult hero centre-half Frank Brennan was also gone, much to the anger of the fans. Brennan was a star of the first two finals but by 1955 had been replaced by Bob Stokoe. Brennan was frozen out, though the conspiracy theorists believed that might have had something to do with the fact that he dared to open a sports outfitter's shop in the shadow of St James' Park, in direct competition to the one owned by club director Stan Seymour.

Former wing-half Charlie Crowe laughed as he told me, 'Frank Brennan's shop was doing great business, so there was bound to be a clash. We used to joke with him about it, and the fans used to chant about Frank and his shop. But the players all got new boots every year from Seymour's!'

In 1957, the break-up of the cup side accelerated. Vic Keeble and cup-final goal-scorer George Hannah were both sold, but the most symbolic transfer of all took place in June when the unthinkable happened: Jackie Milburn left Newcastle and signed as player–coach with Northern Irish club Linfield. Two days earlier, United's other great legend, Hughie Gallagher, whose goals had won Newcastle their last league title way back in 1927, committed suicide on the Edinburgh to London railway line at Dead Man's Crossing near Gateshead. What a week for the club. It must have felt like a part of Newcastle United had died.

From then on, it was pretty much downhill all the way, with the glitter of trophies fast disappearing into the distant past. United were a club in the doldrums on the football pitch and at war in the boardroom.

When I was a young fan, I wasn't interested in men in grey suits, power struggles and balance sheets. I was only bothered about men in black-and-white shirts, 90-minute struggles and goal averages. But the names Seymour and McKeag seemed to crop up all the time when grown-ups talked about what was really wrong with the club. I was vaguely aware that there was more than one Seymour and more than one McKeag, and they seemed to keep sprouting behind the scenes like some many-headed monster. That wasn't far from the truth. The Seymours and McKeags were just two of the families who'd run the club for decades, and the men presiding over the decline in the late '50s were Stan Seymour and William McKeag.

Seymour had earned his reputation as a Newcastle United great. As a tricky winger, he'd helped United win the FA Cup in 1924 and the League Championship in 1927. Shortly after hanging up his boots in 1929, he was elected to the board and was later team manager for two separate spells.

First, he ran the show through the war years. but in his second stint, as 'honorary manager' from 1950 to 1954, Newcastle made Wembley history with those back-to-back cup wins of '51 and '52. When Seymour decided to concentrate on boardroom duties, United appointed a full-time manager, the eccentric Scot Duggie Livingstone. But though Livingstone was notionally in charge for the 1955 cup final, the directors ultimately decided who played. After Livingstone left out Milburn from the side, Seymour famously ripped up the team-sheet, declaring, 'Newcastle don't play FA Cup finals without Jackie Milburn.' (I love this story and often wonder what would have happened in 1999 if Freddy Shepherd had told Ruud Gullit, 'Newcastle don't play Sunderland without Alan Shearer.' How our recent football history might have changed!) After Livingstone's gaffe, the team was selected for two seasons by a 'directorial team', which, in 1950s' Newcastle, was a rather fancy euphemism for Stan Seymour.

One man who remembered Seymour well was former full-back Alf McMichael. Alf was at St James' Park for 14 seasons, racking up a fantastic 431 appearances at full-back. He missed the 1951 final through injury but collected a winner's medal in 1952. He wasn't selected in 1955 but stayed for another eight years, so he was well placed to comment on the comings and goings at St James' Park.

When I called him at his home in Bangor, County Down, I found myself talking to a true football gentleman and one who still had vivid memories of his time at Newcastle. 'Stan was the boss; there was no doubt about that,' he told me. 'Managers and players came and went, but there was no doubt who was in charge. If Stan Seymour didn't like you, he'd tell you, and you probably wouldn't be there very long either! Stan Seymour signed me and was always very good to me. I can't say bad about him. He fell out with other directors, but that was probably because he knew they didn't know as much about football as he did!'

Although he wouldn't say it, I got the clear impression that Alf was referring to William McKeag, who took over from Wilf Taylor as club chairman in the summer of 1957. As Roger Hutchinson puts it so eloquently in his history of the club, 'It seemed to many that McKeag – whose family had a long connection with the club – and Seymour were vying for the title of "Mister Newcastle United". The two men were born to hate each other.'

It was a classic contest but one which would damage Newcastle. Seymour was a shopkeeper and former footballer, while McKeag was a military man and a former Liberal MP and ex-Lord Mayor of Newcastle. McKeag hated the idea of Seymour being director–manager, while Seymour hated the idea of being told what to do by people who weren't steeped in football like he was. Their personal war was carried out in public, even hitting the national press in 1958. McKeag was campaigning for the team to be run by a full-time manager, saying Seymour had 'drifted into the position' of honorary manager too often.

The boardroom civil war set the tone for our forthcoming 50 years of non-achievement. Time and again, the men behind the scenes would be responsible for our failings on the pitch, either through indifference, incompetence or sheer bloody-mindedness. At the start of the '90s, it would almost send us down to the Third Division, but in the late '50s, while other clubs like Manchester United and Wolves were developing exciting, successful sides, Newcastle's egotistical directors had quite literally taken their eyes off the ball.

As season 1957–58 drew to a close, the team was immersed in a relegation scrap. They stayed up by the skin of their teeth, finishing third bottom with 32 points from 42 games. They had the same points as Sunderland, but the Mackems were relegated on goal average. Now I know some people today who would regard that as a brilliant season just for the sheer joy of putting Sunderland down on goal average (or goal difference as it would be now), but this was just three years since Newcastle were hailed as one of the great sides of the century and, understandably, people were slightly concerned.

To make matters worse, the club's reputation as the greatest FA Cup side in the land was getting a bit of a battering. In 1957, United were humiliated in the fourth round, losing away to Millwall of the Third Division South, while the following season was equally embarrassing with a 3–1 home defeat at the hands of Scunthorpe of the Third Division North. Something had to give, and in the close season, it did. McKeag eventually got his way, and the club appointed a full-time manager.

Our recent history is littered with wrong managerial choices, all of which have contributed to Newcastle becoming a trophy-free zone. But the choice of Charlie Mitten was bizarre in the extreme. A club looking for stability and a new start had gone for a 37 year old whose managerial experience was limited to a brief spell in charge of Mansfield in the old Third Division North. Not only that, Mitten was one of football's rebels – as a player, he'd walked out of Manchester United in 1950 and headed for Colombia in South America because there was big money on offer. He'd stuck two fingers up to the FA's maximum-wage system, but it would come back to bite him on the bum during his time at Newcastle.

I can only begin to guess how the fans felt at this time, but I'm sure it was a bit like we felt when the likes of Gordon Lee, Richard Dinnis, Bill McGarry, Jim Smith and Graeme Souness got the job. Your instincts scream 'No!', but deep inside you're desperately hoping that this is a brilliant piece of inspired, visionary thinking by the Newcastle board. And then you realise that the words 'brilliant, inspired, visionary' and 'Newcastle board' have never appeared in the same sentence together before.

Mitten's approach was unorthodox, though there is a case for saying he was a man ahead of his time. He introduced a new strip which included fancy shorts with white edging, designed to make it easier to pick out a teammate. However, the shorts prompted wolf whistles from opposing supporters and embarrassment among the players who had to wear them.

There was also talk of him asking players to learn sword dancing as part of their training regime. Suffice to say the likes of Jimmy Scoular and Bob Stokoe were not impressed. On another occasion, fed up with dodgy refereeing decisions, he called on the Football League to introduce full-time refs and linesmen. It took the football authorities over 40 years to agree with him on that one.

In his first two seasons, Mitten lifted Newcastle to eleventh then eighth in the league, but there was no joy in the cup, with two third-round exits – though at least they were at the hands of Chelsea and Wolves this time.

Mitten actually assembled an exciting collection of players – and the United trio of Ivor Allchurch, Len White and George Eastham were as good as any around at the time. But team spirit wasn't great, which wasn't surprising because, behind the scenes, chaos reigned.

Seymour and McKeag were still at loggerheads, but they soon found themselves on the same side for once as we made history by being the club at the heart of a transfer row which would change football for ever. When they turned down George Eastham's transfer request, Newcastle were dragged through the courts, and the medieval system which controlled wages and transfers in English football was exposed. Eastham won and got a transfer to Arsenal, the 'retain and transfer' system was finished and Newcastle United were acutely embarrassed.

Predictably, with the club in turmoil off the pitch, events on the field took a turn for the worse. First, we found a further way to humiliate ourselves when the Football League introduced a new cup competition. The League Cup was greeted with almost universal indifference, but never mind, perhaps this was an opportunity for Newcastle to forget their league troubles and rekindle some old glories. Fat chance. United took their bow in the inaugural League Cup away to Colchester United of the Third Division South in October 1960 and lost 4–1. It was just five years since we'd been 'Masters of Wembley', but to the faithful, it must have seemed like a lifetime.

There was a flicker of nostalgia in the FA Cup, but progress was halted at the quarter-final stage when Sheffield United won 3–1 at St James' Park. To make matters worse, we were locked in a relegation battle. Attempts to sign new players were proving fruitless as the club's image as one of the giants of the English game was now so badly tarnished that nobody would touch us with a bargepole. United spent season 1960–61 playing cavalier football, scoring goals for fun but conceding them with alarming regularity. Only Newcastle could win games 7–2 (Fulham) and 5–0 (Cardiff), draw 5–5 (West Ham) and lose 6–0 (West Brom), 6–1 (Chelsea) and 5–0 (Everton and Arsenal). By the end of the season, United had scored 86 but conceded a calamitous 109. The theory that goals bring crowds to football is only partly true. The fact is, they need to be scored by the home team at least as often as they are by the away team. So, despite the goal feasts on offer, our average home attendance slumped below 30,000 for the first time since 1938.

Seasoned Newcastle watchers will not be surprised to hear that despite this the Magpies went to London and beat the brilliant Spurs team who were about to become the first side in the twentieth century to win the league and cup Double. However, victory came at a price, with top scorer Len White being carried off injured. White had scored 28 goals in 33 games, but he wouldn't kick a ball again that season, and United slumped to inevitable relegation. Trophy-winning days looked a very long way away indeed.

3

COME BACK JOE (1962–68)

'Joe Harvey, Joe Harvey, is it true what people say? We're
gonna win the Football League?'
Highly optimistic terrace chant to the tune
of the 1967 chart hit 'Excerpt from a Teenage
Opera', aka 'Grocer Jack'

Relegation normally means one of two things for the unfortunate
man in charge: instant dismissal or a chance to quickly get the team
straight back up to the league they've just left. Newcastle chose option
one – except that, in true Newcastle fashion, they didn't really do it
like a normal club would. Charlie Mitten was allowed to plan for the
new season and was even allowed to start it in charge, but a few weeks
later, he was sacked.

This set a trend for something that would become a Newcastle
United trademark. Richard Dinnis, Bill McGarry, Willie McFaul,
Kenny Dalglish, Ruud Gullit and Sir Bobby Robson would all be
allowed to buy players in the summer and begin new campaigns
but all of them would be shown the door before they'd started their
Christmas shopping. This happens from time to time when a club is

in crisis, but the fact that it has happened seven times at Newcastle tells you all you need to know. Too often the club has backed their manager with money in the summer then pulled the plug as soon as we didn't get off to a flying start. 'Panic' is a word that springs to mind. Don't get me wrong, most fans knew that most of the incumbents mentioned above had reached the end of the line. Unfortunately, we usually knew well before the people in charge. If only they'd listen, we could save the club a fortune!

Charlie Mitten's dismissal owed more to skulduggery than panic. He was sacked four days after a 7–2 away win, and not many managers can say that. True, the first season back in Division Two had started badly, but two 4–1 victories and that 7–2 result at Bury meant that United had begun to climb the table. However, when the main man has got it in for you, you might as well start clearing your desk. Stan Seymour certainly had it in for Mitten, and he sneakily waited till his great rival Alderman McKeag was out of the country before calling a board meeting to remove the manager.

United then appointed the oldest man ever to be given a first crack at management, the long-serving 64-year-old coach Norman Smith. Yes, that makes him younger than Bobby Robson when he became boss of United, but this was Smith's first manager's job!

Norman kept us up. Relegation was comfortably avoided with a respectable 11th-place finish. At the end of the season, he retired gracefully after 24 years of loyal service to the club. In an attempt to resurrect the glory days of the 1950s, Newcastle then turned to a club legend. Joe Harvey came back on a 12-month trial, but he'd stay for 14 years, and though he'd never know it, he'd become a very important figure in my life.

Now, fast-forward four years.

Confession time. Up to the age of nine, I supported Manchester United. There, I've said it. But it's OK, I'm fine now. In fact, like a recovered alcoholic, I'm positively evangelical about the ills of the devils of Old Trafford, and I warn all newcomers to the game to avoid them at all costs.

There was a good reason for my wayward start on the football path – and that reason, dear reader, was ignorance. My dad wasn't interested in football. He'd been disabled since his childhood and sadly never discovered the magic of the game, so at the age of six, I knew next to nothing about it. I can actually remember the precise moment when I made the fatal but unwitting decision to stray. Like all kids, I tried to collect stuff from comics and had a handful of crumpled footballer cards which had come free with *The Eagle,* I think. And like all kids, I was desperate to impress my peers and to sound like I knew about stuff – stuff like football.

Alan Richardson lived in the same block of council flats as I did; he had a big brother and a dad who loved football, and they all supported Newcastle. One day, when I was about five or six, Alan and I were kicking a ball about in the square that was actually designed for hanging out washing but was perfect for playing football – what with all the posts and that. Suddenly Alan shouted out, 'I'll be in goal – I'll be Gordon Marshall. Who're you gonna be?'

Now, as I say, I didn't know much about football, but I was relatively quick on the uptake, and I realised that Gordon Marshall *had* to be Newcastle's goalie. The problem was I didn't know any other footballers and suddenly the peer pressure was on. Think fast. Crumpled footballer card in back pocket! Thank you, God. I pulled the solitary card out of my pocket while Alan was taking his position between the posts. Slyly, I read the name underneath the picture and shouted back 'Bobby Charlton, Man United.'

'He's good,' replied Alan approvingly. Phew. Result. From then on, Bobby Charlton became *my* footballer. Man United had to be *my* team. And in the months that followed, I realised that not only was 'Bobby Charlton, Man United' a good player, he was very good. One of the best in England, in fact. While ignorance may have been the catalyst for my interest in the game, it was no longer a criticism that could be levelled in my direction by the time that 1966 came around. I was obsessed with Bobby Charlton, Man United, England and football in general.

World Cup fever gripped the nation. We were in a frenzy of anticipation. 'Look out for Giovanni Rivera, the golden boy of Italian football,' we were warned. 'Flórián Albert is a Hungarian marvel,' they promised. And best of all, 'The world's greatest footballer Pelé is coming to England!' (For some months, I pronounced it 'Peel', but I think I got away with it.)

It was against this background that some sensational news reached our ears. The English League were going to play the Scottish League on the 16 March 1966 – at St James' Park. Alf Ramsey was going to try out his World Cup team! Gordon Banks, Jimmy Greaves, Bobby Moore and, best of all, Bobby Charlton would be running out, all together, onto a pitch near me. I had to go.

Credit to Mam and Dad. They knew that I was desperate to be there, but they also knew that Dad wasn't really up to going. Enquiries were made, and their eight-year-old son was entrusted into the care of some bigger boys who were going to the game. By now, we'd moved from the flats on Windsor Drive and were in a 'proper' council house in Melrose Gardens. The people who lived in the house across the back were called Mr and Mrs Oates, and their son Colin took me to my first-ever match.

We stopped to buy a programme, and when I looked at the line-ups, my heart sank. This was an England reserve team! (I'd soon learn that you'd be more likely to win the treble chance on the Littlewoods Football Pools than find an accurate team line-up in a matchday programme, but this was my debut – what did I know?) I remember the other lads being disappointed, too – it was traditional for the England manager to pick at least one 'home' player in order to swell the attendance, and they'd hoped that maybe Alan Suddick, or even a young forward called Bryan 'Pop' Robson, might have been given a run out.

As we took our places on the 'Popular' – a standing terrace which ran the length of one side of the pitch – I stared around in wonderment at my first view of a football stadium. I also managed to make a complete fool of myself by asking where 'The Circle' was. It's funny what you remember from these occasions . . .

Ramsey actually did pick a couple of local lads as it turned out. When the Tannoy announced the changes to the programme line-ups, the names of Ashington brothers Jackie and Bobby Charlton were read out. I experienced my first football-stadium rush of adrenalin.

In approximately 40 minutes, I received my next one when I witnessed my first-ever 'live' goal. It was scored by R. Charlton, Manchester United. Sometimes football is too perfect to be true. I remember it very clearly – he hit a shot from about 20 yards which was blocked, picked up the rebound, took one step and blasted the ball into the net at the Gallowgate End.

That was the end of the fun. In the second half, the Scottish League team ran amok and ended up winning 3–1. But I went home happy – I'd been to the football, and I'd seen Bobby Charlton score.

Less than two months later, I was back again: this time to watch the penultimate league match of Newcastle's first season back in Division One for three years. The opponents were Fulham and the minder was my uncle Richie, who took me and my cousin Richard to stand behind Gordon Marshall's goal in the Gallowgate End. Again, I remember being disappointed when I heard that England's right-back George Cohen wouldn't be playing, until Uncle Richie pointed out that Newcastle would have a better chance with him not there.

My first-ever Newcastle goal was scored in the Leazes End – over 100 yards from where I was standing. To my young and inexperienced football-watching eyes, it was a visual non-event. A sea of bodies seemed to rise for a corner kick, and the only reason I knew it was a goal was that everyone at the other end made a very loud noise and the blokes in black-and-white shirts jumped up and down while the other lot in white shirts looked sad.

'Suddick!' was the verdict where we were standing, and for the next 20 years, I remained convinced that my first-ever Toon goal was scored by wiry inside-forward Alan Suddick, until I bought *Newcastle United: A Complete Record* and discovered that it was, in actual fact, scored by tough uncompromising centre-half John McGrath. These things are important.

The match ended 1–1, and I don't remember a thing about the other goal – perhaps my first case of football denial. *A Complete Record* doesn't tell you who scored for the opponents, so it was only while researching this book that I discovered that the Fulham goal was bagged by their veteran wing-half, a chap called Bobby Robson. What was that about football being too perfect to be true?

On the bus on the way home, we pored over the league table in *The Pink* (which seemed to come out remarkably quickly in those days – or maybe the buses weren't as frequent) and we worked out the permutations. We agreed we had to beat Leeds in the last game. And we did. We beat them 2–0. Notice that? After one match, I was calling Newcastle United 'we'. Some drug.

As has been well documented elsewhere, the summer went very well. Bobby Charlton was brilliant, and England won the World Cup. I should have been able to watch some of it live, but the Newcastle board were in the middle of an almighty row with Newcastle City Council about the lease on St James' Park. FIFA, who'd allocated World Cup group matches to Newcastle, couldn't wait for them to sort it out, so they took the games to Ayresome Park, Middlesbrough, instead. The Newcastle board would constantly thwart my dreams for years to come.

Still, at the age of nine, I was blissfully ignorant of football politics. All I knew was that this was the greatest sport in the world, that it had changed my life and that I couldn't wait to go to see another 'proper' match.

It was Joe Harvey's Newcastle which became 'my' Newcastle. For the nine years that followed my St James' Park baptism, Joe's teams would give me a rich foundation in the strange but compelling world of football supporting, providing delight and despair, magic and misery. They provided the backdrop to my adolescence and, being Newcastle, helped to magnify the confusion of the already difficult teenage years.

When I came of age, Joe's reign came to an end (though I'm certain the two events were not related). In that time, I'd watched some fantastic players and some dreadful ones, but I was a fully fledged football fan and a dyed-in-the-wool black and white. Looking back, it was a thorough apprenticeship and much of that was down to Joe Harvey. Now rewind back four years.

When Harvey left Workington Town to take up his dream job at Newcastle in 1962, he discovered a club in the doldrums. The fans who'd grown used to feasting on FA Cup wins in the '50s were suffering indigestion from the meagre scraps of Second Division football and were staying away in droves. Harvey felt for them. 'They seemed to me to have lost all the pride and glory I'd known and loved,' he said later. Despite being born a Yorkshireman, his experiences as United's captain for eight years – twice lifting the FA Cup – meant that he was a naturalised Geordie. Years later, another Yorkshireman would captain, then manage, the Toon and also become an adopted Geordie. Like Harvey, Kevin Keegan understood what Newcastle fans wanted.

When Harvey arrived, Newcastle were heavily in debt, and the board hadn't exactly shown great faith in him, offering him just a 12-month contract. But while the first team wasn't pulling up any trees, the youngsters won the FA Youth Cup. Harvey knew that if he could buy himself some time, in a couple of years he might just have the makings of a side.

Joe moved out some of his ageing stars, such as McMichael and Allchurch, and went about buying new players, mainly on the cheap. Names like Dave Hilley, Jim Iley, Ron McGarry, Ollie Burton and

Gordon Marshall were all drafted in. These would be some of the first players I ever saw wearing the black-and-white shirt, and while none of them would get into my all-time Toon XI (or second or third XI come to that), they all have a special place in a box marked 'important' filed away in the back of my sad, anal football brain. In fact, the first bit of football-related graffiti I ever saw was on a board outside a church in Jesmond which you could see if you sat upstairs on the Coast Road bus. A poster read, 'Jesus Christ is alive today and living in Newcastle', and somebody had written underneath, 'Sign him up and drop McGarry'.

Joe got us up to seventh in his first season, but his glorious cup record was taking a battering: knocked out of the League Cup by Leyton Orient and booted out of the FA Cup 5–0 by Norwich. The pathetic attempts to make an impression on the still-new League Cup continued the next year with a 2–1 humiliation at Third Division Bournemouth and Boscombe Athletic (as they were then splendidly called). Then in 1964, Joe experienced the first of three very dark days which would completely shatter his FA Cup reputation.

United were paired with Bedford Town of the Southern League. Ah, the romance of the cup. A once-in-a-lifetime experience for the part-time footballers of unfashionable Bedford, pitted against the famous Newcastle United, 'Cup Kings' of Wembley a mere decade earlier. 'Romance' my bottom. This was a banana skin the size of Brazil waiting for Joe and his boys to do the cartoon arse-over-tit manoeuvre. And, of course, they duly obliged. Bedford won 2–1 (deservedly, by all accounts), the home fans booed and another huge axe was taken to our declining reputation as 'a big club'.

By the end of the season, we'd finished a disappointing eighth, and to make matters worse, Sunderland were promoted. In the modern age, Joe would almost certainly have been sacked, but he survived. In fact, he'd stick around long enough to get a horrible sense of Bedford déjà vu some eight years later. But that's another horror story.

Thank God Joe *was* given another chance because the next season he grabbed it with both hands and finally turned the club's fortunes around. The FA Youth Cup winners of 1963 were gradually working their way into the first team, and names like Bob Moncur, David Craig and Alan Suddick were becoming regulars in Division Two. Youngsters like Frank Clark and Pop Robson were also serious contenders, and Harvey's team had, as all football experts like to say, a good blend of youth and experience.

Before winning the Second Division title in 1964–65, Harvey's heroes had what was becoming a fine Newcastle tradition to carry out. They stormed to a 3–0 defeat at Blackpool in the League Cup and then bowed out of the FA Cup at the first stage, beaten 1–0 at Swansea.

But Joe was gradually starting to get it right. His new-look team had been in the promotion places since October and wouldn't slip any lower. When third-placed Bolton arrived on Good Friday, the Magpies had been top for a month and St James' Park was jammed to the rafters. Geordies know a big game when they see one, and this was arguably Newcastle's biggest since the 1955 FA Cup final. Joe Harvey admitted before the match he felt 'that special tingle' once again. Sixty thousand fans felt it too, especially when Willie Penman and Jim Iley carved their names into United folklore by scoring the goals in a 2–0 win.

Ten years after their last FA Cup victory, Newcastle were crowned Second Division champions for the first time in their history and even got to lift a trophy. Not one of the *real* trophies but a trophy all the same. We were back.

Harvey's first season in the top division was unspectacular, but he did the job and United avoided relegation, finishing fifteenth. There were no cup runs: Sheffield Wednesday putting us out of the FA Cup in the fourth round, while our comedy relationship with the League Cup continued with a 4–3 home defeat at the hands of the mighty Peterborough United – at the first hurdle, of course. But crowds were back above 30,000 with Geordie fans happy to be rubbing shoulders with the big boys like Manchester United, Arsenal, Spurs and Everton once again. And this is where I came in – a St James' Park statistic for the first time for the penultimate game against Fulham on 7 May.

As a new boy, and a mere nine year old, I wasn't really aware of Geordie expectations for the 1966–67 season. But older fans were starting to get impatient, especially after a 3–0 home defeat by Sunderland put us into the bottom three. This despite the arrival of a giant centre-forward called Wyn Davies (soon to become my first Newcastle United hero).

The rumblings of unrest were growing louder, and one night, a group of fans broke into the ground and smashed the posts and crossbars. As the year drew to a close, we were right in the clarts, as we say on Tyneside. A 5–0 hammering at Leeds on Boxing Day was followed by a 4–0 defeat at Spurs on New Year's Eve. Those results sent us to the bottom of the table. If 1966 was a 'Great Year for English Football', then it was a crap one for Newcastle United.

Early in 1967, I reached another milestone – my first game in the Leazes End. So far, I'd been standing either in the Gallowgate End or one of the paddocks in front of the main stand, usually with Uncle Richie and Richard. But on 11 February I went to the Everton match with Vince Rice, who lived two doors from us. Vince was older than me – he was ten, so he obviously knew his way around.

The Leazes was the home end, where the action was. The hardcore fans stood there, singing, swearing and, if the opportunity arose, fighting. It was scary but fantastically exciting to be within spitting distance of the 'Geordie Aggro'. (And I knew we were, 'cause of all the spit.) My mother would've had kittens if she knew, but I figured what she didn't know wouldn't harm her. Another thing – the Leazes had a roof! (At St James' Park, we were deprived of simple amenities – three-quarters of the standing areas were exposed to the elements.)

The atmosphere was noisy but pretty ugly too, and matters weren't helped when it became apparent that a number of Everton fans had got into the Leazes. I have a vivid memory of bottles flying, policemen wading into the crowd and a lad with a blue-and-white scarf being led around the track behind the goal, his blond hair matted with blood. So this was the front line.

When Everton's third goal went in, Vince headed for the exit, and I, of course, followed. We beat the rush and got a train home with ease. We were blissfully unaware that there was a mini riot after the game with the main entrance being besieged by angry supporters.

Crisis is a much-used word when football is discussed on Tyneside. But such was the state of affairs at St James' Park that even people outside the region realised all was not well. The BBC actually sent a reporter all the way up from London to see what was going on, a rare event in those days. The odd appearance on *Match of the Day* (usually when we were playing in London) was all we could expect when it came to national TV coverage. But the midweek sports programme *Sportsview* sent Frank Bough to see if he could find a whiff of scandal. (He'd find his own some years later, but that is very definitely another story and not one for a book about a family sport like football.) Bough did what all good reporters do – he asked the fans:

> Fan 1: 'I blame the board of directors. As long as that board is here, I don't think we will ever have a team as good as Milburn and Mitchell and them.'
>
> Bough to Fan 2: 'What do you think is needed to get this club back on its feet again?'
>
> Fan 2: 'A new set of directors.'
>
> Bough: 'But they're the same directors who were in charge when you won the cup three times in the 1950s.'
>
> Fan 3, interjecting: 'Aye, that's the point. They haven't moved since. They're still living in the past.'

The report suggested that the club had squandered money in the transfer market and criticised the lack of investment in the stadium, revealing that, apart from floodlights, the biggest expense had been for a new directors' suite and main entrance. Everyone agreed that the fans deserved better. Bough's weary conclusion was that Newcastle were 'a great club that will surely come again'. How often would we hear that line in the years that followed?

In 1966, a young goalkeeper arrived from Linfield in Northern Ireland. He'd stay for 22 years, serving as player, coach and manager, experiencing most aspects of the many-headed beast which is otherwise known as Newcastle United Football Club. His name was Iam McFaul, although this mysteriously changed to 'Willie' once he became a coach. While carrying out my research, I tracked Willie down to his native Northern Ireland and had a long chat with him about his time at SJP. I discovered that, like many others I spoke to, his heart still bled black and white. (Something which is very reassuring to a cynical fan like me.) Willie had arrived at a club in paralysis. He told me, 'We never had the players to be in with a chance of the title. Maybe we couldn't get them, but it wasn't down to the finance. The club was actually happy to be midtable – happy to get 32,000 and to finish in the middle of the league. We actually got a bonus for staying up in the First Division, and that established a negative feeling among the team. We would've loved to have done better, but the club was happy the way it was.'

Another man who arrived on the scene at about the same time was journalist John Gibson, who started covering United for the *Evening Chronicle* in 1965. Anyone who makes TV programmes about Newcastle soon gets to know 'Gibbo', and every time I meet him, I realise he's as passionate about the Toon today as he must have been 40 years ago. Gibson is still a prominent figure in the SJP press room, and during the dying days of the Souness regime, I met up with him there to ask him about the problems facing Newcastle United in the '60s. He told me he'd quickly realised that the people running the club in those days were holding it back: 'Old Stan Seymour had run the place magnificently in the 1950s, but despite a fanatical following, the club never pushed on in the '60s. The people on the board had no idea of business, and they weren't all football people, either. Shares had been passed down through families from father to son. They would make the odd big signing to excite the crowd and bring them back if they'd drifted away, but they were not ambitious in their own businesses, so why should they be with Newcastle United?'

Rigor mortis had clearly set in behind the scenes, and things would carry on like this for more than two decades. It was obviously going to take something extraordinary to change it, and Gibson would play his part when the day finally came. In the meantime, managers would come and go, desperately trying to work in this straitjacket environment. No wonder we never won anything.

Joe Harvey's hands were tied more than anyone's, and the chances of him bringing a trophy to Newcastle in this climate were slim. Once again, the cups brought no cheer in the 1966–67 season. We were beginning to wonder why we bothered with the League Cup, knocked out again at the first hurdle, this time by Leeds. Wyn Davies had his best game yet in the third round of the FA Cup, scoring a hat-trick in a 4–3 win at Coventry, but we reverted to type in the next round, losing 3–0 at Nottingham Forest.

We were also locked in a relegation struggle that season which was clearly going to go down to the wire. But back-to-back wins in our final two home games dragged us out of the bottom two and confirmed our First Division status. I have vivid memories of being at the 3–1 win against Southampton, which actually kept us up – though I don't think I appreciated it at the time. I was with cousin Richard, hanging from the orange railings in the 'E' wing paddock in front of the main stand and next to the passageway by the Leazes End where the coppers used to stand (and get paid for watching the match, I seem to recall thinking). It was the first time I'd seen Newcastle actually outplay the opposition and score more than two. We stuffed them 3–1 – Davies, Noble and Robson (B) the heroes whose goals kept us up. This relegation scrapping wasn't good enough, and both

Harvey and the board knew that if they were to avoid a full-scale revolt on Tyneside, things had to get better. Happily, they did.

The 1967–68 season was Newcastle's best in the league for years. 'Fortress St James'' was re-established as we went 19 home games without defeat. Unfortunately, we were dodgy away – something which has plagued Newcastle teams for donkey's years and can only be explained by the fact that we have to travel further than everyone else. I think. (Actually, I haven't got a clue why, and I don't think anyone else has either. But it is bloody irritating.)

I was now watching my football from the Popular, opposite the players' tunnel, going to games with my older cousin Ralph Wilson and his mates from work. We'd travel up in a work's van and park on waste ground near a city-centre pub (usually Rosie's on Stowell Street, I seem to remember). I'd be left in the van with a match programme while the 'men' went through that time-honoured pre-match ritual involving beer. (Which, in order to preserve tradition, is one I practise with my mates to this very day – ironically, at Rosie's on Stowell Street.) They'd then collect me at about quarter to three, and we'd walk up to the ground.

The turnstiles in those days were actually marked 'Men' and 'Boys'. (Women and girls clearly weren't allowed, though I think I saw a few in disguise, sneaking in.) We'd stand in the men's queue, and I'd be lifted over the turnstile. I assume Ralph was giving the bloke a backhander to the tune of the admission price for a boy, otherwise they wouldn't have bothered with the lifting bit, but I never asked questions – all I knew was I was getting in for nowt and that in a few minutes I'd be watching the 'Mighty Wyn', Pop and the rest of the lads.

Despite our new-found league form, we excelled ourselves with spectacular cup exits in the 1967–68 season. The League Cup got beyond a joke when we lost 2–1 at Fourth Division Lincoln City. For God's sake! The FA Cup was no better. Fortress St James' was captured by a visiting band of border raiders from Second Division

Carlisle United, who won 1–0. It was now 13 years since that last Wembley triumph, and people were getting twitchy. Ironically, the supporters had been given a glorious reminder of the good old days at the start of the season. The stingy board had bowed to pressure and finally granted a testimonial to Jackie Milburn, a mere ten years after he'd left. With typical modesty, Jackie assumed no one would turn up, but the Geordies weren't about to forget their greatest-ever hero, and over 45,000 paid more than £8,000 to wallow in black-and-white nostalgia while a couple of fairly meaningless exhibition football matches took place.

This seemed to rekindle some life into the old club, and at the end of January, we went fifth top, only for the wheels to fall off in spectacular fashion. We managed just one win in the last twelve games – and actually lost the last five. The final match of the season saw league leaders Manchester City visit St James' Park needing a win to take the title. Happily, United put in a performance that matched the occasion and gave City a fantastic game before the visitors finally won it 4–3. A trophy had finally been won at SJP but, sadly, not by us. Our disastrous run meant that we finished tenth, but it would prove to be the most significant tenth place in our entire history.

4

EVERY CLOUD HAS A SILVER LINING (1968–69)

'They call us Newcastle United. They call us the team of the land. And there stands Bobby Moncur, the Fairs Cup in his hand.'

Leazes End song, b. 1969

Newcastle United are gloriously unpredictable. The only predictable thing about us is that we can be guaranteed not to win a trophy. However, at the end of the 1960s, we even managed to turn that tradition on its head in sensational style. We'd been trying to win a domestic trophy for 14 years without any joy. So what did we do? We went and won a European one. In 1969, Newcastle United won the Inter-Cities Fairs Cup. Crazy name, crazy story. Now, are you sitting comfortably?

In the days and weeks after the 1967–68 league season ended, West Brom won the FA Cup, Man United (for whom I'd still retained a deep affection thanks to Best, Law, Charlton, et al.) became the first English side to win the European Cup and Leeds United won the

Inter-Cities Fairs Cup. In the wacky world of football in the late '60s, all of this meant that Newcastle United, tenth in Division One, qualified for Europe for the first time.

City as league champions, and United as holders, both qualified for the European Cup, while West Bromwich Albion qualified for the European Cup-Winners' Cup. That's the simple bit. The third European competition was the above-mentioned Inter-Cities Fairs Cup. This weird and wonderful tournament had been devised in 1955 at the same time as the European Cup. The idea was to play football matches between cities which staged trade fairs – hence the 'fairs cup'. When it began, it had nothing at all to do with league prowess – in fact, many cities fielded all-star combination teams representing the various clubs who played within that city's boundaries.

That great European superpower Birmingham City lost two finals before evolving Euro giants like Roma, Valencia and Ferencváros started putting their stamp on the tournament, which eventually became a proper seasonal European competition for the 'next best teams', running alongside the European Cup and later to be known as the UEFA Cup.

Leeds United were responsible for finally getting an English name on the cup in 1968 – their achievement naturally overshadowed by Manchester United's win in the 'proper' European competition that same year. As holders, Leeds would be taking part again, thus possibly increasing the number of English teams in the competition from three to four. I say possibly because UEFA wouldn't announce if this was the case until the day of the draw. Are you still with this?

Liverpool and Chelsea qualified because of their league position, leaving the 'possible' fourth place still up for grabs. The next three highest-placed clubs who hadn't made it into one of the other European competitions were Everton, Spurs and Arsenal, but none of them was allowed to take part because – as the name suggested – it was an 'inter-city' tournament, and the rules stated that only one club per city could enter.

EVERY CLOUD HAS A SILVER LINING

The good men of UEFA met in Copenhagen and dutifully decided to increase the number of teams competing, which meant that there would be a fourth place for an English club after all. The same good men ran their fingers down the English League Division One table looking for someone who would fit their very strict and, it has to be said, bizarre rules. Their podgy digits stopped at tenth place, alongside the name of Newcastle United. The die was cast, and we were all about to go on the most amazing adventure. The chairman of the club at this point was Lord Bill Westwood, who memorably said, 'We're daft enough to go on and win this cup.'

As well as Willie McFaul, I tracked down another of my early boyhood heroes for his memories of this wonderful, crazy season. Only two men have played more games for the Toon than Frank Clark, veteran of over 450 Newcastle matches. And back in 1968–69, Clark was one of the few who agreed with Lord Westwood: 'I don't think anybody else thought we could win the Fairs Cup. Because of the back-door entry thing, we got a lot of stick, mainly from the clubs who felt we'd got their place! We kept hearing how we were going to embarrass the Football League, we were going to get hammered, etc., etc. The pundits, especially the London press, said we were going to be out straight away, so we went in very relaxed. Plus, there was a little bit of, "We'll show the bastards!"'

Few observers gave us much hope when the draw was made for the first round. We drew the Dutch giants Feyenoord, who, along with Ajax, would dominate football in the Netherlands for well over a decade. They would also go on to win the European Cup the next season. They clearly learned a lot from their trip to Tyneside, because on 11 September 1968 Newcastle gave them a football lesson. Beyond all our wildest dreams, in our competitive European debut, we hammered the mighty Feyenoord 4–0. Suddenly, there was an air of excitement all over Tyneside.

The match coincided with my first day at my new school, St Cuthbert's Grammar School in Newcastle, Alma Mater to Lawrie

McMenemy, Sting, Neil Tennant from the Pet Shop Boys, and Dec from Ant and Dec, among others. Quite a catholic collection. Which is good, as it was a Catholic grammar school. Steve 'Blackie' Black, later a fitness coach with NUFC and the British Lions, was in our year, while future Newcastle United coach John Carver was another Cuthbert's old boy.

It was here I met the mates I'd watch Newcastle United with from then on, and their names and opinions will crop up from time to time in the following pages. Mick Ramsey and Chris Baines both went to the Feyenoord game after that first day at school. Mick is one of the most passionate fans I've ever come across – the sort who can't actually enjoy a match until Newcastle are at least 3–0 in front. He obviously enjoyed the last few minutes of the Feyenoord game! Chris still sits next to me at SJP, and is even more cynical than I am. A strictly unsentimental supporter, he has a fascination for football culture, e.g. he's read every book going about hooligans! Simon 'Sime' Malia wasn't a football fan when he arrived at St Cuthbert's, but that changed very quickly. In the years that followed, he'd accompany me to more Newcastle games than anyone else. And Steve O'Brien, who'd actually been at infant school with me in Wallsend, started out a Man City fan but eventually became as committed as anyone – although his provocative and controversial opinions have led to many people saying he *should* be committed!

I was deeply envious of Mick and Chris, who were regulars at the European games. Even though I travelled all the way across the Tyneside metropolis twice a day, I wasn't allowed to do it at night, so Fairs Cup matches were out of bounds for me. But I devoured every word I heard on the radio, saw on the TV and read in the papers, and the games were a burning topic of conversation at school.

The players were also consumed by the tournament, as Willie McFaul told me: 'It suited us to play over two legs, really, because we were very strong at home and were actually quite hard to beat away. No one liked coming to St James' Park. It was always windy with a gale blowing off the Tyne and over the top of the Gallowgate. The pitch wasn't exactly like a bowling green either!'

After surviving a scare in the second leg against Feyenoord (we lost 2–0), we then went on a magical Iberian mystery tour, beating Sporting Lisbon, Real Zaragoza of Spain and Vitória Setúbal of Portugal. Joe Harvey was working some kind of Continental magic, although, as McFaul told me, his 'spying' methods were not what you'd call scientific: 'He'd go and watch opponents in advance, but he'd usually ask taxi drivers who were their best players! That was Joe all over.'

On the domestic front, inconsistency reigned as usual, and by the end of January, we'd been knocked out of both cups. Southampton turned us over 4–1 in the third round of the League Cup, while league champions Manchester City knocked us out of the FA Cup after a fourth-round replay.

We'd finish ninth in the league, but for me, there was another milestone that season – my first away game. Vince Rice, who'd introduced me to the Leazes End, suggested during a Saturday morning kickabout that we should go to the match that afternoon. It was a good job that my mother didn't ask too many questions when I went looking for the cash, as the game in question was a local derby with deadly rivals Sunderland. And it was being played at Roker Park.

Vince and I caught the train and followed the black-and-white herd. Unfortunately, this was one of those occasions when the Toon Army had decided they were going to 'take' the Fulwell, the Sunderland equivalent of the Leazes.

If my Leazes debut was exciting, this was raw seat-of-the-pants stuff. At two o'clock, the 'home' end was a sea of black and white, and suitably offensive songs filled the air. By quarter to three, the home fans had arrived in force, and the songs were being returned. There followed the occasional rush of bodies, flailing fists and flying bottles. Vince even got to throw a full toilet roll into the Mackem ranks! This was spectating on the edge!

The game itself ended 1–1, though my view of the action was negligible. I totally missed our goal, but I did catch a glimpse of Jim Scott getting what I thought was a second, only for it to be disallowed. Eventually, some big bloke moved to let me stand next to the red-and-white picket fence at the front, but all I got was a very good view of Colin Suggett scoring their equaliser. The game was on Tyne Tees the next day, so I did eventually see Bryan Robson's goal, but Dad also saw the trouble and questions were asked in the house.

Months later, Tyne Tees came to my aid once again. The Fairs Cup game with Vitória Setúbal featured in a 'highlights special', so I was able to agree special permission to stay up late *and* see us thrash the Portuguese side 5–1. It was the talk of school the next day. We all knew that, barring a complete disaster in the second leg, we were through to the semi-finals and just one tie away from a European final. The lads duly negotiated the return game in Lisbon, and we were all in Fairs Cup dreamland.

Liverpool, Chelsea and holders Leeds had all fallen by the wayside, but there were still two British teams left in the competition. The semi-finals were to be contested by Újpesti Dózsa of Hungary, Göztepe Izmir of Turkey, Rangers and us. We drew Rangers, with the away leg to be played first.

The match programme for the first leg in Glasgow politely described Newcastle as 'one of the most ambitious, skilful and resolute teams in Britain'. It went on to say, 'Newcastle have come this far by virtue of their pace and action, and believe they have the resources and composure to go through to the final and emulate Leeds United last season in housing the handsome trophy in England.' How language has changed. As have attendances. A Fairs Cup record crowd of 75,580 crammed into Ibrox – 12,000 of them Geordies – hoping for a 'Battle of Britain' epic. What they got was a hard-fought 0–0 draw, which was perfect for Newcastle.

All the reports say that the star of the show was United's keeper Iam McFaul, who, among other heroics, managed to save a penalty from the inappropriately named Andy Penman. McFaul told me, 'I had to save it, really. I'd given away the foul in the first place! But all the defence was outstanding. In fact, all the players were. We really played together as a team and worked hard for each other. We knew the away game with Rangers was the crunch one. We thought, as a team, that if we could get something at Ibrox, then we had a real chance.'

On the day of the second leg, I headed home from school in a fever of excitement. The city centre was awash with Scotsmen, most of whom looked like they'd been drinking all day, largely because most of them had. I still wasn't allowed to go to the evening games and had to settle for kicking a ball against the garden wall, creating my own version of the match (complete with commentary, of course) then sitting next to the radio to listen to the second half live.

A capacity crowd of just under 60,000 filled St James' Park, and what followed has gone into hooligan folklore. McFaul was quite literally on the front line. He told me, 'I have never been so scared in all my life as I was in that game. The Rangers fans had been causing trouble in town all day, and they certainly caused trouble at the ground that night.' Bottles were thrown onto the pitch, and a number of fans followed them. Sure enough, when Jackie Sinclair made it 2–0 with 13 minutes to go, all hell broke loose. McFaul recalled, 'Ollie Burton looked at me and shouted "Run". Of course, I didn't have a clue what he was on about, because it was all happening behind me. But as soon as I looked over my shoulder, I was off like a flash.'

The Welsh referee John Gow took both teams off until order could be restored. McFaul told me, 'The chairman of Rangers [John Lawrence] came into our dressing-room and told us the game was over. He was conceding the match. But the ref said we had to go out and play the last few minutes. We went back out, and I'd never seen so much glass. At the final whistle, we just ran off again. I lost my favourite cap and my gloves because I wouldn't go back for them, but that was a small price to pay for safety. The next day, they cleared the Gallowgate End and took a lorry load of bottles away.'

United were in their first cup final for 14 years, and the club was looking forward to a big pay day – and not just because they got the money back on the empties. No, they were due to face Újpesti Dózsa of Hungary, conquerors of Fairs Cup holders Leeds United. Leeds had just won the English First Division title for the first time in their history, and their manager Don Revie described Újpesti as 'the greatest team in Europe'. Another report said they were 'the best side ever seen in Britain'. Six of their players were Hungarian international regulars, including the legendary Ferenc Bene and János Göröcs, and they'd won their semi-final against Göztepe Izmir 8–1.

This was the fifty-eighth match of United's tumultuous, never-to-be-forgotten season and one I could not miss. Tickets went on sale on the Sunday after the Rangers game, and Richard and I queued for most of the day. The home leg was held the following Thursday, bizarrely enough, but, to be honest, the whole experience felt odd in lots of different ways.

The match was to be televised by the BBC, another rarity. We were used to Tyne Tees turning up on a Saturday for their regional highlights programme *Shoot*. (This title probably accounted for my first experience of feeling 'provincial'. All the other regions seemed to have sensible titles, such as *The Big Match* or *Sunday Soccer*. In the North East, we had *Shoot* with commentators who didn't sound like commentators, and I swear to God they used to stop the highlights to warn you that a goal was coming up!) Whatever the shortcomings of *Shoot*, at least it could be relied upon to show Newcastle on a regular basis. If *Match of the Day* came to SJP, it was a bigger talking point than the game itself.

Matches at Newcastle were *always* filmed from a very low position in the main stand with the Popular in the background, but someone at the BBC clearly thought the Popular would look pretty crap (provincial?) on pan-European TV. As a result, they erected a special gantry and commentary position at the back of the Popular so the good people of Budapest, Milan, Moscow and Madrid could get an eyeful of our dilapidated, antiquarian main stand. But I suppose it made SJP look like a proper football ground, rather than a low-budget council sports facility.

One tradition that wasn't changed on Thursday, 29 May 1969, was the strip. The rule in the Fairs Cup was that the home side changed strip if there was a colour clash, and we'd already turned out in all white against Sporting Lisbon and all blue against Setúbal. However, Újpesti were like Real Madrid in more than just the way they played. Their colours were all white, so there'd be no problems for those Geordies who were easily confused.

For league games, Richard and I would arrive at about half past one and sit on the front wall right up to three o'clock, only for the coppers to tell you to get inside the perimeter wall once the teams came out. So you'd spend the whole match being squashed or, worse still, getting pushed away from the wall into the second 'row' of standing supporters, usually behind someone bigger than you so you didn't get a decent view of the match.

We weren't expecting anything different on the big night. We arrived very early and got a place on the wall. But when the teams came out, the place was so full (59,234 the record books say) that there was no room to get back inside the perimeter wall, and the coppers said we'd just have to stay there. We literally had ringside seats. Result!

It was 0–0 at half-time, and everyone was a bit worried, but this was Newcastle, so it was never going to be straightforward or predictable. And, when the breakthrough came, it came from the least likely source. Skipper Bobby Moncur had never scored a senior goal for the team, but in the space of eight second-half minutes, he got two. Jim Scott added a third in the closing stages, and Richard and I – devils that we were – ran onto the pitch to enjoy the moment. Richard swore he got into the penalty area while I was just delighted to cross the touchline. In the next day's Newcastle *Journal,* there was a picture of some kids in anoraks, jumping for delight after one of the goals – it was us. We were as famous as Bob Moncur!

Two weeks later, it was Joe Harvey's fiftieth birthday. It was also the return leg in Budapest, and Sime's dad actually went! The Supporters Club had advertised a coach trip with overnight stay and match ticket for the princely sum of £37 10s. Michael Malia went one better and shelled out for a flight. He also managed one of the great football blags of all time. Because he knew the club doctor, he somehow wangled it so that he watched the match from a pitch-side bench, right next to Joe Harvey and Co.

Media coverage was minimal. This was 1969, and it was the Fairs Cup, and it was us. So there were highlights on the BBC at about 11 o'clock that night. Before that, there was live second-half commentary on Radio Two. Before *that,* there was nothing. Therefore, we didn't have a clue that the same United XI which had looked so strong in winning 3–0 at St James' Park was being given the biggest tousing in the first half that any of our players could remember.

Willie McFaul told me, 'They hammered us. We were warned that they were different class if they got on top, and that's exactly what happened. We didn't get over the halfway line in the first half.'

Frank Clark agreed: 'I'd spent all season telling everyone we would win the Fairs Cup, and that was the only moment I wavered. They played brilliantly and pulled back two goals. It wasn't that we had played badly. It was just that they had played so darned well.'

And that's what we heard when the radio eventually took us live to Budapest. Two down and hanging on. It was a nightmare. The unassailable lead suddenly seemed very fragile, and I remember banging my head on the wall near the fireplace praying for some kind of miracle, but, deep down, I was expecting the inevitable goals landslide that would shatter the dream.

Imagine my delight – and the delight of thousands of other radio-clutching Geordies – when the commentator announced shortly after the kick-off that we'd scored! Imagine our shock when he said it was Bob Moncur – again. Moncur, the captain and central defender who'd never scored for the first team, had now scored a hat-trick in the club's first-ever European final. As the tabloids might say, you couldn't make it up.

The second half of that match is now part of Geordie history. Ben Arentoft, the busy Danish midfielder, banged in a second shortly afterwards and substitute Alan Foggon turned the game on its head with a third. Bloody hell. We'd done it!

Over in Budapest, it seems the transformation was down to one man, Joe Harvey. Clark and McFaul tell identical stories of the scene at half-time: all the players, heads down, devastated and devoid of ideas. Joe Harvey walked in and said, 'What's the matter? All you've got to do is score a goal. These ******* foreigners are all the same. They'll collapse like a pack of ******* cards.'

Frank Clark told me, 'It seemed daft, but he'd worked out the away-goals situation, which was still a bit of a novelty then, remember. He realised that if we could get one, they'd need another three to win. There was a bit of kidology involved, but it was also logic. And we started thinking, "Maybe we *can* get one . . ."'

McFaul told me that most of the players thought Harvey had gone mad: 'We looked at him and then we looked at each other and shook our heads. But lo and behold, it happened. When that goal went in, we could see their heads go down. By the end, their fans were shouting for *us*.'

Joe Harvey was either crazy or a genius. But whatever he was, he brought home a trophy for the long-suffering Geordie faithful, the only man to do it in the last 50 years.

Sime's dad kept his blag going and got into the dressing-room after the game. He'd also bought a pile of match programmes, which he brought back for Chris, Mick, me and others. I've kept that sacred relic of Toon memorabilia to this day, as has Sime. Though his is even better – it's signed by the team. I've also still got my copy of the following day's *Journal* with the front page headline, 'United Bring the Cup Home: Magyars crushed as Moncur leads his team to Euro glory'. On the back page, the headline is, 'Glory be! They have done it'.

The team flew back to Tyneside and paraded the cup through the streets before arriving at a packed St James' Park. All of us raced down after school to catch our first (and only) glimpse of Newcastle United silverware. We were in the A Wing paddock, and Sime asked me to look after his bag for a second. I thought he must be going to the toilet or something, but a few minutes later, he reappeared to tell me he'd been to get a touch of the cup. If it had been a cartoon, I would have grown a donkey's head, and there would have been a comedy sound effect.

I've also kept that night's *Evening Chronicle* (sad, eh?), which had a special comment piece on our great victory. The closing words were, 'The faithful fans have richly deserved it – and they can now hope that this is but the first exciting page of a glorious new chapter in Newcastle United's chequered history.'

That was exactly how we all felt. It was now the middle of June, and the fantastic season of 1968–69 was finally over. In just over a month's time, Neil Armstrong and Buzz Aldrin would walk on the moon. I was simply over it. I'd been a proper football fan for three years now, and in that time, England had won the World Cup and Newcastle had won a European trophy. All was well in my football universe. This was how it must be all the time, I thought. How wrong I was. How very, very wrong.

5

SUPERMAC, HEREFORD AND MACKEMS (1970–73)

'I am confident that we must go only one way – upwards,
to join Liverpool, Leeds United and the rest at the very
top of the tree.'

Lord Westwood, talking a good game in 1969

By adding a European trophy to our roll of honour, there was a feeling that we had joined some kind of elite. But there was also another feeling – that this had to be the springboard to get us back among the domestic prizes. Joe Harvey certainly thought so. When the dust had settled after Budapest, he came over all 'Churchillian', saying, 'This area of the country has carved out a niche in FA Cup history; we are all aware of that. But no club can live on its past, and all of us are determined to build a new, great team. I am certain that winning the Fairs Cup holds the promise of even greater things to come. There is much to be done, but now we can go forward with confidence.'

John Gibson had written a timely club history called simply *The Newcastle United FC Story*. He'd invited Lord Westwood to write the final chapter, and the chairman showed an ambition (in words at least) that would be echoed by one of his illustrious successors many years later. He wrote:

> Europe, of course, is now vital to our future. We learned that last season. In the glorious '50s, United's name was on everyone's lips, but that was a national success, and now the horizon is much wider. Europe, and even the world, lies beyond.

Most supporters felt that Europe was brilliant but wouldn't it be just as exciting, and a damn sight cheaper, if we could go back to Wembley? It was now 14 years since the last FA Cup triumph. We felt that the cup was our birthright – wasn't it about bloody time we won it again?

And so we prepared ourselves for the brave new era when Newcastle would rise again to the top of the domestic tree and, in true Magpie fashion, pinch every gleaming bit of silver in sight. Of course, it didn't happen. The team sat around midtable for the entire season but shot up to seventh with a late rally of decent results. Seventh was our best final placing since 1951 when Milburn, Harvey and Co. were at their peak, but champions Everton were never unduly troubled by a black-and-white renaissance.

We weren't going to win the league, but we were obviously good enough to win a cup. Sadly, we were knocked out of both of those at the first hurdle. Our dismal League Cup record showed no sign of abating as we were beaten 2–0 by Sheffield United. In the FA Cup, our Euro fighters found that Southampton was just not quite far away enough to bring out the spirit which had prevailed in Budapest. We got beat 3–0.

Ironically, the FA Cup game was sandwiched between two matches against the same team in the Fairs Cup, and when we treated them as European opposition, it was a different story. Having already beaten Dundee United and Porto during our defence of the trophy, our Euro know-how then helped us put out the Saints on away goals.

(Above) 1955: Jimmy Scoular receives the FA Cup from a very young Queen Elizabeth II. It's our third in five years – but there won't be another domestic trophy for at least fifty years. (Courtesy of Newcastle Chronicle & Journal Limited)

(Right) 1969: We'll always have Budapest. The one silver lining in our grey half-century – Bobby Moncur gets his hands on the Inter-Cities Fairs Cup. (Courtesy of Newcastle Chronicle & Journal Limited)

And so does my mate Sime, aged 12. He'd had his eyes on it since the homecoming.

Liverpool's Steve Heighway is walking on air after his goal in the 1974 FA Cup final. Sandwiched between two from Kevin Keegan, it helped turn Newcastle's Wembley dream into a nightmare. (Courtesy of *Liverpool Echo*)

What will we do if we ever win something? Newcastle fans swarm all over St James' Park to greet the team after they didn't bring home the cup in 1974. (Courtesy of Newcastle Chronicle & Journal Limited)

Supermac, Superstar – goals galore but no medals. Malcolm Macdonald comes to terms with his second Wembley defeat in two years. This time it's the 1976 League Cup final, which we lost 2–1 to Man City. (Courtesy of Newcastle Chronicle & Journal Limited)

Kevin Keegan in his first incarnation as an honorary Geordie. Between 1982 and '84, he was our catalyst on the pitch. A decade later, he'd do it again to even greater effect – this time off the pitch. (Courtesy of Les Jones/Covershots Inc.)

So near, yet so far. Keegan salutes the fans at the end of the 1995–96 season. He'd come within an ace of winning the Premiership in the most spectacular fashion, but we lost – and so did football. (© MirrorPix)

1996: The greatest game ever? Stan Collymore scores in stoppage time, and Liverpool win 4–3. But for Newcastle, it's the beginning of the end of the Premiership dream. (Courtesy of *Liverpool Echo*)

Still keeping the faith. My mate Sime (left) and me at Wembley in 1998. We lost, of course, to Arsenal. (Courtesy of *Daily Telegraph*/Russell Cheyne)

1998: Nicolas Anelka shoots past Shay Given and wins the FA Cup for Arsenal. Newcastle manager Kenny Dalglish lost his job three months later. (Courtesy of *Daily Telegraph*/ Russell Cheyne)

(Above) 1999: Teddy Sheringham shoots past Steve Harper and wins the FA Cup for Man United. Newcastle manager Ruud Gullit lost his job three months later. There is symmetry in our misery. (Courtesy of *Daily Telegraph*/Russell Cheyne)

Two Toon fans have the hardest jobs in Britain: Tony Blair has to run the country; Freddy Shepherd has to win a trophy for Newcastle United. (Courtesy of *Daily Telegraph*/Russell Cheyne)

The Toon Army remains as loyal as ever – even if we do have to make our own trophies. (Courtesy of *Daily Telegraph*/Russell Cheyne)

Spot the difference. Jackie Milburn and Alan Shearer are both great Newcastle centre-forwards, but only one has a trophy. Milburn won three FA Cups in five years; Shearer beat Milburn's goals record but retired without winning a medal at Newcastle. (Left: courtesy of the Milburn family) (Below: courtesy of *Daily Telegraph*/ Russell Cheyne)

Some of the greatest names in football have tried and failed to end our 50-year trophy drought. Anticlockwise from top: managers Ossie Ardiles, Kevin Keegan, Kenny Dalglish (with Sir John Hall), Sir Bobby Robson, Graeme Souness and Ruud Gullit. (All © MirrorPix, except Ossie Ardiles, courtesy of Les Jones/Covershots Inc.)

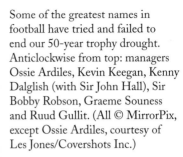

Fifty years of hurt. (Photo montage: Paul Walker)

Anderlecht were next, in the quarter-finals, but after one of the classic European nights at SJP, the spell which had enthralled us all for 18 months was finally broken – and in the most cruel way. Roared on by another 59,000 crowd, the lads overhauled a 2–0 deficit to take a 3–2 aggregate lead, only for an injury-time goal to put us out – our turn to lose on the away-goals rule. Anderlecht went on to the final, which they lost to Arsenal, but all across 'Geordieland' our lads were still heroes.

The seventh-place finish in 1969–70 was seen as a marked improvement. We were definitely moving in the right direction. It also sneaked us into Europe for a third successive year, this time because Arsenal qualified as Fairs Cup holders and because Derby County were banned for 'financial irregularities'. In the first round, we played two classic games against Inter Milan. Wyn Davies scored in the San Siro to earn us a 1–1 draw, but the home leg was the stuff of legends.

I was in the Popular with my elder sister Terry (*everyone* was going to the match at this stage), and we watched open-mouthed as some of the biggest names from that summer's Mexico World Cup were reduced to a rabble in an attempt to stop Newcastle. Inter fitted the classic Italian 'triple D' stereotype of the time – they were defensive, devious and dirty. Their team was full of stars – Fachetti, Boninsegna, Mazzola and Burgnich were walking World Cup bubble-gum cards – but they couldn't handle the Mighty Wyn. When Bob Moncur – him again – put us into the lead, the Italians fell to bits. Wyn Davies had been kicked, punched and spat on, so it was especially sweet when he scored the second and killer goal. But not before one of the most amazing things I have ever seen on a football pitch. *Their keeper got sent off for decking the ref!* It was unbelievable. The police had to come onto the pitch, and we thought they were going to arrest the keeper, a man in a cap called Lido Vieri. Eventually, a kind of calm was restored, Vieri went for his early bath and we went on to win the game.

The contrast in the next round couldn't have been greater. We were the favourites this time, our opponents being little Pécsi Dózsa of

Hungary. We battered them at St James' Park but only managed two goals from Wyn. The second leg was a disaster, and we lost 2–0 before going out in a penalty shoot-out – something we'd perfect in years to come. (The 'going out' bit, I mean.)

Back in the league, we'd gone backwards, finishing 12th. As for the cups, well, I'm running out of ways to describe being 'knocked out of the League Cup at the first stage', but suffice to say we lost 2–1 away to Bristol Rovers of Division Three. The FA Cup saw another flop, beaten after a replay by Ipswich Town. All of this meant our season was over on 13 January. So much for the new era.

Joe Harvey was in his ninth season as manager, and suddenly the pressure was back on him again. For the first time in four years, we hadn't qualified for Europe. Not even the vagaries of the Fairs Cup would admit the team that finished 12th. Harvey realised that the whole thing needed a rethink, and before the season ended, he set about redesigning the forward line. In January, John Tudor arrived from Sheffield United, and in February, top goal-scorer Pop Robson was sold to West Ham. This wasn't a shock, because Robson had fallen out with the management after an argument in which he called the club 'unprofessional'. When he left, most fans were sad to see him go but wished him well, mainly because most of us agreed with him.

Change was happening fast. In March, the unthinkable happened: Wyn Davies was dropped for the first time. Wyn was my favourite Newcastle player, and I was heartbroken. He made a cameo appearance in our final home match of the season, playing on the right wing. I remember thinking, 'Maybe he'll be brilliant on the wing and he can send crosses over for John Tudor and he'll stay and everything will be all right . . .' But he was sold to Man City in the summer, and suddenly we had a vacancy for a hero.

The Fairs Cup team was almost completely broken up – Scott, Sinclair, Arentoft and Foggon all moved on. Newcomers included a teenage winger called Stuart Barrowclough, an Irish midfielder called Tommy

Cassidy, a graduate from the youth team called Irving Nattrass and, more significantly, a Leeds reserve called Terry Hibbitt. But the biggest noise surrounded the arrival of our new centre-forward.

It was the eve of the 1971 FA Cup final, and while Bertie Mee and Bill Shankly were preparing Arsenal and Liverpool for the showpiece game of the season, Joe Harvey was splashing out £180,000 – the second-highest fee ever paid for a footballer in England. It was a huge gamble. The player in question was Malcolm Macdonald – a full-back who'd been converted to a striker by Luton Town. He'd scored 27 goals in his first season in Division Three, another 30 in Division Two and he was still only 21. Harvey was so convinced by his new boy that he tempted fate in the biggest possible way, declaring, 'I just know this feller can be another Jackie Milburn to the supporters.'

Macdonald didn't quite reach Milburn's level, but to those of us who watched Newcastle in the 1970s, he was the next best thing – he'd more than fill the role of hero to me and thousands of other Geordie teenagers. For five seasons, our hopes, dreams and ambitions to win something rested almost entirely on Supermac.

I met him in 2003 when I made the Jackie Milburn TV documentary – Jack Milburn, jun., and I both admitted we'd been slightly in awe of our boyhood hero. I was thrilled when, two years later, Mac agreed to meet me again to talk about his time at St James' Park. First question: why did he agree to come all the way to Newcastle in the first place?

'I didn't hesitate,' he said. 'They'd won the Fairs Cup a few years earlier, and they were a famous club with a big stadium. Joe Harvey was a very impressive man and a great enthusiast of the game.'

When Malcolm Macdonald turned up for his first Tyneside press call in a chauffeur-driven Rolls-Royce, everyone took notice. He announced that he'd score 30 goals in his first season, and the press instantly labelled him 'Supermouth'. By the time he'd burst onto the St James' stage with a hat-trick on his home debut against the mighty Liverpool, the fans had another name for him – Supermac.

Macdonald told me, 'It was one of those life-changing matches, not just for me but for everybody in the ground. It forged a relationship between myself and the Geordies, and I was adopted for ever and a day.' He hadn't lost any of his brashness!

I'll never forget that Liverpool match – because I missed it. Chris Baines and I were away with the school in the wilds of Scotland for the first ten days of the new season. When someone said we'd beaten Liverpool 3–2 and Macdonald had scored a hat-trick, we jeered at the messenger. We weren't born yesterday and all that. Then we found out it was true, and we couldn't wait to get home and hitch ourselves to the new era.

The Liverpool game turned out to be a classic Newcastle false dawn. We won just one of our next twelve games and found ourselves bottom of the table. We were also out of the League Cup, although bizarrely we had managed to beat Division Three giants Halifax Town 2–1 at SJP. A team called Arsenal were next, and they somehow managed to knock us out, winning 4–0 at Highbury.

Joe Harvey then bought a centre-half called Pat Howard to replace the injured Bob Moncur, and a little midfielder from Blackpool called Tony Green. Green was a genius, and he certainly made bullets for Supermac, who scored eight goals in his next six games.

The Toon roller-coaster was in full swing, and we were on the ascent. But the Toon roller-coaster is like no other. Think of that massive thing at Blackpool Pleasure Beach and imagine it ten times bigger – and on the moon. What we didn't realise was that the stretch we were just starting to enjoy was the bit just before the steepest downward section ever built.

We'd been drawn at home in the FA Cup third round to non-league Hereford United. The Hereford episode is very well known – *too* well known if you ask me, thanks to the BBC showing *that* goal every time the FA Cup third round comes along or whenever a little team plays a big team. What most people don't realise is *that* goal was scored in a replay. The first match was played some time earlier at St James' Park. The weather that winter was atrocious and the original game was postponed by nine days and eventually played on a Monday night.

All I knew about Hereford United was that they were top of the Southern League and were quite 'useful', as non-league teams go. But we had Supermac and Tony Green, Terry Hibbitt and John Tudor. We were also in a rich vein of form; it was really a question of 'how many?'

Mind you, when Hereford's big day arrived, there was a hint of Newcastle making their excuses in advance. The match programme said, 'Of course, there is far less pressure on them than on Newcastle United, and don't forget that a heavy ground can help to close the gap between teams.'

It actually turned out to be a cracking cup tie with four goals, all coming in the opening twenty minutes or so. Hereford took a shock early lead, but within minutes, Macdonald had equalised from the penalty spot and Tudor had put us in front. Here we go . . . or so we thought. But just minutes later, Hereford's player–manager Colin Addison hammered in a cracker. We huffed and puffed, but Hereford got their draw.

I remember getting home and my dad winding me up about the score. I also remember my pathetic answer was something like, 'They're not like a non-league team. They're good enough to be in the Third Division, honestly.' The answer actually proved to be quite prophetic, because within 18 months they *were* in the Third Division. The fact that a side like ours shouldn't have had any problems with a Third Division team, let alone one from the Southern League, seemed to have slipped my mind.

Because of the atrocious weather, there were four failed attempts to stage the replay at Hereford. Fans made several abortive trips to the Welsh borders, but the team were stuck there, as Frank Clark remembered: 'We'd stayed down there all week waiting for the game to happen, waiting to be told that the rain had stopped. That wouldn't be allowed to happen today. It was so debilitating. We were just hanging around. We were all in Marks & Spencer buying underpants because we'd only taken enough for two days!'

Eventually, they managed to get the game played on Saturday, 5 February, which was actually fourth-round day. *Match of the Day* sent along a new commentator called John Motson, who entered the nation's consciousness on the same day as Ronnie Radford, the man who hit the infeasible equaliser.

We actually battered them in the first half but just couldn't score. Tony Green was running the show, but chance after chance went begging. We finally got the breakthrough when Macdonald headed in with about ten minutes to go. But then came *that* goal, the one which must have been shown more times than any other goal on the BBC apart from Geoff Hurst's 'They think it's all over' goal in the 1966 World Cup final. While Ken Wolstenholme's famous words bring a glow to every English fan's heart, when United fans hear Motson saying, 'Now Tudor's gone down for Newcastle,' they reach for the off button. Because after Tudor goes down, the ball sits up very nicely, thank you very much, for a joiner and journeyman footballer who hits the most ferocious 35-yarder you've ever seen, right into the top corner of Willie McFaul's net. Ronnie Radford, this is your moment.

'I get a little bit closer to it every time I see it on TV,' McFaul told me ruefully. 'It was a bit special, and we were shell shocked.'

Frank Clark is still bitter about the day: 'I don't believe in curses, but I sometimes wonder about fate. I'm not making excuses, but we started to feel we weren't meant to win that game.'

We weren't. In extra time, Hereford's substitute Ricky George poked in the winner, and United were out of the cup, the first top-flight team to lose to a non-league side for 23 years. The pain. The embarrassment. I remember listening on the radio and, when the final whistle blew, flinging myself full-length onto the settee and crying with shame. Well, I was 14.

If I was embarrassed, imagine how the players felt. McFaul told me, 'It wasn't nice. It goes down on your record, a big blot on your career. But when I think of the chances we had, we should have won that game easily.'

I also spoke to Newcastle skipper Bob Moncur, who witnessed something which clearly showed that the manager felt it worst of all: 'We were travelling back home up the motorway when Joe asked the driver to stop the coach. He got off and threw up by the side of the road. It was awful to see him in such a state, but that's how much it affected him. He was Newcastle daft, and he knew what this would mean to the fans.'

The memories are still painful for Frank Clark. He confessed he still gets reminders when he least wants them: 'In 2005, Colin Addison, who was their player–manager in 1972, invited me to the Hereford United players' reunion dinner. Can you believe that? The non-league team that knocked us out of the cup wanted me to come and reminisce with them. I said to him, "Colin, **** off!"'

The repercussions lasted for years. Willie McFaul remembers 'minnow-phobia' setting in at SJP: 'There was a big fear of minor opposition at Newcastle after that. It seemed to happen so often, and you could feel the fear factor in the crowd. They were so apprehensive every time we played a little team.'

How do you explain it? The 'romance' of the FA Cup? Or the Newcastle United roller-coaster? Another thing that's often forgotten is that the following Saturday we went to Man United in the league and won 2–0. Explain that.

Tony Green eclipsed Best, Law, Charlton and Co. that day and made both goals. He was named our player of the year and was one of the few bright spots in another frustrating season. Macdonald got thirty goals in all competitions, just as he'd promised, but Newcastle finished eleventh, just one place higher than the previous season.

These days, not many managers would have survived something like the Hereford disaster, but the board clearly had faith in Joe. The club was also finally doing something about the ground, with the

Popular closed for demolition at the start of 1972. A 'proper' stand was going to be built at last.

Unfortunately, the start of the 1972–73 season was marred by a shocking injury to Tony Green. During an away match against Crystal Palace, he got 'clattered', to use the Geordie vernacular, and never played competitive football again. Willie McFaul remembers Green with affection: 'That injury was the biggest shame in my time at Newcastle. He was the best player I played with in a black-and-white shirt. I've never seen a player create so much excitement. He didn't know what he was going to do next himself, so obviously no one else had a clue. He was just brilliant.'

Frank Clark shares that view: 'He only played one season, but he was one of the most popular players they ever had at Newcastle. Mind you, he was the worst trainer I've ever known. Ask him to run round a track and he couldn't do it, but put a ball at his feet and it was completely different – he'd run all day.'

The guy only played 33 times for us, but he is a legend. Many United fans who saw him insist he was the best Newcastle player ever, and most will readily include him in their all-time best Newcastle XI. I've never known that sort of reaction to any player before or since. Perhaps it was indicative of the Geordie need for a hero, or heroes. After all, we can't hang our hats on our trophies.

Joe Harvey was gutted. He really felt that Green was the final piece in his Newcastle United jigsaw. But life had to go on. Jimmy Smith, signed after the Fairs Cup win, was finally starting to show some kind of consistency, and in front of the building site which used to be the Popular side, some pretty decent football was being served up. Right up to March 1973, we were in fifth place in the league, the best performance by any Joe Harvey team to date. Both Macdonald and Tudor were banging in the goals, and there were memorable wins over Leeds, Arsenal, Man United and Liverpool.

We were looking good, and the crowd had fallen in love with Macdonald, me included. He was just so exciting to watch, especially when he got behind defences and bore down on goal. 'Climactic' was a word I would use to describe it years later when I'd been to university and drunk lots of beer. What I was rambling on about, in my pseudo-intellectual way, was that you had a few seconds to enjoy the moment as he raced through, there was that 'will he?/won't he?' moment as he got closer and closer to goal, and it usually finished with a huge 'Yeeeeeessss!' as he thrashed the ball into the net.

Mac was the kind of battering-ram centre-forward that the Newcastle crowd loved, and any attempts that coach Keith Burkinshaw made to get us playing with a bit more sophistication were always likely to suffer. According to keeper Willie McFaul, '"Burky" was full of ideas. He wanted me to play through the full-backs and then pass through the team . . . but the crowd always wanted me to kick it up to the front two – get it down the pitch. But we did eventually start to play, and Terry Hibbitt started to run games. Malcolm would show a lot of laziness, and John Tudor would do his work. If we raised this at team meetings, Mac would just say, "Put your goals on the table." And it was hard to argue with him.'

By now, I was a regular in the Gallowgate End. I used to stand with a friend of my mam and dad's called Joe Deighton, cousin Richard and an eclectic collection of individuals who would gather round the first barrier behind the goal. I was also supplementing my pocket money by selling Magpie Bingo tickets. There was a magical number you had to sell each week to qualify for a free ticket for home games, so I developed my own sales patch on the streets of High Howdon. Every other Saturday, I'd go to the commercial department offices at the top of the Leazes car park, hand over my hard earned cash and, in return, get my voucher. Even better, I didn't have to queue at the turnstiles – a bloke on the side gate would let you through in exchange for the voucher. It was brilliant – I felt I was part of it all, a member of the Newcastle United family. (Funny how your mind works when you're a teenager. Nowadays, I'd probably feel it was the least they could bloody do.)

There was another milestone for me that season. In March 1973, some five years after Vince Rice and I took the Fulwell End at Roker Park, I went to my first 'proper' away game. By that I mean travelling miles to somewhere you'd never ever dream of visiting if there wasn't a football match going on. In my case, it was Norwich.

Mick Ramsey and I got on a midnight coach from Gallowgate Bus Station. It was full of 'hard lads' who'd obviously been on the lash all night. We were just 15, and it was dead good. We got next to no sleep on the journey, partly because it wasn't exactly a luxury coach but also because of the hilarious antics of the lads at the back of the bus and the comedy driver at the front. We got into Norwich at the ungodly hour of 7 a.m., and there was little to do apart from try to grab some proper kip in the bus station. We were woken up by some Norwich 'hards' who asked us if we wanted a fight. Not being specialists, we politely declined but cheered them up when we told them there were a few lads down who'd be 'up for a ruck'.

'How will we recognise them? Are they wearing scarves?' one asked.

'Yes, they are. And full-length white butchers' coats with "NUFC" written all over them,' we informed them.

They seemed delighted to hear the news, though having seen both sets of supporters at close quarters, we suspected they wouldn't be quite so happy when the inevitable clash occurred. We then adjourned to the local library to see if we could get some sleep there. Ssssh! Street fighters at rest.

The match itself was a classic Newcastle United performance of the era. Supermac scored a 'climactic' goal, and Bob Moncur and Co. held out until full time. One-nil to the Toon. On the return journey, we quickly established that the Norwich bus station boys had indeed met the white butchers' coats, and all our suspicions had been correct.

Newcastle finished eighth in Division One, three places higher than the season before, and we even won a trophy – the legendary Anglo–Italian Cup. This was basically a contrived competition between also-rans from England and Italy, teams who hadn't qualified for Europe but who either fancied themselves as big European clubs or simply needed the money.

On the way to the final, we beat Roma and Torino, amongst others, and although the football on offer was pretty dull, there were some cracking fights. Six players were sent off during our victorious cup run, including, astonishingly, David Craig, the mildest-mannered man ever to wear the shirt. His crime? To look surprised after being kicked up the arse by a narky Italian. Hilarious. It was Inter Milan all over again, except no one was that bothered if we won, lost or drew. Happily for Craigy, we stuffed Torino 5–1. All the matches were two-legged apart from the final, which we played in Italy in June against Fiorentina. We won 2–0 without Macdonald, who was on England duty, and David Craig scored a rare goal. See, there is a God.

We'd also been semi-finalists in the Texaco Cup for the second year running. The Texaco was another competition for 'nearly' teams who'd just missed out on Europe, but this one featured teams from England and Scotland and was sponsored by an oil company. In 1972–73, we played an extra thirteen games in the Texaco and the Anglo–Italian to go with our forty-two league matches and four in the proper cups – a grand total of fifty-nine matches, with just a Mickey Mouse pizza pot to show for our troubles. On the outside, we were all smiles at our Italian success, but inside, we were seething. Across the Tyne, something had stirred.

If ever there was an incentive to start winning real trophies again, it came in May 1973. That's when the unthinkable happened. Sunderland won the cup. The FA Cup. *Our Cup.*

This little team from down the road had the temerity not only to win it, but to win it by beating one of the giants of the game and consequently win the nation's hearts in the process. As Geordies, we were in turmoil. We had no time for Leeds United and their 'professional' ways. (For 'professional' read 'doing things properly so you win lots of football matches'.) Like most football fans, we thoroughly enjoyed those rare occasions when Don Revie and his boys got a bit of a 'doing'. But it couldn't happen in the cup final, though – not against a Second Division team. Could it?

It could, and it did. Sunderland won 1–0 thanks to a goal from Ian Porterfield, a superhuman performance from their veteran goalkeeper Jimmy Montgomery and a very silly celebration dance from a man in a flasher's mac and a trilby, their manager Bob Stokoe. Oh, yes. The same Bob Stokoe who had helped win the same cup on the same pitch for Newcastle some 18 years earlier. A man who had spent 14 years on the books at the Toon. How bloody ironic.

We, of course, had suffered another embarrassing exit in round four, losing 2–0 at home to Luton Town in front of the *Match of the Day* cameras. Luton were Supermac's old team. They came and did what all teams from lower leagues are supposed to do when they're drawn against 'glamorous' opposition away from home. They ran their socks off, and when their chances came, they took them – twice. Disgruntled United fans even began chanting, 'Supermac is playing for Luton, tra la la la la, la la la la' (as we quaintly used to add in those days). Our hero certainly wasn't pulling up any trees.

The League Cup was no better, of course. Round three, home to Blackpool, Alan Suddick and all. We lost three-nowt. And get this – who was Blackpool's manager? Bob Stokoe, performing his last act before heading off to save Sunderland! You really couldn't make it up. Crap.

So along came Sunderland and their cup final. You could see it happening as well. They kept sneaking through round after round till they had a 'famous victory' over Man City or somebody (I can't even bring myself to check). Well, that was it. They were nailed on to win it.

We'd never actually experienced anything like this before. Sunderland had been useless for years. They were the local rivals, yes, but you never took them that seriously. They were obviously inferior to us but would occasionally put in a big performance in a derby and maybe even win the odd one. But they hadn't won anything for donkey's years. For God's sake, *we'd* won a trophy more recently than they had! But here they were on the most 'romantic' (media word for 'unlikely') cup run seen in years. Geordies were confused. Some got swept up in the local media frenzy, declaring this was obviously 'good for the North East'.

When Sunderland played their semi-final against Arsenal at Hillsborough, they were rank outsiders, but they somehow defied all the odds and won. The frenzy became a hurricane. Suddenly, red-and-white novelty hats were being sold in corner shops on *Tyneside*! Lads at school who'd never before professed an interest in football were turning up in brand new red-and-white scarves. What was going on?

This had to stop. Things were getting seriously out of hand. The natural law of football had to take over, and the mighty Leeds United had to impose their true professional authority at Wembley. Sunderland would have their day in the sun but common sense would prevail. Bremner, Giles, Clarke, Charlton and Lorimer would prove that class always wins through.

Except that it doesn't. One of the great rules of football is that when you really, really, really don't want a shock result, you get one (viz. Hereford). If we'd played Leeds that day, we would have been outsiders but not such big outsiders (we'd already beaten them 3–2 that season in a *Match of the Day* classic). It wouldn't have been David v. Goliath, more like Goliath's smaller cousin v. Goliath, but without the familial bonhomie, if you get my drift.

No, if we'd played Leeds that day, we would have lost. But Sunderland won. It was 'a victory for football', 'a great day for the little guy' and a shit one for Newcastle. But never mind. These things are sent to try us. The next season it would be our turn. Our chance to take over Wembley and show the football world what real supporters from the North East were like. Not ones who get interested for half a season, buy new scarves and hastily learn the names of the players. No, we were proper fans, in for the long haul. We'd been dragging our souls around for 19 years, and we were ready to win the FA Cup again. We never thought we'd say it, but 'Thank you, Sunderland' for giving us back our appetite and reminding us of our rightful place in the football firmament: above you and winning the cup.

And so it came to pass. We *did* go back to Wembley for the first time in 19 years. We did show the football world what real North East football fans were all about. But we didn't win the cup. On 4 May 1974, a new verse of 'The Blaydon Races' would be composed:

> I went to Wembley Stadium 'twas on the fourth of May
> Nineteen hundred and seventy four what an awful* day
> We showed the Scousers how to sing
> We showed them how to sup
> The only thing we didn't do was win the FA* Cup . . .
>
> > (*Some versions replace the words 'awful'
> > and 'FA' with another word. Work it out.)

6

WEMBLEY NIGHTMARE, PART 1 (1974)

'When Moncur goes up, to lift the FA Cup, we'll be there,
we'll be there!'

Pre-match chant, Wembley, 1974

'It's not often I've been ashamed of the Magpies, but I
was saddened and shocked by the performance.'

Jackie Milburn, after the 1974 FA Cup final

The day has passed into legend. It is one of the archetypal Newcastle
United occasions. Build them up high; knock them down hard. Play
like lions to get to Wembley; play like lambs when you get there.

Jackie Milburn was at the game as a journalist. He later wrote:

> Only the goalkeeper and the full-backs played. The rest were
> rubbish. Macdonald had been shouting from the rooftops as
> usual about what he was going to do, but the only thing he did
> that afternoon was tie his bootlaces. It was awful. I could see
> Joe's face, and he was looking sicker with every minute.

Jackie was spot-on. Newcastle were shocking. Astonishingly so. Even hard-bitten experts with very long memories were scratching their heads to recall such a meek capitulation, such a one-sided cup final. And in true Newcastle fashion, the occasion would be laced with rich irony, although we weren't to know it at the time. Our nemesis on the day? Step forward pint-sized all-action-hero mighty-mouse darling of the Kop, Kevin Keegan.

To be fair, it wasn't a one-man show. From one to eleven, Liverpool were better than us. (I would have said one to twelve, but they were so in control they didn't even bother to bring their sub on.) Keegan scored two and broke every Geordie heart that day. Twenty-two years later, he would take us to within a gnat's chuff of winning the Premiership and break many more hearts.

Oddly enough, it was the league that got us all excited at the beginning of the 1973–74 season. We started like a house on fire, and in October, four straight wins lifted us to the dizzy heights of second place. On New Year's Day, we won 1–0 at Arsenal, but once we went on the FA Cup run, our league form disappeared quicker than a Mackem in the Leazes. We won just two more games and finished fifteenth.

Of course, we'd been knocked out of the League Cup pretty quickly as usual, losing at home to Birmingham City in a third-round replay. But our progress in the FA Cup meant that there was a new-found air of excitement around the city. Supermac told me that this enthusiasm filtered through to the players as well: 'There was great optimism around the club. There was a *belief* that our name was already written on the cup, mainly because we had the strangest way of getting into the final itself.' Strange isn't the word. Newcastle's road to Wembley was bizarre in the extreme.

There were horrible feelings of déjà vu when we were drawn at home to non-league Hendon in the third round: same first two letters as Hereford! Nerves were calmed when Paddy Howard put us 1–0 up in the first half, but somehow we let them equalise.

Fortunately, Hendon, fancying a big pay day, kindly moved the replay to a proper ground at nearby Watford, and we duly stuffed them 4–0. Phew.

Next up came Scunthorpe from Division Four, and it was the same story. We drew 1–1 at home but were comfortable 3–1 winners in the replay. We were now in uncharted territory, and some of us were getting nose bleeds. Unlikely as it may sound, those legendary FA Cup fighters Newcastle United had not been beyond the fourth round for thirteen years. Thirteen years! The Beatles had been and gone in that time. Men had been to the moon. Colour TV had been invented. It was most of a lifetime for some of us. And this was a whole new delicious, delirious experience.

We were drawn away to West Brom in the fifth round, and everybody went. I mean everybody. It was one of those occasions when all your mates got tickets so you knew there'd be a good away following, but when we arrived at The Hawthorns, the place was overrun. In the ground, they'd given us the big covered end, and the roof was lifting. It soon became apparent that we had most of one side as well. The atmosphere was fantastic, but nothing could have prepared us for what was about to unfold.

The signs didn't look good when our playmaker, little Terry Hibbitt, limped off with an injury. It was obviously bad – he was immediately replaced by Jinky Jimmy Smith, one of several great enigmas who have worn the black and white. He was a player capable of sublime genius but more often than not disappeared up his own backside. Jinky once said in an interview that he could tell how he was going to play within the first ten minutes of a match. Once he'd realised he wasn't going to play well, he wouldn't bother trying!

At West Brom, he must have had a very warm feeling indeed. Jinky was fabulous. And so was Tommy Cassidy, an unlikely looking trundling lump of a player who quite often defied the laws of athleticism and proved to be a very decent footballer. Along with a rising star called Terry McDermott, they passed Albion off the park.

When Macdonald headed the first, the noise was deafening, and it soon became apparent that we occupied most of the ground. Two more goals followed in the second half from Tudor and Barrowclough, and Newcastle were playing the sort of football most of us had only dreamed about. Wearing the change strip of yellow shirts and pale-blue shorts, the chants of 'Bra-zil, Bra-zil' were inevitable. We were marching, strolling, waltzing into the quarter-finals.

Macdonald, who'd actually had a goal disallowed so the ref could give *us* a free-kick, told me, 'That was probably the finest team performance I've ever been part of in my life. Jimmy Smith ran the whole game. He was brilliant.'

Frank Clark agreed: 'That fifth-round performance against West Brom was absolutely marvellous. We had some smashing players, and we could be wonderful. We could beat anyone on our day.'

Most of my mates still talk about that day. As we reminisced over a few pints recently, Mick Ramsey told me he thought it was the best match he had seen in all his time watching Newcastle: 'Obviously the football we played under Kevin Keegan was the most consistently good, but I think that West Brom game was the single best performance I've ever seen from us.'

That night, *Match of the Day* ended with a tribute, not to the great goals of the day, but to us – the Newcastle fans. Jimmy Hill and Co. were genuinely impressed. We'd been as good as our team, and we were going with them to the quarter-finals. The quarter-finals! It even had the word 'final' in it. There was a palpable feeling that we'd finally broken the jinx. The genie was finally out of the bottle.

Our joy was further enhanced when we were given a home draw against a Second Division team. The quarter-final tie against Nottingham Forest at St James' Park will go down in Newcastle history as 'the match that never was'. It was the most thrilling cup tie any of us had ever seen, but it didn't matter – the game was declared null and void because United fans staged a pitch invasion.

It really was a sensational afternoon. Steve O'Brien and I queued for ages and eventually got into the Leazes End. We were still making our way along the back of the stand behind the crowd when Forest scored. Shortly after we'd taken our place down in the corner near the new East Stand, David Craig hit the equaliser. But the dream rapidly turned pear-shaped when Forest scored again before half-time and converted a penalty early in the second half to make it 3–1. To make matters infinitely worse, Pat Howard was sent off for arguing about the penalty decision.

The pain was almost tangible. We'd all begun to believe that this was the year when the wait would be over, but now the dream was rapidly slipping away – again. For some it proved too much, and a number of fans spilled onto the pitch from the Leazes End.

What happened next has been the subject of debate for a quarter of a century. Depending on your viewpoint, it was either a violent pitch invasion or over-enthusiasm from a bunch of kids. (I lean towards the latter – Millwall this wasn't.) Either way, the ref thought it sufficiently intimidating to take both sets of players off the pitch while the police restored order.

While they were off, the feeling of sheer disappointment got worse. What a bunch of fools we'd been to delude ourselves that this was the year. One good performance at West Brom and we'd bought ourselves a bag full of fool's gold. Suddenly, the delirious optimism we'd allowed ourselves to enjoy at The Hawthorns seemed a million miles away.

The ref asked Forest if they wanted to go back out to play the last half hour. Of course, they said 'yes'. They were 3–1 up away from home, and Newcastle only had ten men. We clapped them back on, unenthusiastically, resigned to another inevitable humiliating exit from the cup.

We should have known better. Nothing is straightforward when you support Newcastle. With 20 minutes to go, we got a penalty of our own, which Terry McDermott duly slotted home: 2–3. Game on. The crowd of 54,000 suddenly realised the dream wasn't dead at all:

maybe we could snatch a replay and maybe, with 11 men, we could beat them down in Nottingham.

Bang. John Tudor's flying header made it 3–3, and the place went nuts. We were still in the cup! But that wasn't all – with time almost up, Bob Moncur knocked in a sensational winner. Cue total delirium. I remember being picked up and hugged by a middle-aged man I didn't know from Adam. Neither of us cared a damn. The Toon were in the FA Cup semi-finals for the first time since 1955!

Our joy only lasted until Monday afternoon when the FA announced, after a protest from Forest, that the match would have to be replayed on a neutral ground because of the pitch invasion. We were devastated. Hadn't Forest been offered the chance of a replay during the enforced break? Of course they had, and of course they'd gambled that they'd win there and then. The gamble had blown up in their faces, and now they wanted another throw of the dice. At the risk of sounding like the stereotypical teenager, it all seemed so unfair!

The match was replayed at Everton's Goodison Park, and the score was 0–0. Bizarrely, they played extra time, even though it was a rerun of the first game and first games don't have extra time. It was still 0–0 after that, so we braced ourselves for a replay at Forest.

The Football Association have always worked in mysterious ways, but what they decreed next was surreal, even by their standards. The two teams were ordered back to Everton a couple of nights later to try to settle it once more. This served to fuel the growing belief at St James' Park that our name was indeed 'on the cup'.

Supermac told me, 'We expected to have to replay at the City Ground, but the FA came out with the most extraordinary decision that Nottingham Forest should be denied a home replay. Nobody at Newcastle could understand it, and certainly nobody at Forest could. But we nicked it 1–0, and I got the winner, so I'd scored in every round.'

He certainly had, and the Toon really *were* in the FA Cup semi-finals for the first time since 1955. So off we all swarmed to Hillsborough, home of Sheffield Wednesday, to take on Burnley. We were given the giant uncovered Kop end, though there were Geordies everywhere as our opponents hadn't sold their full allocation. This added to the sense that we were the big club, finally roused from our slumbers and on the march to our inevitable destiny – a cup-final victory at Wembley.

For an hour we looked decidedly average, nervous even, as Burnley played all the football, hit the bar and generally had us rattled. But Supermac seized the day and scored two typical Supermac goals. Twice he chased long through balls, twice he charged through the middle leaving all in his wake and twice he planted the ball past the keeper.

The great man remembers it well: 'Burnley had battered us for an hour or so, but what happened was just typical of the way we played. We knew if we got the ball to Terry McDermott or Terry Hibbitt they could knock it beyond the centre-half and I'd be away, and that was just how it turned out – twice.'

The Geordies went bonkers. We were finally off to the promised land, and our king had taken us there. There were tears of joy when the team – at the insistence of the fans – returned to the pitch after the final whistle to take an ovation. There would be more tears five weeks later at Wembley, but they'd be cried in very different circumstances.

It was immediately billed as a potential classic. Liverpool were the dominant force in English football; Newcastle were the Wembley specialists with five wins from five cup-final appearances at the stadium. And history beckoned for boss Joe Harvey. If successful, he would become the first man to skipper and manage the same club to victory in two different FA Cup finals.

Malcolm Macdonald told me that the players were optimistic that they'd give Joe his place in the record books: 'Liverpool didn't frighten us. We'd won every game away from St James' Park, so Wembley was fine by us. If anything, we probably went into the final overly confident.'

But it wasn't overconfidence that cost us the cup. If there is one single reason why Newcastle played so badly in the 1974 FA Cup final, it has to be the team's preparation – or lack of it.

Our form was also poor. Since the West Brom cup win in mid-February, we'd played thirteen league games and won just one – dropping from ninth to eighteenth in the table. A run of draws meant we finished fifteenth, but the omens were not good.

The only cause for optimism was that we had a dress-rehearsal cup final, and we won it. We beat Burnley in the Texaco Cup final at SJP. The score was 2–1 with Bob Moncur, hero of the Fairs Cup final five years earlier, getting the winner. With his record in finals, he must have fancied himself to get one at Wembley ten days later.

I asked Moncur if he'd be happy to talk about what really went on back in 1974, and he readily agreed. As I sat in his Gateshead living room, he revealed that stories of unrest behind the scenes were accurate. He told me, 'There was actually a split in the camp. Not an open one but enough to cause a bit of friction. I was approached by some of the players, as captain, to go and ask management for a bigger bonus. Some of them were talking about going on strike!

'I told them that was ridiculous – the time to ask for a bigger bonus is when you're negotiating your contract, not just before you play in the FA Cup final. The ringleaders were Malcolm [Macdonald], John Tudor, Terry Hibbitt, Alan Kennedy and Terry McDermott. They gave me the impression that *all* of the players were in on it.

'I couldn't believe that my old mates Frank Clark, Willie McFaul, David Craig and Tommy Gibb would go against me, so I called a meeting of all the team, and, of course, they agreed with me.

'I told the others that I would go and see Joe Harvey, but I'd make it clear that I disagreed with what they were asking for. It was daft – I was just happy to be in the cup final! It all blew over, but that kind of split meant that there were always murmurs in the camp. It was definitely something we could have done without.'

This was typical Newcastle: on the verge of the biggest game in nearly 20 years and something has to happen to take our eyes off the ball. We've had more than our fair share of bolshy players down the years, and the football equivalent of the militant tendency would emerge at St James' Park a few years later in one of the most extraordinary examples of player power ever seen in the British game. Why is it always us?

With a week still to go before the big day, the club decamped to the Selsdon Park Hotel in Surrey – the same base Sunderland had used the year before. Frank Clark wasn't impressed: 'It was important to get away from Newcastle, because the hype was building up like mad, but if you do go away, it has to be structured, and, above all, you need good training. I believe we went away with no clear idea of what to do.

'Looking back, it was pathetic. We trained on a sloping bit of grass in the hotel grounds, which would have been fine for someone with one leg six inches shorter than the other! This was the club's biggest game in years, but the preparation was hopeless. I don't think any other club in the First Division would have prepared like that.'

By 1974, Joe Harvey's relaxed management style meant some players were beginning to take liberties. 'By then, Joe had a very laissez-faire approach to management,' Clark said. 'He allowed the senior players freedom and responsibility, and hoped they'd use it wisely – but some of them didn't. Let's say some used the occasion of our week in London to enjoy themselves socially. There's nothing wrong with that, but it is a question of how much.'

Alan Kennedy, who'd just broken into the team that season, agreed: 'We didn't focus on the match. It was like something from *Hi-de-Hi!* We were playing snooker and golf, and then, in the evening, we'd have a few beers and Frank Clark would get the guitar out. We were eating well, and we did more or less what we wanted. All those decisions were taken by Joe Harvey – he said, "Enjoy it." The longer the week went on, the less we focused on the game.'

Then there was the case of the official 'cup-final tracksuits', which turned out to be a classic Newcastle cock-up. 'They had contracted

Burton to make them, and they were going to be designed by Hardy Amies,' Bob Moncur told me. 'As cup-final day got closer, we were all wondering where they were. They finally turned up two days before the match, and you've never seen such a mess in your life! They were made out of towelling material, and they had huge black-and-white flared trousers – really trendy. But everyone took one look and said, "We're not wearing them!" The club had to go out and buy some new ones, and we ended up walking out in purple tops. What a fiasco that was.'

Back on Tyneside, the build-up was reaching fever pitch, and the fans were being swept along by the sheer excitement of it all. The demand for tickets was phenomenal. The club had decided to issue vouchers at the first home game after the semi-final – even though the opponents were Everton. This was another typical bit of daft Newcastle administration. Everton fans were paying to go in twice, realising the vouchers would prove extremely precious on the black market back home on Merseyside. Really, our lot couldn't have organised a booze-up across the road at Scottish & Newcastle.

A whole bunch of us sent our vouchers to the club in one envelope. We decided that either we were all going to London together or we were all staying at home to watch it on TV. Eventually, the envelopes arrived from the club – we'd all got tickets. In the weeks before the final, Supermac had been telling anyone who'd listen just what he was going to do at Wembley. You couldn't blame him for that – he thrived on the attention and the pressure, and he'd scored in every round so far. Unfortunately, we weren't playing Hendon, Scunthorpe, West Brom, Nottingham Forest or Burnley this time. We were playing Liverpool, the reigning League and UEFA Cup champions and 'the best team in England and probably the world', according to their legendary manager, Bill Shankly.

Moncur wasn't pleased with a number of the boasts that were making headlines on the back pages: 'All the players who had never been to Wembley before were talking about what they were going to do to Liverpool. Malcolm, in particular, was getting headlines, talking about how many he was going to score. John Tudor said something as well, and Alan Kennedy made a great remark about how we'd beat the old men of Liverpool. I kept saying, "Isn't it best if we just keep our mouths shut?" Me, Willie [McFaul] and Clarkie had been before. We knew what it would be like – that's why we were keeping quiet.'

Frank Clark was secretly worried going into the game: 'Our form wasn't good, and you can't just turn it on like a tap, especially against a side like Liverpool. I never went into any game thinking I was going to lose, but I was apprehensive, and I know our coach Keith Burkinshaw was very worried and quite upset about the way the build-up had gone. I didn't repeat my fears to anyone, because I knew many of the lads were upbeat, and I didn't want to bring down the atmosphere.'

When I asked Willie McFaul if complacency had begun to creep in, he said, 'We might have been overconfident. Mac definitely was. He was in the papers all week, and that was daft. You just don't do that against Liverpool. Joe tried to stamp on it, but he didn't want to wind the rest of us up as well. His attitude was, "Let the players sort it out themselves."'

Supermac denies that he ever made the remarks which, even today, are still talked about with great amusement on Merseyside. He told me, 'I used to write a column in *The Sun* and kept certain aspects just for them. The story everyone refers to appeared in *The Mirror*, which was *The Sun*'s biggest competitor. They literally made up the quotes to make it look like I was giving them better stories than I was giving *The Sun*.'

True or not, Bill Shankly famously pinned the reports on the Liverpool dressing-room wall and told his players, 'There you are, boys. I don't need to say any more than that. It's all been said.'

Macdonald, however, points to team selection rather than overconfidence when asked to single out the one thing that caused United to play so badly on the big day: 'For some extraordinary reason, our coach Keith Burkinshaw decided to change our system on the Thursday morning before the final. We'd been playing 4–4–2, with Stuart Barrowclough becoming an outside-right when we had the ball. He was quick, and he hit fantastic crosses which were like shots – John Tudor and I loved them.

'But Burky persuaded Joe to leave Stuart out and play four recognised midfield players instead, meaning Stuart missed out altogether. He must have been thoroughly annoyed, and he had every right to be, because he'd played most of the season and done brilliantly for us.'

Frank Clark didn't see it as a major problem: 'I was a bit surprised that Stuart Barrowclough had been left out, but we had Hibbitt, McDermott, Cassidy and Smith in midfield, and they weren't bad!'

To complicate matters, Northern Ireland full-back David Craig, one of United's unsung heroes, dislocated his elbow just weeks before the final. This led to a reshuffle in defence – Clark moved to right-back, and young Alan Kennedy was drafted in to replace him at left-back.

Moncur wasn't phased by the defensive reshuffle, but he'd have preferred it if the sub had been in the starting line-up. 'The fans always used to have a whinge at Tommy Gibb, but he would always have been in my team. He always kept going, just the type we needed in our side. Jinky [Smith] had been brilliant at West Brom, but he was a one-game-in-ten man.'

Back on Tyneside, we were booked onto a coach organised by the Lindisfarne Catholic Club in Wallsend. It seems remarkable now, but there I was at the age of 16 about to go to London for the first time. Steve O'Brien, Mick Ramsey and cousin Richard were also on board, along with my other Wallsend pals Brendan Egan and Vin McDonald. I'd also managed to get Mick a ticket because of my status as a Newcastle United Bingo ticket-seller.

We set off after closing time on the Friday night and arrived as the capital was waking up. The sun was shining, and all over London, groups of bleary-eyed Geordies were tumbling off buses and onto the streets. Soon we were wide-eyed tourists, wandering around staring at anything that looked vaguely familiar, very much the provincial boys just arrived in the big city. I even got searched by a policeman outside 10 Downing Street (in the days when you could actually stand outside No. 10). The constable found an offensive tube of Toffos in the top pocket of my Wrangler jacket, realised that I wasn't a threat to Harold Wilson or to national security, and allowed us to move on.

None of us looked 18 – indeed, some of us struggled to look 16 – so there was only limited pre-match boozing. But the capital was a sea of red and black and white as Geordies and Scousers took over London. The *craic* was mighty, and there was good-natured banter between opposing fans, exchanging predictions and idle boasts.

We got to Wembley ages before kick-off in order to soak up yet more atmosphere. Girls were handing out flyers, advertising two new records about to be released by Warner Brothers: 'Liverpool Lou' by The Scaffold and 'Jarrow Song' by Alan Price. It was as if Liverpool and Newcastle were competing on every available stage. (The Geordies won that one by one chart place, pop pickers.)

Then we were all distracted by the sounds of a 'rumble' going off in the Wembley car park. A bunch of Scousers were getting a bit of a kicking by a gang of marauding locals who burst into cries of 'The London!' A bunch of Geordie storm troopers rushed to the aid of their fellow northerners and redressed the balance. The locals were soon in retreat while Black 'n' Whites and Reds united for a chorus of 'We hate the cockneys!' It was all part of the buzz and thrill which made it such an awesome day for a teenager at his first FA Cup final.

When I finally got through the turnstiles, I remember sprinting up what seemed like miles of stairs before emerging high above the goal at the opposite end to the tunnel. I gazed in wonder. This was where England had won the World Cup in my first year as a serious football fan. I also remember thinking the pitch looked bloody miles away.

Before kick-off, there was an exhibition 3,000 metre race around the edge of the pitch which was won, to the delight of everyone down from the North East, by Geordie hero Brendan Foster, wearing a black-and-white vest.

As the teams emerged, the scene was set for a classic cup final. Frank Clark was as excited as we were: 'Wembley was a magnificent sight. The atmosphere and the noise and the passion were fantastic. The two sets of fans were probably the best in the land. What a mixture!'

Unfortunately, the football match spoiled everything.

Incredibly, it was 0–0 at half-time. Everyone connected with Newcastle was thinking exactly the same thing. 'I remember saying to Frank Clark as we walked off, "We've been dire. There's no way we can play as bad as that in the second half." The irony is we played worse,' recalled Malcolm Macdonald, who hadn't had a sniff of the ball let alone a shot on goal.

'I had our only shot on target,' said Clark. 'It bounced about 15 times before it got to Ray Clemence. Now, if *I* had the only shot on target, you know we were in trouble!' His club record at that time read: 12 seasons, no goals.

Bob Moncur was hopeful: 'I thought we must still be in with a shout, because we'd been outplayed. But we were still level, and we had players in our team who could win the game for us.'

Young Alan Kennedy wondered what had hit him: 'In the dressing-room, I was looking around and people were having a go at each other. The manager or the captain should have been strong enough to say, "This is what we've got to do." It wasn't for the players to have a go, but there were some pretty strong characters in that dressing-room.'

Liverpool came out in the second half, went up another gear and simply blew Newcastle away. 'They just steamed through the middle of us and down the sides,' said Macdonald. 'They were skinning us, and we were allowing them to get to the deadball line, and that's exactly what you had to stop Liverpool from doing.'

Macdonald's view that Barrowclough should have been in the team was supported by what happened next. 'Their left-back Alec Lindsay was as slow as a carthorse,' he said, 'and Stuart would have frightened him to death. But he was bombing up and down. He had the freedom of the left wing, and he actually scored a perfectly good goal that was disallowed.'

Shortly afterwards, though, Keegan got one that did count, and it was then a question of how many. Steve Heighway ran on to a John Toshack flick for the second, then Liverpool started pulling out their party tricks to open us up for Keegan's second and their third. Unfortunately for Alan Kennedy, it was orchestrated by the experienced Tommy Smith, who took great delight in reminding Kennedy about his pre-match jibes about Liverpool's 'old men'. Kennedy remembers the match only too well: 'We were not right in our minds in that second half, but the goals came from rank bad defending. We were cavalier in our play. We played as a bunch of individuals, not as a team. We'd been caught up with the euphoria of being at Wembley. It's a wonderful day out, and I thought we'd be able to look after ourselves, but the writing was on the wall pretty early on.'

The story of the match was succinctly put by the BBC's poet laureate, David Coleman: 'Keegan two; Heighway one. Liverpool three; Newcastle none.'

Grown men cried. The dream was over, along with the club's 100 per cent record at Wembley. We'd climbed to the top of the mountain and fallen off. And it bloody hurt. Still Geordie voices rang out, and as Liverpool received the trophy from Princess Anne, all that could be heard was 'We'll support you ever more!' from the black-and-white end.

My mate Sime (the only one of us who bunked off school to go to both Nottingham Forest replays in the quarter-final) is convinced that the 1974 final was a turning point in the modern history of the club, a moment when everything changed at Newcastle United. He argues, 'Clubs definitely have a psyche – Man United and Liverpool always play a certain way. We had this tradition of being a wonderfully barmy, somewhat chaotic club that always produced a side with a fantastic centre-forward, we always won cups and we always did the business at Wembley. That tradition and that myth got annihilated that day, which I believe was ground zero for Newcastle United.

'From that day on, instead of going in hope to watch them, it became a case of going with fingers crossed and girding yourself in preparation for another heavy defeat. Ever since then, for me at least, there's always been a fear that Newcastle will get slaughtered and you as a fan will be shown up. For me, that feeling was born on 4 May 1974 and still exists to this day. I'm rarely confident about our chances on the big occasion and usually feel that the only thing we've got going for us is the Newcastle support, with our passion, loyalty, dignity and defiance.'

He's so right. For 50 years, the fans have been Newcastle's greatest asset, drawing admiration from all quarters of the football world. But why on earth do we keep going? Is it fabulous devotion, blind loyalty or plain stupidity? Is defiance part of the Geordie DNA? All my mates see it as part of the price on the ticket. You're born a Newcastle fan, so you support the team. Don't get me wrong, we're not entirely uncritical. Just ask any Newcastle player who didn't give 100 per cent at St James' Park what sort of treatment he got from the fans. But when the occasion is bigger than the individuals involved, criticism of our own players can wait till we get back home. When we're on that big stage, we revert to type, and our support, as Sime says, is passionate, loyal, dignified and defiant. We sing our hearts out for the lads.

Following the cup final, the papers ripped into United. *The Mirror's* vitriolic columnist Frank McGhee ran a piece under the headline, 'What a load of rubbish – I wouldn't watch Newcastle if they were playing in my back garden'. And in his article, he wrote, 'Newcastle United should today be prosecuted under the Trades Descriptions Act for masquerading as a first-class football side.'

The game was famously Shankly's last as Liverpool manager. It is less well known that it was also Bob Moncur's last for Newcastle.

After 12 seasons and 343 appearances, the only man to lift a major trophy for United in the last 50 years called it a day and moved to Sunderland. But not before one last emotional day at St James' Park. 'I was dreading the homecoming,' he says. 'But we were absolutely staggered by the reception.'

As the train pulled through Darlington station, Moncur saw a young United fan with a banner saying 'We still love you' and cracked: 'That got the tears out of my system, but the others were in bits as we went through Newcastle on the open-top bus. Malcolm, Willie and lots of the lads were crying.

'At the ground, I really made the most of it. It was my last time on the pitch, and I remember doffing a black-and-white cap in front of the main stand like a farewell. It was very emotional.'

Supermac admits he was 'humbled' by the homecoming experience and is still amazed at the Geordie obsession with the FA Cup: 'It's a local phenomenon which you don't get anywhere else. It certainly didn't exist at Arsenal when I was there. It's peculiar to Newcastle, but it puts huge pressure on the players.'

Macdonald vowed he'd never leave till he'd helped to win something for the fans. He'd still be the star man at St James' Park for the next two seasons, and he'd come close to keeping his promise – but as every centre-forward knows, a miss is as good as a mile.

Frank Clark stayed on one more season before being handed a free transfer to Nottingham Forest. Remarkably, he went on to win the League Championship, League Cup and European Cup in one of the most sensational career twilights in the game's history. Thirteen years at Newcastle and he only had one Inter-Cities Fairs Cup to show for it; four years at Forest and his sideboard was creaking. Why could unfashionable Forest do it, yet we couldn't? Well, for starters, says Clark, they were managed by Brian Clough: 'Cloughie ran the whole thing with a rod of iron. The set of players I joined couldn't hold a candle to the players I'd just left at Newcastle, but Cloughie got the best out of them all, and everyone reached their maximum potential. Losing league matches like we did in the run-up to the cup final wouldn't have been tolerated. We weren't even allowed to lose testimonials! I had four very good years at Forest, but it hurts when people think I didn't have a career before that. I wouldn't swap my 13 years at Newcastle for anything.'

The cup-final experience left Joe Harvey in a state of shock. Some years later, he said, 'May fourth, 1974, will haunt me for ever. I felt sick and embarrassed. We never got started, and I can't understand it.'

If anything, he was even more shocked by the homecoming: 'Our supporters have moved me to tears on many occasions, most of them winning ones. But this time I knew they were entitled to show their anger, even disgust. They did no such thing. They gave us a heart-warming return which staggered me. I have never felt so humble.'

Humiliated one day, humbled the next. It was now 19 years since the last domestic trophy . . . 19 years and counting.

7

GORDON WHO? (1975–77)

'He was dull in a new way, and that made many people think him great.'

Samuel Johnson

Joe Harvey had one more season in charge. When he stepped down, loads of fans were pleased, saying he'd had his time and had failed to take Newcastle to the very top. That was true. The highest we'd finished in Joe's time was seventh, and the best we'd done in the FA Cup was one disastrous runners-up performance, while we'd consolidated our reputation as the lepers of the League Cup.

Joe *had* won a trophy, albeit not a trophy that the rest of the world seemed too impressed with. But Newcastle fans felt that the Fairs Cup win should have been a springboard to domestic success. The FA Cup final should have been the next peak on Newcastle's climb back to the football summit, but the humiliation we suffered at the hands of Liverpool was, instead, a dramatic fall from grace and the beginning of the end for Joe Harvey.

His final year was another season of desperate underachievement – 15th in the league and another FA Cup embarrassment. There was, however, a club best in the League Cup when we finally got to the dizzy heights of the fifth round (or the quarter-finals in old money). But even this was put into dismal perspective when we were knocked out after a replay by Chester City of Division Four.

The team was again in transition. Moncur had gone, replaced by a raw (some would say useless) centre-half called Glen Keeley. Full-backs David Craig and Frank Clark, who'd served more than a decade together, were supplanted by youngsters Irving Nattrass and Alan Kennedy. Micky Burns arrived from Blackpool in the close season, and there was a flurry of transfer activity before Christmas.

At least one of our players had managed to impress Liverpool at Wembley because Terry McDermott returned to his native Merseyside to wear a red shirt. In turn, Harvey had clearly been impressed by Burnley's Geoff Nulty in the semi-final – he came in as McDermott's direct replacement. Tommy Craig arrived from Sheffield Wednesday, slotting into the gap on the left side of midfield vacated by the injured Terry Hibbitt.

In December, we beat Southampton 3–1 over two legs to retain the Texaco Cup. This was our third trophy in eighteen months – two Texaco Cups and an Anglo–Italian. And there was you thinking Newcastle were an underachieving club.

The Nottingham Forest pitch-invasion drama during the previous season meant that we were banned from playing FA Cup ties at home for a year. So off we trooped to Maine Road to play Man City despite having been drawn at home. Happily, we won 2–0 with McFaul playing an absolute blinder. The City fans weren't pleased, so we travelled home with one of the windows missing on our coach. Ah, the joy of away trips in the '70s.

Obviously, if you can beat Man City on their own patch, then Third Division Walsall in the next round should be a doddle. Er, no. This is Newcastle we're talking about. We lost 1–0 in the mud, Macdonald was awful and Sime got chucked out of Fellows Park by the coppers for being the tallest person singing a rude song about the ref. Ten minutes later, he was back, having climbed over a wall with the rest of the evicted Geordies. Gluttons for punishment, all of them.

One of the most annoying things about Newcastle United – and believe me there are lots to choose from – is their knack of playing brilliantly when it doesn't really matter. Or, at least, shortly after it really *did* matter. Hereford was a classic example. Seven days later the team went and beat Man United at Old Trafford, which was fantastic but all we really wanted was a cup run or, at a minimum, to avoid national humiliation.

In 1975, we did it again. On a Wednesday night in February, nine months after the international humiliation of Wembley, we absolutely hammered Liverpool at St James' Park. Macdonald did what he said he'd do in the cup final, terrifying their defence and scoring two. The whole team was magnificent, and we won 4–1.

Don't get me wrong, it was a brilliant night, and I was dancing like everyone else. But you couldn't help feeling even more gutted about the cup final because we'd proved that we really *could* do it. The same thing would happen 21 years later against Man United when a 5–0 win would make us happy for a day but would never really undo the trauma of losing the Premiership title to them the season before. As everyone always says, 'Newcastle can beat anyone on their day.' Unfortunately, we just can't seem to beat anyone on the *big* day. There appears to be something in the fabric of the club that allows us to put on a big sideshow, but when it comes to the nitty-gritty of winning trophies, we bottle it.

The 1974–75 season petered out in alarming fashion, and we won just one of our last eleven league games to finish a miserable fifteenth. Chants of 'Harvey Out' were commonplace in the final weeks of the season. It was about this time that the *Match of the Day* opening titles included a banner draped on the new East Stand at St James' Park which stated simply, 'We Want Success'. Perhaps, after watching every Saturday night for a year, the message finally got through to the board.

Coach Keith Burkinshaw was sacked, and Joe Harvey resigned. At least that was the official version. Those who were there are adamant that Joe was sacked, but it suited the board to announce that it had been a bloodless and amicable severance.

Malcolm Macdonald was, and still is, furious at the decision: 'Joe Harvey *was* sacked, and we were horrified. I think it ranks alongside the FA sacking Alf Ramsey after the job he did. Only the year before, we'd got to the cup final. The one after that was a bad year, but you have to put it into context. Joe was no tactician, but he knew how to build a club, put together a side and work the transfer market. He was sacked by directors who should've known better.'

The *Chronicle*'s John Gibson agrees: 'It was very sad because that man had nothing but success on his CV. He'd won promotion, the Fairs Cup, got to Wembley and won the Anglo–Italian Cup. People laugh at that, but it was no mean achievement. Joe had no minuses, but any manager is vulnerable if he's been there a long time. In hindsight, it was a desperate decision, but, at the time, some people thought it was a good idea.'

Frank Clark recalls the fateful day: 'I was in the dressing-room after the last game of the season, just me and Burky. Joe came in and said, "It's bad news – we've all been sacked. I'm being moved upstairs, Burky, you've been sacked and, Frank, you've been given a free transfer." I couldn't believe it. The club had been in disarray when Joe took over in 1962. They were near the bottom of Division Two, they had a lot of poor players and they were £100,000 in debt, which was a serious amount of money in those days. He turned them round without spending a fortune. It was very sad the way it finished.'

For Frank Clark, it was the start of a glorious new chapter, but for Newcastle, it really was the end of an era. The statistics say that, domestically, Joe was a failure, but those of us who witnessed it will never forget the Fairs Cup victory. Thirty years after Joe Harvey's reign ended, it was still the only cup we'd seen Newcastle win. We never thought we'd say it, but by the standards of modern-era Newcastle United, Joe Harvey was a rip-roaring success.

For those of us who'd only ever known one manager at Newcastle, this was uncharted territory. There was an air of excitement and anticipation. Who would it be? Brian Clough? The best manager in the land had very strong North East connections. Lawrie McMenemy? He was making a name for himself at Southampton, and he used to go to our school! Or big Jack Charlton? A World Cup hero from 1966 and a Toon fan as a kid, he was performing minor miracles at Middlesbrough.

We couldn't have been more underwhelmed when the news came through that our new manager was to be Gordon Lee, who'd just won the Third Division Manager of the Year award for getting Blackburn Rovers promoted to Division Two. John Gibson broke the news to Supermac by phone, prompting the response, 'Gordon who?'

Lee had been a full-back with Aston Villa and Shrewsbury in the '60s. His first management job was at Port Vale, where he'd won the Fourth Division title before he moved to Blackburn. He was a dour kind of character with a broad Staffordshire accent and a face which was a cartoonist's dream. If I say some fans called him the 'human skull', you get the picture. He'd stay less than two seasons, but we'd never forget him. Lee would get results, but he'd alienate the fans with his style of football. He'd take us back to Wembley, but he wouldn't bring home a trophy. Worst of all, he'd sell Supermac, and then he'd walk out without finishing the job.

Nowadays, Gordon Lee spends his days playing golf near his home in Lytham St Annes on the Lancashire coast. It felt odd to be speaking to him 30 years later and asking him about his short and controversial reign at the club. I thought I'd hate him – he did sell my favourite player, after all. But he was quite charming, and all his answers seemed perfectly reasonable.

Lee has a clear recollection of what he thought about the

opportunity being put his way in the summer of 1975: 'Newcastle was a well-supported First Division club with potential, and I knew there was a chance for me to do well. They'd always been in the bottom half of the First Division – they'd enjoyed a few cup runs, but they'd never been successful, certainly not enough for a club of that size. For a club who were so well supported, they underachieved.'

Lee quickly worked out who was to blame for that state of affairs: 'The board had got used to that way of life. Staying in the First Division was the important factor for them. I never felt they had the ambition to be top of the table. Lord Westwood, Stan Seymour . . . they were an old-style board. They'd been there a long time, but their routine was staying up, and the cup was seen as a bonus. It had been like that at Newcastle for far too long.

'I tried to get them to think my way, but when it came to buying players, they were reluctant to compete with Man United and Arsenal. All right, they had to be careful financially, but there was a bit of fear there as well. This applied to transfers *and* wages.

'I remember Brian Clough visiting our training ground one time and saying we really should spend money on it. It was ramshackle, and it wasn't much better at St James' Park either.'

The main thing everyone associates with Lee's reign was his 'clash' with Malcolm Macdonald. Lee was quoted as saying he didn't want 'superstars' at Newcastle. Macdonald, quite naturally, took this personally. He was one of the most feared and flamboyant strikers in the game. At the end of the previous season, he'd scored five goals in one match for England against Cyprus, equalling the national record. He remains the only man to have scored five goals in one match at the old Wembley Stadium. So, if Newcastle had ever had a 'superstar', Mac was it. Macdonald v. Lee was a car crash waiting to happen.

Lee, however, denies ever uttering the infamous phrase. 'I can't ever remember saying those words,' he told me. 'I'd always thought the term "star players" was a misused phrase anyway. I believed in *good* players.

'On the pitch, I wanted to change the system. Macdonald had scored twenty goals a season for four years, and the club still seemed to be in relegation trouble. I genuinely believed that the club had the ability to win the title. That was all I was interested in, and it didn't matter who scored the goals.'

Lee insists that he and Macdonald got on fine from the start and results certainly seem to bear him out. Supermac started the new season like a man possessed, scoring eight goals in United's first six games.

Things were looking promising despite a number of unpopular transfers. Lee rubber-stamped Frank Clark's move to Nottingham Forest, signed the gangly striker Alan Gowling from Huddersfield for £70,000 and then sold Terry Hibbitt to Birmingham just a few weeks into the season.

But despite the grumbles, we were soon off on another adventure. Newcastle were finally going to shake off their League Cup jinx, and five months later, we'd all be heading off to Wembley once again.

The League Cup had now been in existence for fifteen years, and only once in that time had Newcastle got past the third round. But in round two, we were drawn at home to Southport, who were still in Division Four in those days. We hammered them 6–0, and new boy Alan Gowling scored his first goal for Newcastle. (And before the night was out, he'd scored his second, third and fourth goals for Newcastle.) In round three, we got a late equaliser at Bristol Rovers and won the replay. QPR in London was next, a match we won in some style, Macdonald getting his only goal of the League Cup campaign in a 3–1 victory. Notts County at home in the quarter-finals proved more difficult than it looked on paper, and our 1–0 win had a hint of good fortune about it. One of Supermac's more unusual talents was for taking prodigiously long throw-ins, and when the County keeper flapped at a Supermac special and knocked it into his own net, we were in the semis.

Sadly, I was missing out on all of this because, in the autumn of 1975, I'd flown the nest and gone to Liverpool University to study English. (The joke at the time was 'What's a Geordie doing studying English in Liverpool?') I would plan my weekend visits home around Newcastle matches – obviously – but these midweek League Cup ties were beyond me.

As 1975 drew to a close, we were in the semi-finals of the League Cup, but we were still decidedly average in the league, sitting in 12th place. No change there then. The two cups were different, however, and the next couple of months turned out to be cup-tie heaven with Newcastle progressing to the League Cup final and playing eight FA Cup ties before being knocked out in the quarter-finals.

First up was QPR in the FA Cup (won after a replay), and next came Tottenham in the two-legged League Cup semi-final. As luck would have it, my new best mate at university was a Spurs fan. (I'd been getting worried that there weren't any normal blokes at uni, but I breathed a sigh of relief after spending an afternoon talking to Geoff Fieldsend about football chants, flair players and our all-time England XI. These things are vitally important when you move away from home.)

I watched the highlights of the first leg of the semi on TV, and although we lost 1–0, I felt quite happy about it. So, it turns out, did Gordon Lee. He told me, 'As we walked off, I looked at the Spurs players, and I could tell they thought they were going to lose at our place. My players knew they were the better team.'

Geoff was more confident than his team's players, but Lee's prediction proved to be accurate. We tore into them at St James' Park with Gowling cancelling out their goal as early as the third minute after being set up by Macdonald's perfect through ball. (Supermac the provider? Lee's master plan was obviously working!) Glen Keeley and Geoff Nulty added goals in the second half to wrap up the game. Spurs got a late consolation, but we ran out convincing 3–1 winners.

I'd joined the Liverpool University Geordie Society, which seemed to exist purely to try to get Newcastle Exhibition Ale installed in the student union bar and to organise occasional away trips. The weekend after the Spurs game, we set off in a minibus to the FA Cup fourth-round game at Coventry. A great trip was spoiled by Coventry, who cancelled out Alan Gowling's opening goal and forced a replay. Once again, I missed the fun as we hammered them 5–0 at SJP.

However, two weeks before the League Cup final, we played another cracking FA Cup tie, and this time I was there. We were away to Bolton, and I made the journey from Liverpool with a good Geordie lad called Brian Hall from Washington. The match was a classic. There was a great old-fashioned cup-tie atmosphere, both in the pubs and in Burnden Park. There were 47,000 in the ground, and our lot filled the old uncovered away end. I somehow managed to meet up with my old school mates Mick Ramsey and Chris Baines (which was always a minor miracle in the days before mobile phones), and even today, we still talk about the 3–3 draw at Bolton.

Match of the Day was there to capture the drama, the highlight of which was a pair of superb Macdonald goals. Unfortunately, we still had a bit of a soft centre at the back, and a bloke called Sam Allardyce was among the three Bolton scorers that day.

Once again, I had to miss the replay at SJP on the Wednesday, but when it ended 0–0, a few of us decided to head to Elland Road, Leeds, which had been picked as the neutral ground for the second replay the following Monday. One of the lads from our Geordie Society was that very rare animal in 1976 – a student with a car. Mind you, it was a typical student's car, and the bonnet was raised a couple of times en route along the M62. It got us there eventually, though.

Elland Road was heaving with 43,000 inside and what seemed like another 5,000 outside, including us. We ran round and round the ground, trying to get in anywhere we could, only to be greeted by a procession of 'Ground Full' signs. We 'heard' the first goal (which, happily for us, was scored by Micky Burns) while we were queuing in the car park. We eventually gave up and headed back to Merseyside where we heard the good news. Alan Gowling had also scored, and we'd won 2–1 without the injured Supermac. Bloody hell. We'd become a real cup team! Five days later, the Geordie nation headed to Wembley once again – this time for the League Cup final against Manchester City.

The team had been too busy playing cup matches to get involved in the idle boasts which accompanied them to the FA Cup final of 1974. Malcolm Macdonald was older, wiser and more experienced this time and claimed he'd learned the lessons of two years earlier. He told the *Sunday Sun*:

> We are there to play football, and if I see one of our boys looking about them, they will get a rollicking from me. The time to look for your wife is when you have a winner's medal to show them. They can do what they like when they've got that, because being a loser at Wembley means nothing. Worse than that, it means failure.

However, he still managed to do his own impression of Muhammad Ali by predicting that he'd score the first goal in the tenth minute!

He was very confident that United's build-up was right this time. Ironically, City were based at the same Selsdon Park Hotel where Newcastle's preparations had gone so badly wrong two years earlier. Mac told the paper, 'Manchester City are building towards this final just the way we did in 1974, while our preparations are similar to Liverpool's . . . We have had no problems, Manchester City have had lots.'

That wasn't strictly true. Our skipper Geoff Nulty had broken his jaw against Bolton and was already out of the final. Tragically, so too was David Craig, who'd damaged knee ligaments against Liverpool. 'Craigie' was one of my favourite players, a classy full-back who'd missed the 1974 final in similar circumstances. Now here he was missing out again. Irving Nattrass and keeper Mick Mahoney were also carrying injuries. But even worse was the news that the club had been hit by a flu epidemic which put half of the team in bed. Six players were left behind when United travelled to London on the Thursday before the match. They eventually followed on in ones and twos.

I had a ticket for the game because my dad, God love him, had kept up my Newcastle United Bingo round when I went to uni. Good old Dad: he was only the slightest bit interested in football but still sold Newcastle Bingo tickets every week on the off-chance that I'd need to apply for a cup-final ticket!

It was an odd day for me. I caught the train down from Liverpool on my own and arrived in Euston, surrounded by Man City fans. I travelled to Wembley and looked in and around one of the big pubs near the stadium on the off-chance that I'd meet up with some of the lads. I saw Steve's brother-in-law but no sign of anyone else. I knew that none of my pals had a ticket for the section I was standing in but was cheered up when I saw a familiar face from Wallsend in a neighbouring pen. Ray Blackburn, a regular at our unofficial HQ, the Lindisfarne Catholic Club, climbed over the wall, and, at last, I had someone to talk to.

When the teams emerged, it was clear that the club had put the Lemsips to good use and had managed to patch up the squad, so we put out something like our first XI. But when Peter Barnes scored for City after 11 minutes, every Geordie in the ground must have thought, 'Here we go again.' However, Newcastle were in no mood to lie down, and their subsequent performance was a million miles better than the abject surrender we'd witnessed two years earlier against Liverpool.

Ten minutes before half-time, we got the moment we'd been waiting for. Macdonald burst past his man on the right-hand side of the box, whipped in a low cross and Alan Gowling stuck out a boot to deflect the ball past Corrigan and into the net. Cue mayhem in the black-and-white end – it was an emotional release of volcanic proportions. In that moment, all the expectation and frustration of '74 combined with the hopes and dreams of '76. My chest was bursting, my legs were 'pogoing' and my arms were punching the air. *We'd scored at Wembley!* It was as if a curse had been lifted and we could now go on and finally win a domestic trophy for the first time in 21 years.

Unfortunately, in that wacky Geordie way, there was to be a very cruel twist to the tale. Sixty seconds after half-time, we witnessed one of the most spectacular goals Wembley has ever seen. It was scored by a bloke from Newcastle – for Manchester City. Dennis Tueart, one of the heroes of Sunderland's 1973 FA Cup-winning team, performed the most acrobatic overhead bicycle-kick you'll ever see to put the ball into the bottom corner of our net. It was right in front of us, and I vividly remember my jaw dropping and uttering some profanity.

We never recovered, although we gave it a helluva good go. We went close on a number of occasions, but the flu epidemic took its toll, and by the closing stages, the players' legs had visibly tired. It had been a cracking game – in fact, it was acknowledged in some quarters as the best League Cup final to date. Both sides were adventurous and played good football. But only one team won the cup, and, once again, it wasn't us.

However, we'd purged some of the demons from our last trip to Wembley, and Gordon Lee echoed all our thoughts when he said afterwards, 'We ran out of steam in the second half, but we are going back to Newcastle with our heads up.'

Thirty years later, his pride is undiminished. When I contacted him, he told me, 'We knew it was a very important game for us. We went into it knowing we could win something and that it would also be financially good for the club. Walking out at Wembley was a wonderful feeling and a great experience for all of us. We were very disappointed to lose, but the big fact was that we got there. In my heart, I knew we weren't quite ready to be successful. We were a couple of players short.'

My mate Sime summed it up: 'We were unlucky to lose, and it was great to get some pride back. If we'd won that cup, our history might have been a bit different. But it was a kind of false dawn. In the end, all it did was put a Band Aid on the wound left by 1974 – and that was a very big wound.'

A week later, we played our FA Cup quarter-final at Derby County. The injuries incurred from playing eleven cup ties in two months had taken their toll once again. Mahoney, Nattrass and Tommy Craig were all missing, and their places were taken by a trio of youngsters: Eddie Edgar, Ray Blackhall and 'Rocky' Hudson. We lost 4–2, and our season had effectively ended in the space of seven days.

There was a huge backlog of fixtures to play in the league, and after a mixed bag of results, we ended up in 15th place, precisely where we finished under Joe Harvey the previous year. The next stage of the Gordon Lee plan needed to be put into operation, and we were about to witness the biggest casualty of all.

Supermac had now been at Newcastle for five seasons, playing two hundred and twenty-eight games and scoring one hundred and twenty-one goals. The season just ended was the first one where he hadn't been our top scorer. His total of twenty-five was eclipsed by strike partner Alan Gowling, who weighed in with an impressive thirty, with thirteen coming in the two cups.

Possibly, Macdonald felt a bit miffed that his position as the goal king of Newcastle had been usurped. It certainly made the manager smile – his philosophy that hard work would be rewarded appeared to have been vindicated. Lee told me, 'Alan Gowling was a wonderful team player. He made a major contribution to getting us to the League Cup final, and he scored more goals than Malcolm Macdonald.'

To say that Lee and Supermac were like chalk and cheese would be to neglect the fact that cheese begins with 'ch' and is occasionally hard and white (and, I daresay, a useful writing implement in the correct circumstances.) No, Lee and Macdonald were like chalk and jam. The only amazing thing was that they survived a season together.

When the news came in the close season that Newcastle had agreed to sell their superstar striker to Arsenal for £333,333, most of us were devastated but not totally surprised. Some accounts say that the seeds for the transfer were sewn on a close-season tour of Majorca when a clique of players who had the manager's ear developed the confidence to openly discuss Macdonald's role within the team. It seems the comments went further than the usual dressing-room banter, and the management team did little to stop it. As soon as he returned to England, Supermac was on his way.

When he left, he fired a parting shot at the boss, telling one paper that his first four years with Newcastle had been 'like a honeymoon', but 'After Gordon Lee arrived as manager, the honeymoon for me was well and truly over.'

When I asked Lee about the situation, he said, 'He had all the equipment to be a great player, and he should have played for England more, but he never made the most of his assets. You couldn't play to his feet, because he needed space to hit people on the break. So, when we started getting the better of teams, it didn't suit him.

'The problems started at the end of my first season when it became apparent he wanted to leave. He'd got his house up for sale before he came to see me. It was the easiest decision I've ever had to make, and we got over £300,000 for him.'

When I spoke to Macdonald, he, not surprisingly, saw it differently: 'They appointed someone with no track record at the top level, and we soon realised he'd never understand it as long as he drew breath. I kept my head down so there were no rows, but there were piss-takes. People like me, Paddy Howard, Terry Hibbitt, Tommy Cassidy, we knew the business, and we'd take the piss. His training sessions were childish in the extreme. They were fine if you were looking to impose a little bit of discipline in a secondary modern but utter stupidity for a First Division football team. Things that were said at those sessions would have us bursting into fits of laughter.

'One day, he told us, "I've just signed the new Bobby Moore!" It wouldn't have mattered who he'd brought in – there was only one Bobby Moore! He'd lifted the World Cup for England. I'd played with him, and I knew him. But the player he was referring to was Graham Oates. You never make comparisons – it's one of the most dangerous games you can play. It always rebounds on you.'

When I spoke to Alan Kennedy, he said that he was still finding his way in the professional game at the time and was uncomfortable at the clash between the manager and players: 'We didn't like the style at first and some rebelled, especially Malcolm and Terry Hibbitt. That wasn't good for the team, and Malcolm said too much at times.

'They used to call him "Leapy Lee", which I thought showed disrespect. [Leapy Lee was a one-hit wonder who had a chart hit called 'Little Arrows' in 1968.] I was always taught to be respectful to older people and people who you worked for. I fell out with Malcolm and Terry one time when I said, "You shouldn't talk to him like that, he's the manager." Terry Hibbitt just gave me a right mouthful.'

On the day Macdonald left, my mate Steve actually bumped into him at the Fox and Hounds pub on Westgate Road, which was close to the club's Benwell training ground. As Mac got up to leave with centre-half Paddy Howard, Steve – never slow at coming forward – handed Mac his season ticket. 'No thanks, I'm trying to give them up,' came the reply. Mac's tongue was almost as quick as his feet.

The Lee–Macdonald conflict was the talk of the Toon, but there was no doubt which camp most Newcastle fans were in. They'd had five years of goals from Supermac and were gutted to see him go. My mate Brendan Egan was one of many who stopped going to St James' Park after the transfer.

But Lee insists he'd do it again: 'Of course, I knew what the fans' reaction would be. Newcastle supporters love centre-forwards who score goals and wingers who beat people. They'll idolise whoever they want, but I knew – I was 100 per cent certain – that we'd be better off without him. Managers have to make decisions. You only get a job at a place like Newcastle because you know what the game's all about.'

There was another factor. Lee says he and others inside the club thought that Macdonald had a suspect knee and it was worth cashing in: 'I knew with the injuries he was getting that he wouldn't last another two years.' (Macdonald was forced into premature retirement three years later.)

When the dust settled, Lee's 'all-for-one and one-for-all' philosophy began to pay immediate dividends. Despite all the experts making Newcastle one of the favourites for relegation in 1976–77, we actually began the season playing slick, attractive and winning football. Micky Burns had been handed Mac's No. 9 shirt, but the goals were being shared throughout the side, just as Lee wanted.

'We were actually a better side without Macdonald,' Lee said. 'He'd been getting more money than the other players, and that's OK if you're winning. The others sensed that this was their chance to prove themselves.'

As December dawned, we were in third place, just behind Liverpool and Ipswich. Then United travelled to Highbury for a date with destiny – our first showdown with the new Arsenal centre-forward. Arsenal won 5–3, and, inevitably, Malcolm Macdonald scored a hat-trick.

Despite the surprisingly good league form, we quickly restored our noble tradition of escaping reasonably early from the League Cup. This time we got to the fourth round, and although there was no giant-killing involved, we still managed to exit in style, losing 7–2 to Man United.

In the FA Cup, we knocked out Sheffield United after a replay, setting up a fourth-round home tie with our League Cup final conquerors, Manchester City. However, all thoughts of revenge disappeared when Gordon Lee dropped his next bombshell. He was leaving.

The story goes that Lee had agreed to meet Everton officials after the game to discuss taking over from Billy Bingham at Goodison Park.

The bad news for Lee was that the news leaked out, and the mood turned nasty before the Man City cup tie. The game was held up by demonstrations and pitch invasions, and, not surprisingly, the players were affected by the atmosphere and duly lost 3–1.

Within hours of the final whistle, Lee was Everton's new manager, and we didn't know whether to laugh or to cry. To those fans who despised the man's dour personality and star-less football, it was definitely a case of 'Ding dong, the wicked witch is dead'. But to others, it was their worst nightmare – here we were at the business end of Division One for the first time in living memory and the bloke who got us there had walked out.

I felt angry on all those levels that football fans feel angry. First, we'd been dumped. Our manager was saying he wanted to manage Everton more than he wanted to manage us. Second, he'd dismantled our team and pissed off before he'd rebuilt it. Third, he'd sold my favourite player.

When I asked him about why he left mid-job, Lee told me, 'The main reason I left was because my kids were down here in Lancashire. We'd had to break the family up because of their schools situation. We'd left them behind [at boarding schools] and that was difficult for us. We spent a long time getting a house, and we never really settled. I wasn't actively looking to leave, but I knew I would go if I got the chance.'

But if Gordon Lee was a big family man, he was also very ambitious: 'Professionally, Everton were as big a club as Newcastle, and I thought I could do it again. Expectations were greater at Everton – they had had more success.'

The thought that he might have let us down didn't seem to have crossed his mind: 'I think I did very well at Newcastle United. The directors made it difficult for me at times – it was always a fight to get things like bonuses, etc., for players – but I did OK. We got to Wembley, and I got them into Europe and did good business, transfer-wise.'

There is a bit of mythology about Lee's last few months at Newcastle. The man himself says 'I got them into Europe'. In his excellent book *Forever Everton*, Stephen Kelly writes, 'He steered the north-eastern club to the League Cup final and a place in Europe . . .' And many United fans remember Lee as the bloke who 'got us back into Europe'. Well, that's not strictly true. Lee took the HMS *Newcastle United* halfway across the North Sea and then abandoned ship. OK, the ship was definitely on course for Europort when he jumped, but we were lying in seventh place and still had to play twenty-two more games. After his departure, we climbed back up to fifth, and only then did we qualify for the UEFA Cup (the fancy new name for our old Fairs Cup). But how we managed to finish in our highest league position for 26 years is one of the minor miracles of '70s football.

8

HARD TIMES (1978–82)

'The fans had to grin and bear it because the football was shocking at times.'

Alan Kennedy

What occurred after Lee left was completely farcical. If it happened today, the tabloids – and *Sky Sports News* – would have the club for breakfast.

Lee's deputy was a 35-year-old, quietly-spoken, former PE teacher called Richard Dinnis, and he duly took charge as caretaker manager while the board considered their options. Then, one of the strangest episodes in the history of the strangest club in the world began to unfold: the story of player-power. I spoke to Alan Kennedy, one of the players thrust reluctantly into the spotlight at the time, and asked him how it all came about. He told me, 'When Gordon Lee went to Everton, we all wondered "Who's next?" Some of the lads were bothered when he went – his lads, the ones he'd signed – but not the rest of us. But we did all agree that we wanted to keep Richard Dinnis.'

A players' delegation visited the home of chairman Lord Westwood and told him they wanted Dinnis to be given the job full time. The only other witness to this odd meeting was Stan Seymour, jun., son of 'Mr Newcastle' who had now retired from the board due to ill health. The story goes that Westwood agreed to their wishes, but when there was no official announcement within three days, the players decided to take matters into their own hands. The media gathered on the steps of St James' Park to hear Newcastle footballers issuing a statement publicly endorsing Dinnis and calling on the board to give him the job. But, instead, the board signed a new player (Ralph Callachan from Hearts) without involving the caretaker manager, and the players then issued *another* statement, this time issuing a vote of 'no confidence' in the directors. There were even veiled threats of a players' strike.

We watched the TV news in disbelief as the normally quiet Irving Nattrass, flanked by two other local lads, Kennedy and Paul Cannell, read out the statement which made our team the pride of the trade unions. But while having soft-voiced Geordie spokesmen standing up to the cameras made the exercise look very reasonable, there was something Machiavellian about the whole thing. Standing in the shadows were the real organisers, Geoff Nulty, Micky Burns, Alan Gowling and Tommy Craig.

Alan Kennedy was very definitely a reluctant front man: 'Alan Gowling and Micky Burns were more political than the rest of us. Look where they ended up – they both got involved in the Professional Footballers' Association [PFA]. Us young local lads were thrust to the front, but I didn't want to say anything. I was cringing. It's true that we all wanted Richard Dinnis, but us young lads were definitely being used.

'The chairman and the directors might have thought it was us who were behind it all, and, sure enough, we all left within the year. It was our strong feeling at the time, but I regret it now – we should have shown more sense.'

The unlikely militants soon got their way. Within 24 hours of the latest players' statement, Westwood made Dinnis 'acting manager' until the end of the season.

Of all the episodes in Newcastle's recent history of underachievement, this may well be the most bizarre. Our initial amusement at the players' humiliation of the directors was soon replaced by disbelief and anger. This sort of thing just didn't happen at successful clubs. It was a classic case of the tail wagging the dog and was doomed to end in failure. We'd known for some time that our long-established board of directors lacked ambition, but we'd now discovered they were also spineless, caving in under pressure from a group of pretty ordinary players. It was pretty obvious where the root of all our problems lay, and it wasn't on the football pitch.

As if to prove a point, the players then went on an 11-game unbeaten run (without the help of poor Ralph Callachan, the board's February signing, who wasn't wanted by Dinnis and consequently never got a kick). We finished fifth – our highest league placing since Jackie Milburn and his mates got to fourth in 1951.

It also meant that we were back in Europe, and, more importantly, Richard Dinnis got the manager's job. Still the club dithered over the appointment, and there was yet another very public boardroom row. Eventually, Westwood – who'd been won over by the acting-manager – got his way and gave Dinnis a two-year deal. The summer also saw a series of public disputes over player contracts, and the club's reputation took another battering. This airing of dirty washing in public has long been one of Newcastle's big problems and has clearly contributed to the instability which has so often beset the club. You'd think they'd learn, but, sadly, they never do.

One man who watched in disbelief at what was going on was former goalkeeper Willie McFaul, who'd moved onto the coaching staff after his retirement in 1975. He told me about one disturbing incident he witnessed in the summer of 1977: 'I went to Malta on a pre-season tour to help Richard Dinnis, and I just couldn't believe some of the stuff I overheard from the players. Some of them were actually talking about taking the club over! David Craig and I could hear these conversations going on around the pool. We couldn't believe it.

'When we got back, they refused to wear the kit provided by the new sponsors and refused to do pictures at the photo call. It got to the stage where a group of players were actually picking the team. I told Dinnis, "Look Richard, these guys got you the job. Now they're going to get you the sack. You have to pick the team yourself." It was getting completely out of hand.'

Alan Kennedy didn't agree that it had gone that far, but he did admit that some players had more sway than others: 'People like Alan Gowling and Micky Burns were very intelligent people, and they could articulate their opinions quite well. I'm sure they could have influenced team selection, but the team picked itself really.'

Player-power came crashing to earth in the 1977–78 season, the most desperate I'd witnessed to date. We won our first match, 3–2 at home to Leeds, but then lost our next *ten* to put us rock bottom of the league table. At the same time, we restored our proud tradition of being put out of the League Cup at the first stage by a club from a lower division, going down 2–0 at home to Millwall.

Our return to European football was equally unimpressive. After beating the Irish team Bohemians over two legs, we lost home and away to the French side Bastia from Corsica. The Dutch World Cup star Johnny Rep hit two fantastic goals at SJP as they cruised to a 3–1 win. Dinnis admitted that Bastia had given us a football lesson. Afterwards, he got the harshest lesson of all – he was sacked.

The players – despite being the chief culprits in this desperate run – were not happy with the manager's dismissal, but the board had had enough of player-power and weren't going to let them call the shots any more. Surely the time was now right to finally bring in a big-name manager with a proven track record of success. Clough and McMenemy both had North East roots and had both won trophies in recent years. However, there was an inevitability about the next managerial appointment.

Bill McGarry was hard. As a player, he'd even kicked people for England. His middle name was 'discipline'. If ever there was a knee-jerk managerial appointment at Newcastle, this was it. Twenty-seven years later we'd do it again with Graeme Souness, appointed primarily to sort out a supposedly 'unruly' dressing-room. Fat lot of good that did.

The players behind the revolt must have been bricking themselves. There'd be no picking the team, votes of 'no-confidence' in the board or talk of going on strike from now on. The men behind the Dinnis mutiny were swiftly moved on or silenced. Tommy Craig was gone by January, Gowling by March, while Burns and Nulty both moved at the end of the season. Local boys Rocky Hudson and Paul Cannell jetted off to try their luck in the North American Soccer League before the season was out, and Alan Kennedy got a dream move to Liverpool in the summer. Like McDermott before him, he'd one day make his mark on the European Cup final.

Unfortunately, the disciplinarian couldn't get any better results than the PE teacher, and apart from one brief run in December when we strung three wins together, we were never out of the bottom two. Alan Kennedy's memory of that time is just like mine: 'The fans had to grin and bear it because the football was shocking at times.'

At such times, the side changes from week to week, desperate signings are made, kids get pitched in and names appear on the team sheet which make grown men shudder for years to come. These were the Graham Oates years, the days of Andy Parkinson, Dennis Martin, Mike Larnach and Jamie Scott. A club record of 35 different players had a go at saving us from the drop in 1978, as compared to the 21 who'd got us to fifth place the previous season. You know you're in trouble when you use three goalkeepers and they all get into double figures on the games-played chart.

We were finally relegated along with Leicester City, a good ten points behind third-bottom West Ham – and this in the days of two points for a win. I remember watching the penultimate home game against QPR and thinking this really was the end of an era. The club had shut down the Leazes End so they could make a start on long-overdue ground improvements, and the team played with no heart, no guts and no character, meekly surrendering 3–0. The last home game was the following Wednesday against Norwich, and the faithful finally showed what they thought of the whole sorry mess. Just 7,986 turned up, Newcastle's lowest home gate for 40 years.

They were responding to these damning statistics of shame: the club's lowest-ever points total (22), fewest wins (6) and most defeats (26). Add to that our longest run without a win (21), record number of consecutive defeats (10), lowest number of home wins (4) and most home defeats (11). Oh, and I forgot to mention, we were knocked out of the FA Cup in the fourth round 4–1 by Wrexham of Division Three after a replay. I wanted to cry.

I'd now been a football fan for 12 years. For the first nine I'd only known one manager, one division (the top one) and one trophy (a European one). They say that you go to university to get experience, and that was certainly true for me. In three years, I'd experienced another three managers, lots of new grounds and dozens of new players, many of whom would appear in some of my worst nightmares for years to come. However, I still hadn't experienced the joy of winning a major domestic trophy, and I have to admit that, back in 1978, the prospect seemed a long, long way away.

At least I would be able to witness the curious world of the Second Division at close quarters. Having completed my degree, I was now back on Tyneside seeking gainful employment and standing on the Gallowgate End once again. (It had to be the Gallowgate – the Leazes End as we knew it no longer existed. There was now a low terrace with no roof at the other end of the ground. It looked awful, and it would stay that way for a long time.)

McGarry brought in a number of new players, the most significant being the return of Terry Hibbitt from Birmingham City and the £200,000 club-record signing of Peter Withe, who'd just won the league title with Nottingham Forest. So, while all his old mates at

Forest (including Frank Clark) were about to go and win the European Cup, Peter Withe committed himself to trying to get Newcastle out of Division Two. (He'd be rewarded with his own slice of European Cup final glory a few years later. Not with us, of course. That would have been ridiculous.)

Newcastle fans are quick to appreciate such personal sacrifices and quickly adopted Withe as the new hero of Gallowgate. Not long into the season he got himself an unlikely striking partner. Alan Shoulder was a North East fairy story. Like Jackie Milburn before him, he was a miner, working long hours at Horden Colliery and playing football in his spare time – in his case, for Blyth Spartans. Like Milburn, he made the jump from the pit to big-time football, but what was even more remarkable about Shoulder was that he was almost 26 before he was spotted. Also, it was more than 30 years since Jackie went from coals to goals, and that sort of thing just didn't happen any more.

At the same time as Shoulder arrived, McGarry also convinced West Brom midfielder Mick Martin to forsake European football and drop a division to come and lead our promotion fight. But when Martin arrived, the club was definitely still in the aftershock of relegation, and, apart from our 'little and large' double act up front, there was little to cheer us through the long, hard winter of Division Two. We were low on expectation and suitably low on delivery. A traditional exit at the first stage of the League Cup (away to Watford) was followed by a shock in the third round of the FA Cup when we actually *beat* Fourth Division Torquay 3–1. We then went out in the fourth round, losing to Wolves after a replay. The game at SJP was the first match I ever took a girl to. Poor lass – but at least she saw Peter Withe score a goal.

We finished the 1978–79 season in eighth place in Division Two. More significantly, 1978 saw the death of Stan Seymour, the self-styled Mr Newcastle who'd brought glory and chaos to the club in equal measure. Most fans my age couldn't stand him, but we were too young to appreciate that the bloke was a Toon legend. As a player, he'd won the cup and the league; as a manager, he was in charge for two of our '50s cup wins. He was also the man who overruled the manager who didn't pick Milburn!

However, much of our predicament could be traced back to his personal feud with Alderman Bill McKeag, a bitter battle that formed the eye of the storm which seemed to continually rage within the boardroom at Newcastle. That internal strife somehow defined the club as it stood in the late '70s – devastated and rudderless. By then, their places in the boardroom were occupied by their sons, Stan Seymour, jun., and Gordon McKeag. The fury may have dissipated but the incompetence hadn't. The decline of the previous few seasons had seen the advent of a rebel fans group – the Newcastle Supporters Association (NSA). For years, they were no more than an irritant to the long-established families who'd enjoyed power at St James' Park, but their day would eventually come.

McGarry almost did it the following season (1979–80). With a few astute if unspectacular signings, he moulded a team that was soon top of the Second Division table. At the end of January, we were looking good – top of the pile with sixteen games to go. But we crashed and burned in spectacular fashion – it was even more dramatic than Kevin Keegan's team's fall from grace in 1996. McGarry's team won just one of those sixteen remaining matches and eventually finished ninth. To add insult to injury, Sunderland were promoted.

It was the season during which our hatred for Sunderland was rekindled big style. We'd never liked them, of course, but they'd never really bothered us that much, mainly because we hardly ever played them. They've always had a habit of hiding in the Second Division whenever we've had a decent side. Poor Malcolm Macdonald, for example, would have filled his boots against Sunderland, but he never ever played against them for Newcastle.

In 1979–80, we played the Mackems four times. In the League Cup, we drew them in the second round. The first leg was at Roker

Park, and loads of us went over. I remember inventing a new insult for them, screaming 'southerners' at every opportunity. A few people near me smiled the first time, but I think it was wearing thin by the end. Still, the unlikely names of Peter Cartwright and Ian Davies etched themselves into Geordie folklore by scoring our goals in a 2–2 draw. Job more or less done, we thought. Wrong.

At SJP, it was the same score, Alan Shoulder and Stuart Boam getting the goals. Enter the penalty shoot-out. As far as I can remember, this was my first experience of the dreaded 12-yard lottery, and I don't remember enjoying one to this day. Newcastle are crap at penalty shoot-outs, though we didn't know it on the night of 5 September 1979. We lost something like 7–6, and Jim Pearson went down in history as the bloke who missed the vital penalty against Sunderland. It was his last-ever kick for Newcastle – poor sod. (I always had sympathy for Pearson as I distinctly remember some seasoned professionals refusing to step up and be counted that night.)

Revenge was gained at SJP on New Year's Day when we gave them a right going over and won 3–1 thanks to another goal from Peter Cartwright (the boy from North Shields was developing a very good habit), a penalty from Shoulder and an absolute raker from Tommy Cassidy which flew in from about 30 yards. The match has gone down in North East folklore – both sets of fans sing a version of 'Hark! The Herald Angels Sing' which ends with ' . . . and we will fight for evermore, because of New Year's Day'. *This* was the New Year's Day in question. What a way to start the new decade. (It was also memorable for the complete and utter drunken state that Sime got into. I have never seen him so close to oblivion, and I've seen him very close to it on many occasions.)

The final encounter with the great unwashed of Wearside ended in a 1–0 defeat at Roker, thanks to a midget in white boots called Stan Cummins. But the good news is that it was the last time we'd ever lose at 'Joker Park'.

When I asked Mick Martin about the problems at Newcastle in

that era, the spectacular crash of 1980 was still fresh in his mind: 'Sunderland were second when we beat them on New Year's Day, and we went about seven or eight points clear at the top. It was shattering watching what happened after that.

'Everybody blames everybody else, but certainly the club were not ambitious enough. They were always happy to sell someone who'd bring in a bit of money. They'd sell someone for £250,000, but they wouldn't spend £300,000 on a replacement. They'd rather get two new players for £80,000. They were nice enough people, but they were not aggressive business-wise in the boardroom. It seemed so obvious – you only had to look at the gates. If you could get success, you'd double the gates at Newcastle.'

The FA Cup saw another one of our, by now, almost ritual humiliations. We lost 2–0 in the third round at home to Chester City of the Third Division. We were abysmal. And one of their goals was scored by a gangly kid with a big nose called Ian Rush. (The kid, not the nose.)

The upshot of all this was that McGarry, from being within touching distance of hero-status, was now hated even more because of the manner in which we'd caved in. And his predicament had been magnified ten times over by the fact that the Mackems had been promoted. It was now 25 years since our last domestic trophy. He had to do something special the following season or he was out.

Guess what? He was out.

McGarry started the close season by losing his best player. Peter Withe couldn't be blamed for wanting First Division football again, and we made a hefty profit when he went to Villa for £500,000. Withe would immediately win another league title with his new club and then score the winner in the European Cup final the following season. How he must have regretted leaving the Toon!

By now I was a season-ticket holder. Mick Ramsey and I had taken the plunge the previous season, investing in tickets for the paddock in front of the East Stand, not a million miles from where I'd watched the Inter-Cities Fairs Cup final back in 1969. Standing tickets, of course.

Newcastle kicked off the new season with a blue star on their shirts (due to the club's first-ever shirt-sponsorship deal with Scottish & Newcastle breweries) and the dream-ticket front three of Ray Clarke, Billy Rafferty and Bobby Shinton. You can guess the rest. When the first league tables were produced on 23 August, United were bottom of Division Two with one point from three games. Since the euphoria of the Sunderland game on New Year's Day, we'd won just two league games in 1980. Next up was the dreaded League Cup, and when, true to form, we were knocked out on away goals by Fourth Division Bury, McGarry got the bullet.

It was hard to find anyone with any sympathy for McGarry. I asked John Gibson, but his verdict was damning: 'Bill McGarry was a disaster. He could knock down a wall, but the problem was he couldn't build a new one in its place.'

Mick Martin was less critical and also made a pertinent point about managers and the Geordie faithful: 'In the end, there was a bit of a campaign to get rid of him, but, then again, there's always a campaign to get rid of the manager at Newcastle!'

Joe Harvey, who'd been moved upstairs, popped back down for a couple of games – which we promptly won – while the board lined up McGarry's replacement. Still we craved a Brian Clough or a Bobby Robson, but the club managed to gobsmack us once more by appointing Arthur Cox of Chesterfield.

For the fans, Cox was hard to love. First of all, it turned out he'd been coach to Sunderland's 'famous' 1973 FA Cup team, not a good calling card for those of us with black-and-white blood. Second, he was a miserable-looking bugger with a dour Midlands accent.

The new boss set about putting his stamp on the side, but it wasn't an easy task. He was our fifth manager in six years, and he was working with the remnants of three previous regimes. The chart which shows the players used that season looks like a patchwork quilt, perfectly illustrating what was going on. Cox was chopping and changing players and positions, desperately trying to find a formula that worked. Perhaps the most significant entry is for 22 October in a match against Shrewsbury in which the new manager blooded a young sausage-factory worker turned footballer called Chris Waddle at centre-forward.

The New Year also brought a mini FA Cup run with Waddle the man of the match in our third-round win over Sheffield Wednesday. Next we beat Luton at home and then got another home draw against Exeter City. This was more like it. We cheered up enough to invent a cup song for Arthur Cox, who had just been named Manager of the Month. But with his gruff sergeant-major demeanour and crew cut to match, he wasn't exactly pop-song material. Appropriately, we nicked 'Sgt. Rock (Is Going To Help Me)' by XTC, which became 'Arthur Cox Is Going To Wem-bley'. He wasn't, of course, and well we knew it, but just to confirm it, we got a severe dose of FA Cup-itis when Exeter came to town and did the time-honoured thing. A goal five minutes from time gave them a well-deserved 1–1 draw at St James' Park, and we then travelled all the way to the other end of the country to get hammered at the *other* St James' Park.

Where were you when we got beat 4–0 at Exeter City? I was at a shorthand class. Yes, a shorthand class. I was now a trainee journalist with the *Shields and Wallsend Weekly News*, and trainee journalists have to do these things. Three of us were in the Whitley Bay suburban home of a very nice old chap called Mr Price trying to work out the finer points of Pitman New Era when one of us muttered something along the lines of 'Wonder how the Toon are getting on?' Always ready to oblige, Mr Price switched on his transistor radio (no doubt after making us take down a fictional speech by a fictional borough surveyor at speeds of up to 40 words per minute), and we heard the grim news. We were 3–0 down at half-time. It finished 4–0. Newcastle United was fast becoming shorthand for 'FA Cup disaster'.

We finished 11th but don't be fooled – we were six points off a relegation place. This was the infamous season when our top scorer was Bobby Shinton with seven goals. No wonder then that our average crowd dropped below 20,000 for the first time since the outbreak of the First World War. One day they'll build a memorial to the 17,350 unsung heroes who made the fortnightly pilgrimage. 'Above and beyond the call of duty' the inscription will read. Dear reader, I was one of those soldiers.

Why did we go back the next season? Why do we always go back? Mick's opinion is typical of most fans: 'There are lots of reasons: habit, genuine devotion and a fear that if you stay away, you'll miss something special. Having said that, if someone said that Newcastle would definitely win a trophy next season but only if I stayed away, I wouldn't go within a mile of the place. The club winning is far more important than me being there to see it.'

But no one made such a promise back in 1981, so Mick and I rolled up yet again for another season with expectations set suitably low. However, things got slightly better. Chris Waddle was now a regular up-front, playing alongside our new centre-forward – Imre Varadi from Everton. Varadi was quick, and he scored goals, which was a bit of a novelty at that time. He was soon dubbed 'Olive' by the Gallowgate End (work it out) and even got his own song, courtesy of an Elvis Costello tune: 'Olive Varadi is here to stay!' Post-punk irony hits SJP.

Unfortunately, our new-look strike force had little impact in the cups. The League Cup was sponsored for the first time and was now the Milk Cup, and we appropriately bottled it at the first hurdle. We were beaten by Fulham, who were on their way to promotion from Division Three under their new bright young manager. His name? Malcolm Macdonald. Oh, how football is laced with such rich irony.

We *did* win an FA Cup third-round match against lower-league opposition, beating Colchester United of Division Four 4–3 on their own patch (after a replay *and* extra time). But then we were knocked out at home by Grimsby Town, who were a very average Division Two side. But, then again, we were also a very average Division Two side, so we couldn't really grumble.

League form was erratic, and we eventually finished ninth with sixty-two points. This was actually the highest points total in our history – but, then again, they had just introduced three points for a win!

The Geordie faithful were in a state of gross disillusionment, and crowd levels were pretty alarming. Just 9,419 turned out for the last, meaningless, home game of the season against Wrexham. Something had to be done. But not even the most optimistic Newcastle fan could believe what happened next.

9

KEVIN (1982–84)

'I was standing waiting to kick off, and I was in a daze – there was Kevin Keegan playing in the same team as me!'

Chris Waddle gets caught up in the excitement

Even by Newcastle United standards, 19 August 1982 was an extraordinary day. Arthur Cox started talking in sound bites. 'You don't win the raffle if you don't buy a ticket,' he said. But even the dour sergeant-major's sudden burst of quotable prose was trumped by the headline-inspiring verse uttered by our usually unobtrusive club secretary Russell Cushing. 'We're in heaven – we've got Kevin,' he said. Cue explosion of flash bulbs and jaws dropping to floor level as England's most famous footballer entered the press conference at the Gosforth Park Hotel.

Kevin Keegan. Yes, Kevin Keegan! Twice European Footballer of the Year, the England captain, the reigning top scorer from Division *One* and the bloke who destroyed us in the 1974 FA Cup final – but we were prepared to forgive that minor indiscretion because . . . he was signing for *us,* and he was only costing £100,000.

It was nothing short of miraculous. Here we were, four years in Division Two and still no sign of being able to get out of the damn thing, and the nation's top player wanted to join us. Was he completely mad? Fortunately, he'd put pen to paper before his advisers had been able to contact the psychiatric unit at the Royal Victoria Infirmary, and he was now an honorary Geordie.

I'd never been able to work out how Arthur Cox pulled off this miracle. Throughout his two spells at Newcastle, as manager and coach, he'd always struck me as dour and uninspiring, yet everyone who knew him well (especially Keegan) spoke incredibly highly of him. But I never got it. Not until I spent an hour chatting to him on the phone while researching this book. The bloke is just about the most committed football person I've ever spoken to, and I could happily have talked to him all day.

This is Cox's account of how he bagged the most famous player in the country for a midtable Second Division side: 'At the end of my first year, I arranged to have a meal with Harry Swales, Kevin's agent. I took Joe Harvey with me, but neither of them had a clue why we were meeting. After the meal, I told Harry, "Look, I've got the best supporters in the country and a massive club. I want a player to do for us what Dave McKay did for Derby County. I want Kevin Keegan to come to Newcastle but only when the time is right. And if this gets out onto the street, forget it. I don't want anything improper going on. You call me when you are ready."

'Next close season, I saw one or two reports that Kevin might be going here or there, so I rang Harry and said, "What's happening?" There was lots of publicity about other clubs being interested, especially Man United and Sunderland. Things developed from there, and the rest is history.

'Nobody in our boardroom knew anything about this until I asked to see them. One or two thought I was pulling their legs, but I said to them, "You support me and it will happen." So, along with Mr Seymour, Russell Cushing and Alastair Wilson of S&N breweries, I met Kevin Keegan in the Swallow Hotel in London. I told him at the start of the meeting, "Nobody leaves here until you sign for Newcastle United." He said he couldn't stay long because he wanted to watch his horse run later that day! I said, "That's fine, just sign before you leave!" He went off to discuss personal sponsorship terms with Alastair Wilson, and I said, "The pressure is on you, Alastair – it's all up to you." Little did he know, Kevin had already shaken hands on the deal with me and the board!'

Keegan, it seems, had only talked to two clubs once he'd decided to leave Southampton – Man United and us. The Newcastle delegation played a blinder and convinced Keegan to come 'home'. It turned out that Kevin's grandfather Frank Keegan had been a miner in County Durham. And more than that, he'd been a hero in the West Stanley colliery disaster of 1909.

Keegan was born and raised in Doncaster, but his dad Joe taught him 'The Blaydon Races' and told him all about Jackie Milburn and Hughie Gallagher. As Kevin himself said in his autobiography, 'Your roots are your roots, and there was a tremendous pull, an inevitability about me coming at some stage to Newcastle United. It was always going to happen, and now it had.'

It certainly had, and if we were shocked, imagine how the players felt. They were on a pre-season tour of Madeira, blissfully unaware of what was going on back home. Mick Martin told me that, as club captain, he was the first to be told: 'We were in the hotel, and I got a call from Mr McKenzie, the director, asking me to come up and have a chat with him in his room. I went up, and he told me they were signing Kevin Keegan the next day. I was shocked – it had come completely out of the blue, and I hadn't heard so much as a whisper about it.

'The next day, Arthur Cox called me from England – he hadn't come to Madeira as he was trying to tie up the transfer – and he told me that part of the deal was that Kevin would be captain. It didn't bother me in the least – my attitude was that it didn't matter if it helped us to get promotion.'

Chris Waddle is another former United great I spoke to. He said the players were incredulous at the news: 'When Kevin's name was mentioned, we started laughing. We were convinced it was a wind-up. He was captain of England! What did he want coming to play with us?'

Mick Martin confirms that the man was as good as the myth: 'When we finally met, Kevin spoke to me and said he wasn't the best captain in the world and hoped I'd still help out. I told him we were all captains on the pitch – and we became friends.'

Actually we *all* became friends with Kevin, every Newcastle supporter on the planet. We were in a state of complete shock, and, of course, we were counting the days to the start of the season. We didn't have long to wait. Nine days after he signed, he led out the team for the first game of the season, a home match against QPR.

The game was a sell-out with 35,718 squeezing into the underdeveloped, partly closed-off SJP. The crowd was immediately more than double last season's average, something Keegan had been smart enough to predict. It turned out that he'd negotiated himself 15 per cent of any increase in Newcastle's attendances. Clever boy. But we didn't give a damn about that – he was here, and he was playing for us.

The atmosphere was sensational with Keegan's name ringing out around the ground for almost an hour before kick-off. When Keegan emerged from the tunnel with his teammates in tow, the place went barmy.

By a complete stroke of luck (or else fate was finally rewarding us for our long-suffering and dedication), shortly before Keegan arrived, Mick and I had upgraded our season tickets to seats in the East Stand. I can still remember my seat number: G133. And that was my vantage point for a little slice of Newcastle United history as Kevin Keegan marked his debut by scoring the only goal of the game at the Gallowgate End. We went mental. We love our heroes at St James' Park, and it had been a long time since we'd had one.

'They are far and away the best supporters in the land,' Keegan said afterwards. 'I've enjoyed the roars of the Liverpool Kop, but I've never known anything like today. It was stereo with four speakers. In that split second when I was on my way to scoring, I knew I dare not miss. It was the proudest day of my life.'

We won our next game 2–1 away at Blackburn, and Keegan scored again, along with Mick Martin. However, Martin told me that the match served as a rude awakening for our superstar striker: 'Division Two was a culture shock for Kevin. I remember at Blackburn we spent the entire second half camped in our own half lumping the ball forward. Kevin came into the dressing-room at the end and said, "I can't be doing with that all season!" He just wasn't used to it.'

Cox had admitted to Keegan that we weren't a good side but was confident that the new captain could provide the catalyst that was needed to finally launch us back into the top division. And at the end of September, there was a reunion which would make Kevin feel a little more at home. Eight years after leaving for Liverpool, where he and Keegan had helped win the European Cup amongst other odd bits of silverware, Terry McDermott rejoined the Toon.

His first match back couldn't have been better scripted. *Match of the Day* picked our away game at Rotherham for its once-in-a-blue-moon trip into the Second Division. It was easy to see why. The cast list was vintage Liverpool. Keegan and McDermott would be doing battle against their old mate Emlyn Hughes, now captain of Rotherham. We battered them 5–1, and Keegan scored four. This was the stuff of dreams. We just didn't win away matches – let alone 5–1. In fact, I remember one of my mates was on holiday in Crete at the time, and when he asked a bloke with an English newspaper how Newcastle had got on, the bloke told him, 'Won 5–1, mate.' Pete's response? 'Piss off. What was the real score?'

But now it seemed anything was possible. The pied piper had well and truly arrived, and everyone wanted to dance to his tune. A week later, the ex-Man United midfielder David McCreery arrived. He would prove to be a vital cog in the promotion wheel.

I had become a 'long-distance' supporter by 1982, travelling up from Darlington for home matches. Just as Keegan was making the switch from Southampton to Newcastle, I moved from the *Shields and Wallsend Weekly News* to the *Darlington Evening Despatch*. I was now a qualified journalist, and writing for a daily paper was a big deal at the time. Under previous circumstances, the 35-mile journey to home games may have been a bit of a hike, but in these new crazy days of St Kevin, it was more like a pilgrimage.

I even got to meet the great man on an unusual assignment. Keegan had agreed to open a new swimming pool for a special-needs school near Darlington, and I got the job of covering the story for the *Despatch*. He was everything the pre-publicity said and more. Not only did he declare the pool open, but he even borrowed a pair of swimming trunks from one of the teachers so he could have a swim with the kids. The photographers loved it! I got ten minutes for a one-on-one with him afterwards, and whether he was talking about the school or football, he was brilliant.

Alan Oliver has been the main Newcastle man at the *Evening Chronicle* since 1977. When I talked to him about his time covering the Toon, he was quick to flag up the Keegan years: 'We were going nowhere till Kevin Keegan came – he changed it all. On and off the field, he was sensational. He was captain of England, and we'd never had anyone like that before. I was an unknown journalist, but suddenly I was getting calls from all over the world, simply because Kevin Keegan was at Newcastle. Nobody in modern times has had as much influence on Newcastle United as Kevin Keegan, and he's done it twice. They were amazing days.'

But it wasn't all sunshine and light. Keegan announced his international retirement after being unceremoniously dropped from the England squad by the new national manager Bobby Robson. And his arrival also seemed to have a negative effect on young Chris Waddle, who looked a bit like a rabbit caught in the headlights. Waddle told me he was a victim of Keegan mania: 'I got caught up in it, like everybody else. I was 22, but I was new to football. I was used to smaller crowds, and suddenly we were playing in front of 34,000 every week. And I thought I had to give the ball to Kevin Keegan every time I got it!'

His form suffered, and Waddle was dropped by Cox. I have a fantastic memory of an away game at Oldham when Waddle showed that he was basically just one of the lads. En route to the match, we pulled into Hartshead Moor services just past Leeds on the M62. On the way into the toilets, I bumped into my mate Chris Baines, who had a huge grin on his face. He said, 'Chrissy Waddle's in there, and he's mortal drunk!' Sure enough, our boy-wonder winger was out with his mates on an away trip and was obviously under pressure to keep up on the lager front. He was struggling. When we got to Boundary Park, he popped up again at the front of a conga dancing along the terraces.

Surprisingly, he remembers it well: 'I'd been left out, so I was at home when my mates pulled up at 9.30 in a minibus and shouted, "Howay, we're gannin to the match." I jumped in, and, of course, we had a few beers in the back. It was a good day out – the fans started putting scarves and hats on me, and I remember going to the fence at the front when our keeper Kevin Carr had come to get the ball. I shouted, "Howay, Carrsey – sort it out, man!" I could see him telling the lads, "Look, Waddler's in the crowd!"

'Anyway, Arthur Cox pulled me in on Monday and asked where I'd been on Saturday. I said I'd been at a local game, but he knew I'd been at Oldham – he just couldn't prove it.'

Cox also remembers it well: 'After the Oldham game, I gave him a strong talking to. I asked him, "You'd rather be on the terraces than on the pitch? You'd rather be with the punters than with the players, eh?"'

Cox then gave Waddle the fright of his life by telling him, truthfully, that Brighton wanted to take him on loan. Waddle quickly learned the errors of his ways, although Cox admitted to me that he still regrets just how tough he was on him at times.

Keegan or no Keegan, we still couldn't make any headway in the cups. We were hammered by Leeds in the Milk Cup and then lost to Brighton in a third-round FA Cup replay. I would never blame a ref for us not winning a trophy, but there are fans of a certain age who hyperventilate at the name of Trelford Mills, an alleged referee who managed to disallow not one but *two* Newcastle goals in injury time. Brighton went on to reach the FA Cup final, losing to Man United after a replay.

We missed promotion by three points that season, finishing in fifth place. And if Keegan hadn't picked up a freak injury in a testimonial game, which caused him to miss five games mid-season, we might just have made it.

Keegan was only on a 12-month contract, but he'd been bitten by the bug and agreed to sign up for another season, although not before getting assurances from the board. As he told the *Chronicle*'s John Gibson, 'I'm not holding a gun to their heads, but I want to see some movement from the club. I want to play with a better all-round squad next season so we gain more success. It's as much for the benefit of the fans as for myself. They deserve so much after all this time.'

At last, someone at the club understood us.

And so, in the summer of 1983, we started our sixth attempt to get promotion. Arthur Cox worked hard on the fine tuning, controversially selling Imre Varadi and Mick Martin. Several new faces arrived, but the biggest surprise and best signing came from the other side of the Atlantic.

Peter Beardsley was a local lad who had played for Wallsend Boys Club. He'd once had a trial with Newcastle, but we let him go. (A brilliant decision we'd repeat with a kid called Alan Shearer some years later.) Somehow he'd ended up at Vancouver Whitecaps in the North American Soccer League via Carlisle and Man United. But now he was coming home to Tyneside to link up with Kevin Keegan.

Beardsley didn't actually join us until half-a-dozen games into the season, but his arrival sparked lift-off. We won six games off the belt, charged up to second in the league and Beardsley was an instant hero. The fans loved him. He could dribble for England (and later did). Chris Waddle was also playing out of his skin, and with these two in the same forward line as Kevin Keegan, we were irresistible. One game against Manchester City summed it all up. They were serious promotion contenders, but we ripped them to bits, beating them 5–0 with Beardsley scoring three and Keegan and Waddle one each. This was as good as anything I'd seen in my 18 years as a Newcastle fan, and everyone was on a permanent high all season.

Even first-round knockouts in both cups didn't seem to dampen our enthusiasm, although losing over two legs to Oxford United in the Milk Cup would normally have resulted in ridicule and general grumpiness. The FA Cup, however, put us in the national spotlight and had more significant consequences than simply our annual early exit.

We were drawn away to Liverpool. Kevin was going back to Anfield, and, of course, the media couldn't resist it. It was on a Friday night, and it was live on the BBC. Being a cup tie, we got a 25 per cent ticket allocation, so the place was swarming with Geordies. Unfortunately, our penalty area was swarming with Liverpool players, and they stuffed us 4–0. But the significant moment came when Kevin Keegan slipped past Mark Lawrenson and set off for goal. Keegan was mortified to find that in the space of about ten yards Lawrenson had not only regained the ground but had won the ball back off him. It was a defining moment for Keegan, and he realised it was time to quit.

And so it was that a month later, on his 33rd birthday, Kevin Keegan announced that the 1983–84 season would be his last in professional football. We knew then that we'd better get promotion this time or else we might be down in the Second Division for ever.

After Keegan's announcement, we stormed to promotion, finishing third behind Chelsea and Sheffield Wednesday. Our cause had been helped by the arrival before Christmas of Glenn

Roeder, a classy central defender from QPR, who gave our defence a lot more assurance. Keegan, Waddle and Beardsley scored a fantastic 66 goals between them, Keegan leading the way with 28. The dark days of 'Shinton, seven' were a dim and distant memory. Thank God.

Criminally, I wasn't there on the day we clinched it. It's a long story, but in short, it was all down to Elton John and a woman – not a sentence you read very often. Suffice to say, the woman and I didn't last, and every time I hear Elton John, I want to vomit bone marrow.

Fortunately for me, the extended carnival continued the next Saturday when Brighton and *Match of the Day* came to town for Kevin Keegan's last ever game of professional football. It was an amazing atmosphere with a typical swashbuckling performance from Newcastle. We won 3–1, and, of course, Kevin scored and so did Waddle and so did Beardsley. Beardsley's goal was unbelievable and is one of my favourites of all time.

But the day belonged to Kevin. After the final whistle, despite being submerged by fans at the mouth of the players' tunnel, he took a microphone and issued a typically heartfelt Keegan message to the supporters who'd been with him on the last leg of his fantastic football journey. We couldn't see him, but we could hear him, his voice cracking with emotion as he said his piece. He'd done what he said he'd do, and we were truly grateful. We were back in the big time, with average gates of just under 30,000 – the third best in the country that season.

The carnival wasn't quite over. A few days later, Keegan had a 'farewell' match against Liverpool to give him a proper send-off – and to raise money for the new players we'd need in the First Division. Not too many people remember the match but everyone remembers Keegan's departure. He left the pitch in a white helicopter, taking off from the centre circle with everyone waving goodbye as he disappeared into the night sky, turning his back on professional football for ever. Or so he thought.

10

OLD WAYS (1984–88)

'Fly away Peter, fly away Paul.'
Nursery rhyme which predicted the transfers of
Beardsley and Gascoigne but forgot to mention
Chris Waddle

It's impossible to underestimate Kevin Keegan's contribution to Newcastle United in the seasons 1982–83 and 1983–84. The club was going nowhere when he arrived and was back where it belonged when he left – in the top flight of English football.

When I asked Arthur Cox to sum up what Keegan the player meant to the club, he put it very simply: 'He was the catalyst, and that club has to have a catalyst.' This tells you as much about Cox as it does about Keegan. Like Keegan, Cox understood the club and its fans. He was the one who had the mad, but brilliant, idea to go out and get Keegan in the first place, and now he had to manage without him. Life after Kevin was not going to be easy.

There was a very telling comment from Keegan in the Tyne Tees Television programme which was made to celebrate the promotion season. Right at the end of *Going Up* he says, 'Now is the time to go into debt because they have got a great chance. With three good signings, this club could not only go into the First Division and hold its own, it could challenge everyone bar Liverpool and Man United.'

Keegan was not only a great footballer, he was also an astute businessman, for example, the '15 per cent of the gate' arrangement which he'd negotiated for himself when he first joined. He knew what the club needed at the start of our first season back in the top division, but I suspect he also knew what the club was like at heart.

Just about everyone I've spoken to in connection with this book said the same thing about the board of directors during this era and the one which preceded it. Malcolm Macdonald said, 'We always felt they were small time. That seemed to be the outlook in the boardroom. They wouldn't go the extra penny. If there was an extravagance to be had, it was one which suited the board of directors, but it wouldn't be a professional extravagance.'

Bob Moncur agreed: 'In our day they were quite happy to accept second best. The club lacked ambition, and the directors were less inclined to take risks. They bought Jimmy Smith with the money they made from the Fairs Cup but only because they were due to pay corporation tax. They bought Jinky rather than give the money to the taxman!'

Alan Kennedy also spotted a lack of drive: 'We were getting big crowds, regardless of the way we played, but the board sat on their policy of not investing too much in the club. We knew we were never going to challenge Leeds or Liverpool. The board were nice men, but they were not willing to see the future.'

Mick Martin felt they couldn't see the wood for the trees: 'As a club I always thought they were not strong enough or determined enough to build on what they had. They probably didn't know what they had – perhaps the knowledge wasn't there. The ambition certainly wasn't.'

And ambition was the key. Arthur Cox, it seems, had certain plans for the assault on Division One. The board obviously had other ideas.

Perhaps they didn't believe Cox could do it without Keegan. Perhaps Cox didn't believe *the club* could do it without Keegan. Whatever the reason, it became clear that there was a dispute going on from the moment we won promotion. But, of course, this was Newcastle. When we should have been building for the bright new dawn, the house came tumbling down around us. Twelve days after the season ended, Cox resigned.

Clearly a man of principle, Cox explained to me precisely what went on that summer: 'I'd thoroughly enjoyed those four years, but I didn't feel the directors respected what we'd achieved. They had asked me what the plans were, so I said I wanted the following three players: Steve Bruce, Kevin Sheedy and Mark Hately. They were all gettable; there would have been no problems signing them. But we never got round to talking about transfers.'

The reason for that was the board's reluctance to give Cox the contract he felt he deserved. 'When I first joined Newcastle, I met the board for 15 minutes,' he told me. 'They offered me a four-year contract on the spot. In my fourth season, we got promoted with all tickets sold for home games, and then they offered me a three-year contract. I said, "No. It took you 15 minutes when you were in real trouble and now the club is back on the map, everything in the garden is rosy and you've just had your most exciting season for years. I'm not going to argue – I've got too much dignity. I'm going to leave." Some of them thought I was joking, but, no, they'd had their chance. One of the directors, Sir George Bowman, said to me at the time, "You've just created the biggest wave that's ever come down the Tyne."'

Now this all sounds very melodramatic, maybe even petty, but Arthur Cox is a man who wears his heart on his sleeve; he is a man who sees things – and not just affairs at St James' Park – in black and white. The board must have known how he'd react, yet still they offered him a smaller contract than the one he'd been on. Were they actively trying to push him away? Were they afraid that Cox without Keegan would struggle in the First Division? Were they put off at the thought of having to spend money on the calibre of player Cox clearly knew was needed? Boldness was not something associated with the men who ran Newcastle United, as Cox told me: 'I always thought they would be happy in the middle of the league, but I just wanted to go forward and keep climbing.'

Which is surely what we would have done with the emerging Waddle and Beardsley, especially if they'd been assisted by Bruce, Sheedy and Hately, as Cox planned. At the time, we were all furious (though not shocked) that Newcastle had managed to undo all the good work that Cox and Keegan had done, but we were about to be playing Man United, Arsenal and Liverpool in the league for the first time in six years, and we needed to get our act together sharpish. Once again, a host of names were trotted out. Many fancied the idea of Supermac returning to lead us to glory, others wanted the return of former coach Keith Burkinshaw, who'd had some success at Spurs. But the man who got the job was one who'd been in the frame each time it had become vacant since Joe Harvey left nine years earlier – Jack Charlton.

'Big Jack' was a North East football legend, largely because he and brother Bobby had both been part of England's famous World Cup-winning side of 1966. The brothers were from Ashington in Northumberland and were second cousins of the great Jackie Milburn. Jack had spent his entire career at Leeds United and had won a sackful of medals. As a manager, he'd done the business at Middlesbrough and Sheffield Wednesday. But Jack was very much his own man and was prone to falling out of love with the game from time to time. He'd quit Wednesday to concentrate on his other loves – shooting and fishing. When the Newcastle job became available, he simply wasn't interested, but in the unlikely setting of a Consett Double Glazing factory (which Jack had been invited to open), he was persuaded to talk to Newcastle by his silver-tongued second cousin, one J. Milburn, Esq.

I spoke to Charlton and asked him if it was true that he wasn't really interested in the Newcastle job at first. He told me, 'To be honest, I was quite enjoying my summer off, and I didn't want another job at the time, but Jackie talked me into meeting the board. I said I'd do it for a year to try to keep them in the First Division, which was basically what they wanted. I didn't want a contract, but I asked if there was any money to buy players. They told me there was but only what I could raise through selling.'

This might go some way to answering the questions about Cox's departure. Arthur would have bristled if he'd been told to sell before he could buy any of his high-quality targets, especially having seen the ground packed to the rafters for most of the previous season. The board must have loved the idea of Big Jack looking after the purse strings. He wasn't one for the transfer market; he liked building sides from the tools at his disposal, and the statistics showed he was pretty successful. Jack signed up for 12 months, and any fans hoping for more of the cavalier football which had taken us to promotion were in for a rude awakening.

Astonishingly, when the new season kicked off, we hadn't replaced Keegan and had sold Terry McDermott. What's more, David Mills and John Trewick had left, and we hadn't replaced them either. Jack simply rejigged the defence, moved Kenny Wharton into midfield and recalled young Neil McDonald. Waddle and Beardlsey were left to play up front on their own. Remarkably, it worked.

Chris Waddle described to me the Charlton formula for success: 'Jack didn't want to play through the middle; he liked to hit the front men early and get us turning opponents. We caught teams by surprise in the first half of the season, and we were even top early on.'

We certainly were. Thanks to three straight wins at the start of the season, we were in top spot for the first time since Jackie Milburn and his mates got us there for five short weeks in 1950. It didn't last, however. Once we started playing the big boys, we got our backsides kicked. We then played our part in one of the strangest games in the modern history of Newcastle United (or the Football League, come to that) when we drew 5–5 at QPR after being 4–0 up at half-time.

I received the details of this bizarre game while sitting in the press box at Goodison Park, Everton. Like Terry McDermott and Alan Kennedy before me, I'd moved to Liverpool, the city which has been my home ever since. Having completed two years at the *Darlington Evening Despatch,* I'd joined Mercury Press, a news agency which covered news stories all week and Liverpool and Everton at weekends.

And so, while Newcastle were having fun at QPR, I was covering Everton versus somebody else (come on, I only have a photographic memory for one team, and it's not Everton!). As usual, I was desperately trying to keep in touch with events elsewhere, on this occasion at Loftus Road. The radio boys were always pretty reliable at feeding latest scores along the line, so imagine my delight when I heard 0–1, 0–2, 0–3 then 0–4 all before half-time! This was it – Big Jack's cracked it, I thought.

Imagine my horror when the second-half goal flashes kept coming: 1–4, 2–4, 3–4. It was pretty hard to concentrate on what was going on at Goodison, that's for sure. With a few minutes to go, the news came that we were now winning 5–3, so at last I could relax – we'd got the points. Wrong again. Next up was the full-time score, and it was 5–5. We'd blown it big style.

Despite the brilliant form of Chris Waddle, who'd scored a hat-trick at QPR, the team were starting to find the big league a bit of a struggle. Big Jack then made his first foray into the transfer market – 'swooping', as the papers liked to say, for Sheffield Wednesday's Pat Heard and then Gary Megson from Nottingham Forest. Let's just say they were OK but didn't quite evoke the spirit of the Keegan era. By the turn of the year, we were in the relegation zone.

As for the cups – don't make me laugh. Milk Cup: beat Bradford, lost to Ipswich at home after a replay. FA Cup: lost to Nottingham Forest at home after a replay. Hey, at least we were finding some sort of consistency.

Before that, we had our 'game of the season' – a relegation six-pointer on New Year's Day at SJP with the great unwashed from Wearside. I was back home for the holiday and was delighted to be at a proper derby – blood and thunder, lots of goals, penalties, sendings off, the lot. And, of course, we beat them. Peter Beardsley scored a hat-trick and even missed a penalty in our 3–1 triumph, while the Mackems had two sent off. 'Hello, hello, Happy New Year, Happy New Year . . .' Fantastic.

Our centre-forward that day was a physical lad called Ian Baird who Big Jack had taken on loan from Southampton. He only stayed for five games, but it was obvious which way Jack's mind was working. Weeks later, he signed not one, but two big centre-forwards and completely altered the way we played. Tony Cunningham and George Reilly were the new spearhead of the team, which just a few short months ago was led by Keegan, Waddle and Beardsley. Long ball replaced short pass and dribble. Grumbling was in vogue again.

At Newcastle, we don't just like to win, we have to win with style. I honestly believe if we'd had a run of success like Don Revie had with Leeds or George Graham had with Arsenal, the Toon Army would have been unhappy. 'One-nil to the New-cass-ell' isn't our idea of an anthem to be proud of. This, of course, has contributed to the problems facing anyone who's tried to end our trophy drought. Lots of managers swear that you've got to start building a successful side from the back, grind out results and, hopefully, win your first cup by playing stifling football. Only once you've learned the art of stopping others, they say, can you start thinking about expressing yourself. 'You've got to earn the right to play football,' is their mantra. At Newcastle, we say, 'Bollocks to that.' If you can't win with flair, then you're at the wrong club. (Jack Charlton would soon learn *he* was at the wrong club.)

I'm delighted to say that Chris Waddle backs me up on this! He told me, 'Newcastle fans insist on good football, they want 4–3 every week. Jack brought in Tony Cunningham and George Reilly and put Peter

Beardsley and me on the wings, and our game suffered as a result. The direct play was exciting at first, but teams worked us out and we hit a brick wall. It disillusioned the fans. They started wondering, "Where are we going?"'

Jack gave me his reasons for the switch in style: 'We didn't have a big lad up front. Chrissie Waddle and Peter Beardsley were the two front players, and they needed someone up front with them. You can only buy what you can afford, and I had £60,000 to spend, not £200,000.'

I also spoke to Peter Beardsley, who agreed with Chris Waddle: 'When Jack came in, everyone thought he'd be great for us. He'd had great success as a club manager, and his tradition and his qualities were good, but it didn't work out for me and for Chris. We started to play a system which didn't suit either of us. But it was successful to a point, and we survived that season quite comfortably in the end.'

He's right. In the second half of the season, we were never in real danger of relegation and eventually finished fourteenth – a small crumb of comfort as we reached the thirtieth anniversary of our last FA Cup win. There were, however, a couple of bright spots: Chris Waddle became the first Newcastle player to be picked by England since the days of Supermac, and there was also a surprise trophy – United's youngsters won the FA Youth Cup. The youth team had one shimmering talent, a chubby kid with skill to die for. On 13 April, Charlton unwittingly made a small piece of football history when he gave the kid his debut as a sub for the home game v. QPR. Gazza had arrived.

Meanwhile, in Liverpool, I was witnessing something I'd never ever experienced at first hand – a league-championship win. Everton won the title in some style, finishing thirteen points clear of neighbours Liverpool, who'd won it for the past three years. Every week, I was at either Goodison or Anfield, reporting on top-quality football while my heart was somewhere else, praying that somehow the modest stuff being served up by Big Jack's army would evolve into something special.

But when they came to Merseyside, I was, inevitably, embarrassed. There were nudges and sniggers from my colleagues in the press box as my usually professional, impartial exterior was hideously exposed. For the record, Everton hammered us 4–0, and Liverpool won 3–1.

I was also watching European football again with Everton winning the European Cup-Winners' Cup and Liverpool reaching their fifth European Cup final in nine years. But this was the year of the Heysel Stadium disaster, and while I wasn't in Brussels – the agency only covered home matches – we all worked overtime reporting the aftermath of the tragedy.

My flatmate was Russell 'Rusty' Cheyne, a young photographer just down from Scotland after working for *Rangers News*, the official publication for all things Ibrox. He didn't stay in Liverpool for long: the quality of his pictures ensured that. Eventually, he ended up as chief sports photographer at the *Daily Telegraph*. Great snapper; top bloke.

Back home, the natives were restless once again. One factor was Sunderland's return to Wembley – in the Milk Cup final. Fortunately, they lost in comedy fashion, an own goal giving Norwich the trophy. But their presence at the Twin Towers only served to magnify our underachievement. Attendances at St James' Park spoke volumes: in Division Two, our average home crowd had been just under 30,000. In our first season back in the big league, average gates dropped to below 26,000. This despite the attractions of Man United, Liverpool and the rest.

Time and again, Newcastle fans have voted with their feet. If we're not being entertained on the park, lots of them don't want to know. In the summer of 1985, the Toon Army were still decidedly in favour of 'flair or else', so we waited with interest to see how – or if – Jack would develop the team. But we were gutted when the only significant transfer was the outgoing one of Chris Waddle to Spurs for £590,000. This was the proof, if proof were needed, that we were officially a 'selling' club.

Jack Charlton insists to this day that he didn't want to sell Waddle: 'I got him his first England cap. I told Bobby Robson he should play him, and he picked him for a game over in Northern Ireland. But when Chrissie Waddle came back, I knew he'd made a deal with somebody, and it turned out later it was Tottenham. Several clubs wanted him, which wasn't surprising because he was a very good player. It depressed me a bit that he was leaving. The club tried to offer him a new deal, but Chris had made up his mind, even though I tried to talk him out of it.'

Chris Waddle gave me his own account of the move and doesn't deny Jack's claim that he was 'tapped up' on England duty: 'I had four or five England players telling me their manager wanted me. That always happens, and Jack knew that. That will never change.'

But for him, there were more compelling reasons to move, reasons with their roots a lot closer to home: 'When you get promotion, that's when you've got to spend, and Newcastle didn't. They were happy just to stay in Division One. I started thinking, "Are we going to have a relegation battle every season?" It was obvious to me that Newcastle lacked ambition. They'd also left it to Jack to make me an offer, and he treated it like it was *his* money, not the club's! Jack offered me a contract, and it was a poor offer, so I was even more disillusioned. Put it this way, he was offering me less than George Reilly was on. I'd started playing for England by then and felt I was worth more. Stan Seymour came in late and offered me over four times more – I couldn't believe it. But by then I'd made up my mind.

'I got on fine with Jack as a person, but his style of play also had a lot to do with my decision to move on. When Newcastle played at White Hart Lane, I got all the chants of "Judas" from the Newcastle fans. I thought, "If only they knew how much more money I could have made if I'd stayed."'

No new faces arrived, and to rub salt into the wound, Sunderland's new manager, Lawrie McMenemy, signed the Ipswich forward Eric Gates, a player we'd been linked with. That same day, it all went pear-shaped. We had a pre-season friendly against Sheffield United at St James' Park, and a section of the crowd turned on Charlton; after the game, he walked out.

Peter Beardsley recalled, 'He came in at the end of the game and said, "That's it – I'm off." We thought he was kidding. He literally went out, and we never saw him again.'

I asked Jack for his memories of the day he walked. He said, 'The crowd were getting onto me 'cause I didn't sign Eric Gates. I'd turned him down on the Thursday because we couldn't agree terms. On the Saturday morning, Lawrie McMenemy signed him for Sunderland. Once the crowd started, it became an excuse for me to get out of a job that I was getting stuck into. Remember, I'd only said I'd do it for a year. I walked up to the boardroom and said, "I'm leaving. I'm not having that from a crowd."'

Jack stormed out of the ground but not before Jackie Milburn had a stand-up row with him in the foyer. Milburn saw this as treason – no one should ever walk out on Newcastle United. But although they came from the same stock, they were made of completely different material.

Charlton told me he actually came back to the ground for a second opinion two days later. He'd been to his farm in the Yorkshire Dales and had driven back to St James' Park on the Monday to empty his desk. He found a welcoming party in the car park: 'There were loads of fans there, and they got upset with me the way that Newcastle fans do. Inside, I saw Joe Harvey and asked him, "What would you do?" He said, "Once they get into you like that, then you might as well go." That was it. I'd done what I said I'd do – I'd kept them up, and I wasn't going to get trapped into a job I didn't really want to do.'

And so we were in limbo once again when we should have been building for an assault on the upper reaches of the First Division under Arthur Cox. Changing managers regularly is never the way to find success. Only Newcastle would agree to take on a manager for just 12 months 'to keep us in the First Division'. Surely that's the sort of thing you do when there's only a few months left of the season and you're deep in relegation trouble? Maybe they thought Jack Charlton would fall in love with the idea of managing Newcastle and want to stay long-term. If that's the case, then it shows how little the board knew about Big Jack and about their own supporters. Newcastle fans were never going to embrace a manager who had learned his trade under Don Revie at Leeds. We were back to square one, but this time the new season was just days away, and there was no time to start a long search for a new boss. Instead, Willie McFaul was promoted on a caretaker basis.

McFaul was our seventh manager in ten years. He'd been at the club since 1966 – just like me. Twenty years of living and breathing Newcastle United had given him some idea of what the fans wanted – and what club tradition demanded.

He told me that the failure to keep the promotion momentum going and the fall-out with Arthur Cox were major blows to Newcastle's progress: 'We should have gone on from there – Newcastle should be bigger than that. Jack did it his own way, but it wasn't the Newcastle way. We had Waddle, Beardsley, Keegan, McDermott, Glenn Roeder and Davy McCreery in one season, then we got Tony Cunningham and George Reilly. They weren't Newcastle type of players. I was determined to do it the way the fans would appreciate.'

McFaul didn't have much cash to play with and brought in some low-budget recruits for the 1985–86 season. Fortunately, he had the courage to play the most exciting kid the club had produced in decades.

Paul Gascoigne was just 18, but he put down a marker in his third full game, running the show against a Liverpool midfield which contained Jan Mølby, Ronnie Whelan, Steve Nicol and Craig Johnston. We won 1–0 against the team that would go on to win the title. Gazza played 35 times for Newcastle that season and was one of the key reasons why a limited squad finished 11th. 'Gazza was just a kid, but he had to be at the forefront; he loved the limelight,' McFaul said. 'He was a great talent. We had our ups and downs, but I loved him.'

Throughout the season, the manager was still trying to find his own winning formula. He got rid of big George Reilly but replaced him with Billy Whitehurst. Whitehurst became a bit of a legend on Tyneside but in an ironic kind of way. He looked more like a hod-carrier than a footballer, but that was because he actually *was* a hod-carrier who'd become a footballer. The affection for him merely served to illustrate how immune we'd become to mediocrity.

Once again, there was no cup joy. In the Milk Cup, we limped past Barnsley on away goals only to lose 3–1 at Oxford in the next round. Oxford then went on to win the trophy that year, joining the litany of clubs who have lifted one of the three domestic trophies since we last did.

In the FA Cup, we lost 2–0 at home to Brighton of the Second Division, and this time they didn't have Trelford Mills on their side. By now, I'd concluded that we'd never win a trophy in my lifetime. We never even had 'accidental' victories in cup ties, which most other sides seemed to from time to time. No spawny flukes, no blind refs who gave us a penalty we didn't deserve against the run of play. Nothing. It was thoroughly depressing.

We also seemed to have the knack of featuring in the strangest games in history, albeit usually in a negative kind of way. That season we lost 8–1 at West Ham and used *three* different players in goal. One of them was Peter Beardsley, who played in all 45 games that season and was easily our top player. He was rewarded with a place in England's World Cup squad for Mexico and scored in the 3–0 win over Paraguay.

By now, I was getting used to seeing other teams win silverware. In my second year on Merseyside, Liverpool, with their new player–manager Kenny Dalglish, won the League and FA Cup Double. I'd moved to a job at Granada Television's 'state-of-the-art' News Centre in Liverpool's Albert Dock, working as a journalist on the local news programme *Granada Reports,* and one of my early assignments was the first-ever Merseyside FA Cup final. I worked with the crew following Liverpool, spending the weekend in London and filming all things red. Being the junior member of the team, I didn't actually get into the match but got some kind of compensation by travelling on Liverpool's team bus through London after the final. I even got to touch the FA Cup. 'Toon man gets hands on silverware shock!' We stayed at Liverpool's hotel that night and flew back to Merseyside with both teams the following day. This was work?

When the new season arrived, rumours were rife that Everton were about to make a bid for Peter Beardsley to replace Gary Lineker, who'd departed to Barcelona after his sensational World Cup. My old mate Sime had now followed me to Liverpool and was actually working for Mercury Press as well. The Beardsley question was put to Everton manager Howard Kendall in a press conference. Kendall said something like, 'No, I'm not interested in Beardsley. Why should I be? We've got Adrian Heath, who is a better player.'

A lone voice shattered the decorum of the press conference: 'You're cracking jokes!' It was Sime, who, like me, always wore his black-and-white heart on his sleeve and couldn't help but express his astonishment that a manager of the calibre of Howard Kendall could be so ignorant about football.

Fortunately, the Everton boss saw the funny side. 'It's a good job I recognise that accent,' said Kendall, who was born and raised in County Durham.

As often happens, a new season brought new hope for the eternal optimists who follow Newcastle. But when Gazza got a serious injury at the start of the 1986–87 campaign, we were in big trouble. McFaul turned to Gascoigne's FA Youth Cup teammates and made a clutch of new signings, but by the end of February, we'd won just five league games and were deep in the relegation mire. Miraculously, we turned it round by going on a nine-game unbeaten run, largely thanks to Gazza, back after a four-month absence, and Paul Goddard, who scored in seven consecutive games, a club record. We finished seventeenth in the end, five points off the drop.

The Milk Cup was now the Littlewoods Cup, but there was no jackpot for the Toon, Bradford City (Division Two) knocking us out at the first hurdle. In the FA Cup, we beat two Fourth Division sides, Northampton Town and Preston North End, both at home, but then lost at Chris Waddle's Spurs, courtesy of a dodgy penalty.

We weren't kidding ourselves. We knew we were a desperately ordinary First Division side with two shining lights called Gascoigne and Beardsley. McFaul needed the board to change the habits of a lifetime and invest heavily in the playing side, but there was more chance of the country electing a Labour government. In the summer of 1987, Geordies got a double dose of déjà vu: Margaret Thatcher was re-elected for a third term, and Newcastle sold their best player.

Liverpool had agreed to sell Ian Rush to Juventus, so Kenny Dalglish was rebuilding his forward line: John Aldridge, John Barnes and . . . Peter Beardsley. To get Peter, he broke the British transfer record.

Following on just two years from the sale of Chris Waddle, the Beardsley transfer infuriated Newcastle fans. How could we ever hope to be a half-decent side if we continually sold our best players? The board was accused of both incompetence and greed. OK, we knew smaller clubs had to sell their better players just to break even, but we were continually among the best-supported teams. Most fans suspected that the club was more interested in paying the bill for ground redevelopments than it was in building a trophy-winning team.

Willie McFaul was the man who had to appease the board, the fans and the players. He's still convinced he couldn't have done any more to hang on to our star player: 'We got £1.9 million from Liverpool for Peter Beardsley. I was so disappointed to lose him, but it was already done and dusted. I kept asking myself, "Did Peter really want to leave?" And if so, why?'

Beardsley gave me his own account of the controversial transfer: 'I left for two reasons: first, I loved playing for England, and I didn't want to lose that; and second, I had the chance to go and play for the best team in the country. You've got to remember there was no one to touch Liverpool at that time. For me to go and replace Kenny Dalglish, to be asked by Liverpool's best-ever player, in my opinion, to come and wear his shirt, was just too good to turn down.'

Beardsley insists it wasn't 'a done deal' and that he could have stayed if the right circumstances had prevailed: 'Willie McFaul called me in and asked if I'd sign a new contract. I still had two years to go on my existing one, but I said to him, "Once you show me that your ambition matches mine, then I'm happy to stay, because I don't particularly want to go anywhere." Willie said, "If you're not going to sign, then we want you to go." It was the club's lack of ambition, not Willie's, really – Willie's hands were tied. I just wanted them to buy some players – money wasn't an issue.'

Strangely, I found myself with a ringside seat at this latest miserable chapter in Newcastle's colourful history. Me and my mate Dave Stewart did all the sports stories on *Granada Reports*. There was no way Dave would be doing this one!

And so it was that I found myself at Liverpool's transfer record-breaking, Beardsley-unveiling press conference, interviewing Kenny Dalglish and the departed Geordie hero himself. I remember it for two things in particular, the first being that Dalglish took the piss out of me in front of all the other journalists when I stumbled over a question. (I was dying to hit back with an Oscar Wilde-style riposte, perhaps about how crap Kenny had played in the Littlewoods Cup final, but I knew it was more than my job was worth, plus, unlike Oscar Wilde, I always tend to think of my best lines about 20 minutes after the event.) The other thing I remember is that I interviewed Peter Beardsley and, contrary to all my instincts, managed to retain some sort of composure. (A reporter down on one knee asking a player to think again and go back to the Toon might have been frowned upon by the assembled media, to say nothing of Kenny Dalglish.) Hey, I was becoming a real media professional. In fact, I even managed to sign him up as the judge for a kids' football competition we'd been running on the programme.

A week or so later, when the time came for him to do his judging, I collected Peter from the main reception at Anfield and drove him down to our studio at the Albert Dock. We talked about his first impressions of Liverpool and how he was settling in. Then we chatted about the transfer. In the cold light of day, 175 miles away from the passion of St James' Park, it all seemed so logical and obvious. We actually had a lot in common. We had both moved away from our spiritual home to better ourselves, to make a go of our careers and, hopefully, to achieve the goals we'd dreamed of achieving when we each started out. There was one major difference – the entire population of Tyneside didn't give a stuff about who Ged Clarke worked for.

And so a new season dawned. Peter Beardsley had joined the club with the biggest, shiniest trophy cabinet in football, and he'd help to fill it even further. We were gutted, of course, but strangely not in the way we were when Supermac left, or maybe even when Chris Waddle left. Because now there was an inevitability about us selling our best players, a certainty about our true place in the grand scheme of things. We were a bottom-half-of-the-top-division club who could easily drop into the second if we weren't careful. As fans, we were fast becoming resigned to our fate. Twenty-one years after I'd first pushed my way through the St James' Park turnstiles, we were no nearer winning the league, the FA Cup or the League Cup. If anything, we were further away. Our club had no ambition, our ground was a mess and the one great talent we had left would be sold as soon as everyone realised how brilliant he was. We knew Gazza would be next. It was just a matter of time.

Bizarrely, we then proceeded to have our best league season for 11 years. Not that it was spectacular stuff – we'd made a miserable start but then a bit of Brazilian magic started to kick in. McFaul had gambled almost £600,000 on Beardsley's replacement – a little Brazilian called Mirandinha. (Note a recurring theme here – club receives £1.9 million for star player and replaces him at less than one third of the price.) The fans were aching for Mira to be a success and hung their hats on him – or, in this case, their sombreros. For the next two seasons, all our games, especially away matches, were coloured by the sight of dozens of sombreros among the Toon Army. The wee man also inspired one of the best terrace songs to be devised in years:

> We've got Mirandinha
> He's not from Argentina
> He's from Bra-zil
> He's f***in' brill

He *was* 'brill', but only in fits and starts. Sime and I made the short journey along from Liverpool to Old Trafford to see his first goals for Newcastle in a 2–2 draw with Man United. We were thrilled and exasperated in equal measure (and so, I suspected, were his teammates). In true Newcastle fashion, we weren't pulling up any trees, but with the little Brazilian and our own Geordie genius Gazza alongside, it certainly wasn't dull.

Granada sent me to cover our Littlewoods Cup second-round game at Blackpool, and I got to interview Alan Suddick and Tony Green, who'd each played for both clubs. (I got paid for this as well!) I then watched in horror as a dreadful Gazza back-pass gifted Blackpool a 1–0 win. Fortunately, it was a two-legged tie, and we hammered them 4–1 at SJP, only to be knocked out in the next round by Wimbledon, who would later put us out of the FA Cup as well.

We beat Palace and Swindon before drawing the Crazy Gang in the fifth round. We actually played them four times that season, including one match famous for a picture of Vinnie Jones getting to grips with Gazza's tackle – if you know what I mean.

Gazza was by now the talk of the nation. The brightest young talent in the game. An England star of the future. But still they scoffed when Jackie Milburn told Bob Wilson on the BBC's *Football Focus* that he thought Gazza had the potential to be one of the best players in the world. Wor Jackie was getting on a bit, but he still knew what he was talking about.

Wimbledon arrived on Tyneside for the FA Cup match, and I remember thinking this was make or break for us and Gazza. I was sure that only if we got to the FA Cup final would he consider staying. If we went out, he was as good as gone. My worst fears were realised as we lost 3–1, and Wimbledon went all the way to Wembley to beat Liverpool in one of the most famous cup-final upsets of all time. My poor consolation prize was that I was there to see it – working for Granada.

Despite the cup exit and the gathering gloom over the seemingly inevitable departure of our boy wonder, we managed to finish the 1987–88 season in eighth place. We'd been hearing that the board had been negotiating with Gazza for months in an attempt to tie him to a longer contract, but you'll not be surprised to hear that most of us didn't get too excited. These were the same people who'd negotiated with Chris Waddle and Peter Beardsley after all. Spurs weighed in with a £2 million-plus offer, and you could almost picture our directors' faces. Along with the usual 'we desperately wanted him to stay' noises came the announcement that Gazza was off to London to team up with Chris Waddle.

One man who *was* desperate for him to stay was boss Willie McFaul. He told me, 'As a manager, do you want to sell Peter Beardsley or Paul Gascoigne? No way. I tried very hard to keep them both, and, in the end, Gazza went for not much bigger wages than he was offered by Newcastle. But it was all about ambition – he thought the club had none.

'The club gave me the impression that they tried hard to keep them both, but their big fault was that they were not good at PR. But it's also true that the money was important to them.'

Arthur Cox believes that Newcastle's modern history would have been very different if he'd stayed: 'Had I still been manager, then neither Beardsley or Waddle or Gascoigne would have been allowed to leave, make no mistake about that. Those boys were very close to me. I think they left because the club was not as ambitious as they were.'

No doubt aware of the anger and resentment festering on Tyneside, the board, for once, gave the manager all of the money from the transfer to spend on new players. McFaul brought in four: goalie Dave Beasant and centre-half Andy Thorn from Wimbledon, winger John Hendrie from Bradford, and striker John Robertson from Hearts. What tends to be forgotten is that we also sold Paul Goddard to Derby and Neil McDonald to Everton.

Any hopes that our new Gazza-less team could do the business was rudely shattered within 34 seconds of the new season. That's how long it took Tony Cottee to score the first goal of his hat-trick in our 4–0 defeat at Everton. Once again, I had a front-row seat (or rather a press-box seat) as the alarm bells started to ring among the faithful. Having four new players was one thing, but a straight replacement for Gascoigne was clearly missing. Our first home game fitted neatly into the 'you couldn't make it up' category. We were playing Spurs.

It was the day of the Mars bar, frozen or otherwise. 'Fat boy', as Gazza was now known in Geordie circles, was pelted with them at throw-ins and corners. But Gazza, who was always emotional as well as being a very proud Geordie, was probably more upset by the ferocious verbal reception he received rather than the confectionery one. Chants of 'Judas' and even 'yuppie' also hit the spot, and Gazza was substituted during the 2–2 draw.

The treatment Newcastle fans give to star players who leave tends to be, appropriately enough, black or white. Malcolm Macdonald was booed mercilessly the first time he came back to St James' Park and so was Chris Waddle. Peter Beardsley seemed to escape the vitriol while Gazza clearly didn't. It's generally motivated by the player's perceived keenness or reluctance to leave. This was never better illustrated than in the late '90s when both David Ginola and Les Ferdinand left for Spurs. Ginola made some scathing remarks about Newcastle and was clearly desperate to move on. Each time he returned, the booing almost lifted the roof off. 'Sir Les', on the other hand, didn't want to leave and let it be known. On *his* first return, he ended up doing a lap of honour! The blame is almost always laid squarely at the door of the board, and occasionally the manager, but the ritual of slaughter or praise seems to be something we have to go through with our departed heroes. They have deserted the fight to make our club great again, so they'd better have a bloody good excuse!

Life after Gazza was proving very difficult for Willie McFaul. After five games, we still hadn't won, but, sensationally (or typically, in Newcastle's case), we then went and won 2–1 at Anfield on McFaul's birthday – the first time I'd seen Newcastle win on Merseyside. But the following week, it was business as usual. We lost 3–0 at home to Coventry, and Willie became another boardroom statistic.

When I asked him about his departure, he said he felt the odds were stacked against him: 'There was a lot going on behind the scenes, and that does affect you when you haven't got experience in the team. The season before, I'd basically been using the team that won the FA Youth Cup, and we still managed to finish eighth and beat Man United and Arsenal. But this time I got five points from seven games and was sacked.'

The stuff going on 'behind the scenes' was the first rumble of a revolution that was to rock the club to its very foundations, as they say in the best newspapers. 'Young' Stan Seymour had stepped down as chairman in the close season, handing over the reins to Gordon McKeag. For years, the clashes between their fathers had torn the club apart, but now the names Seymour and McKeag were about to feature on the same side of a new battle for control of Newcastle United. It was a battle they were doomed to lose, because finally, after more than 30 years of hurt, the supporters had been stirred into action. And this time the natives weren't just restless – they were revolting.

11

REVOLUTION (1988–92)

'The fundamental premise of a revolution is that the existing social structure has become incapable of solving the urgent problems of development of the nation.'

Trotsky, 1932

'Sack the board, sack the board, sack the board.'

Toon Army, 1988

This won't surprise you by now, but the way Newcastle United went about appointing a successor to Willie McFaul was shambolic in the extreme. Their ruthlessness had not been accompanied by foresight, and the club spent two months trying to find someone to take permanent charge. Youth-team coach Colin Suggett, along with former skipper Mick Martin, held the fort for eight games of which we won one and lost five. We were also knocked out of the Littlewoods Cup by Sheffield United in the second round (again).

Several potential managers were approached – the board even went cap in hand to Arthur Cox, who'd dramatically walked out more than four years earlier. But Cox was having none of it. As he explained to me: 'I was invited to go back three times during the time I was at

Derby, but I wasn't tempted. I had an obligation to remain loyal to Derby County, and that's what I did. I knew after what had happened before that the trust and respect could never be the same again.'

United were publicly turned down by the former Everton manager, and well-known Geordie, Howard Kendall and then got themselves into the farcical position of giving the job to former Celtic boss David Hay, only to withdraw their offer at the eleventh hour. Eventually, early in December, they appointed Jim Smith, the king of the wheeler-dealers, who quit QPR to come north.

Smith started a flurry of transfer activity that had the revolving door at St James' Park flying off its hinges. Suddenly appearing in the black and white were former England full-back Kenny Sansom and ex-Man City veteran Ray Ranson. It was the start of Geordie careers for Liam O'Brien and Björn 'Benny' Kristensen, but others will be remembered with rather less affection (and those fans who were there at the time may want to look away now): Lee Payne, Rob McDonald, Archie Gourlay, Paul Sweeney, John Cornwell and Frank Pingel, to name but a few.

Willie McFaul had used seventeen players in the first seven games of the season, caretakers Suggett and Martin used another six in their two months, and Smith tried out another twelve. That's a total of thirty-five players in one season – precisely the same number we used when we were relegated in 1978. You're ahead of me here, aren't you? We were relegated again, only this time we were rock bottom, nine points adrift of the rest.

People often joke that it's best to be knocked out of the cup so you can concentrate on the league. In our case, that actually might have helped, but in 1989, we couldn't even get knocked out properly! It took us four games to lose to Watford in the third round, games which Jim Smith could certainly have done without.

The pain among supporters was now almost tangible. Most football fans have spells when they stop going to the match, usually for domestic or work reasons, but occasionally they get to the point where they just can't take any more. My mate Mick Ramsey, who I'd sat with before I moved to Liverpool, is one of the most passionate Newcastle fans I've ever known. But the state of the club at the end of the 1988–89 season got too much even for him. Like many others, he'd moved into the brand new Milburn Stand (or 'Peter Beardsley Stand' as it was known among the supporters, convinced that his transfer had funded it) which had opened at the start of the season. He'd paid a 50 per cent hike on the price of his old season ticket in the East Stand for the pleasure but has painful memories of his move: 'The seats were great, but, unfortunately, the football wasn't. We saw three home wins all season, and we ended up getting relegated. I thought, "I've had enough of this," and after 25 years, I stopped going.'

Mick wasn't alone in his discontent. Rebel shareholder Malcolm Dix and the NSA pressure group had suddenly enlisted some real heavyweight support in their battle to finally wrest control from the old guard, the dynasties who'd controlled the club since time began. John Hall, a local property developer and self-made millionaire, had been coaxed into getting involved by North East sports journalist Bob Cass. Cass had argued that the club needed Hall's kind of 'vision and clout to pull it out of the shit'. Reluctantly, Hall agreed to act as a catalyst. (And, as Arthur Cox said about Kevin Keegan, 'That club has to have a catalyst.')

The Magpie Group, as the rebels called themselves, wanted democracy – power for the people – and they weren't going to rest until they got it. Their cause was helped when the city's local paper, the *Evening Chronicle*, pledged full support for the takeover group. John Gibson, by then the *Chronicle*'s sports editor, told me that the paper took a huge risk at the time: 'As a paper, we'd got so sick of reporting failure that we stuck our neck out and backed John Hall to overthrow the board. It was hugely controversial – I've certainly never known a local paper do anything like it. I was told by the directors at the time that I would never be welcome back inside St James' Park again. I said, "Actually, I'm not sure *you* will be welcome here again when we win the fight!" Of course, it compromised the information we were getting from the club, but the bigger story was the takeover.'

It certainly was. I was still at Granada TV, but I remember being glued to my TV when BBC2 screened a network documentary called *Newcastle Dis-United*, which followed the battle for power. Producer Ray Stubbs and reporter David Taylor explained how Gordon McKeag had received death threats from angry fans and that John Hall had to stay at home and listen to the match on the radio as his very presence could start a riot.

The case for the prosecution was pretty compelling, especially when the star witness was wheeled out; Peter Beardsley told the cameras that the club had made little effort to keep him. Then, Jeremy Beecham, the leader of Newcastle City Council, weighed in, claiming, 'The club is run by a handful of people basically in the interests of themselves as directors and shareholders and, frankly, with little or insufficient regard for one of the most loyal bands of supporters in the country.'

John Gibson was as pithy as ever: 'The players have changed regularly. The managers have changed regularly. But the board has remained basically the same – handed down from father to son . . . It has been their own private little club, and they find it very difficult to accept that it can no longer be like that.'

The board appeared to be on the run. Owning only 13 per cent of the total shares, they were certainly vulnerable. The fight for control escalated into a full-scale bidding war with both sides determined to buy up shares, even at vastly inflated prices. The Magpie Group offered £500 a share; the board matched it. Next it was £1,000 and eventually £5,000, and both sides were still buying.

As the battle raged, the documentary team managed to get an interview with our eccentric Brazilian striker Mirandinha. Through an interpreter, he told the camera, 'The great majority of the fans are against the board and most of the players are as well. They don't speak up because they are frightened.' Frightened, and not mad. Unlike Mira!

Chairman Gordon McKeag showed remarkable tenacity in the face of the onslaught and a welter of personal abuse, telling reporter David Taylor, 'It is no fun being spat at, having one's car spat at, to have people shout abuse and seeing hatred in their faces. It's no fun seeing one's friends and relatives abused and shouted at. That's no fun at all.

'I don't walk away from it, because I've got a job to do. It's a job that I think I'm doing well, given the difficult circumstances. It's a job I think I can do a good deal better than John Hall could do. I don't like bullies, whether they are financial bullies or otherwise. I don't believe it would be in the best interest of Newcastle United if Mr Hall were to take control.'

Eventually, McKeag and his board bought their way into a majority shareholding position, which meant that the only way the rebels could succeed was to pick off directors with offers they couldn't refuse. They had some success but never got into a full takeover position.

As the season drew to a close and relegation was confirmed, Hall told his troops, 'Maybe we've lost the battle, but I tell you this – we're going to win the war. Because our cause is just. We are not going away . . . I issue this challenge to the board: are you afraid of real democracy? Because we aren't.'

The first battle was over, and the casualties were many, including the club, the team and the fans. Millions had been spent on the share-buying spree which could have been used to buy new players or to make ground improvements.

While the battle raged at St James' Park in this most desperate of seasons, two of the club's greatest names passed on to that great stadium in the sky. Jackie Milburn and Joe Harvey were spared the ignominy of seeing their beloved black and whites relegated once again. Jackie died of lung cancer in October 1988, and the streets of the city came to a standstill as his funeral cortège wound its way up the hill to Gallowgate and past St James' Park.

Four months later, Joe Harvey died of a heart attack. For some time, he'd been receiving treatment in Newcastle's Royal Victoria Infirmary, which is a goalkick away from the ground. Willie McFaul remembered visiting his old boss on a match day: 'He could hear the crowd chanting "sack the board" from his hospital bed. He looked at me and said, "It's the likes of that that puts you in here. Controversy – you don't need it." Joe didn't last much longer.'

The passing of these two great heroes from an era when Newcastle United were a force in the land seemed symbolic at this miserable time. It was now 33 years since the last FA Cup win and 20 years since Harvey's great Fairs Cup victory. Once again, our club was on a downward spiral, seemingly miles away from winning something for the long-suffering and now actively agitated fans. Hope was in short supply.

Football had also changed for good. In April 1989, 96 Liverpool fans died at the FA Cup semi-final at Hillsborough. The disaster shattered the people of Liverpool, and as a news editor at Granada TV living in the city, I was closely involved in the day-to-day coverage. This was one front-row seat I didn't want. But it certainly helped put my own football disappointments into very sharp perspective.

Jim Smith later admitted that the battle for power behind the scenes had made his job almost impossible, saying, 'If I had known in advance of the two years of heartache I faced, I would never have taken it.' He made plans for a swift return to the top division by shipping out a whole team and bringing in another. Of the 11 who lined up on the opening day of the 1989–90 season, only Andy Thorn had played in the disaster at Everton 12 months earlier, and even he would be gone by October. The opening match was against Leeds, and we had a new strike partnership in place: Mark McGhee and Micky Quinn. We won 5–2, and Quinny got four. A new hero had landed.

The pair were virtually unstoppable in the Second Division, and their goals helped drive us into the promotion places. After a blip at the end of 1989 (and defeat in the third round of the Littlewoods at the hands of West Brom), Smith brought in former Scotland skipper Roy Aitken from Celtic and immediately gave him the captain's armband. Soon we were back up near the top, and promotion was definitely 'on'. The football was good as well, including a classic home game with Leicester when we were 4–2 down and won 5–4 in the dying seconds. There was even a mini-FA Cup run to enjoy, with wins over Hull City and Reading bringing Man United to St James' Park. We gave Fergie's boys a decent game but lost 3–2. No matter – we had more pressing matters to think about.

The race for promotion was tight, and we just missed out on an automatic spot, which meant the play-offs and a two-legged encounter with the great unwashed from Wearside. It was us or Sunderland for a place in a Wembley promotion decider. It was a match made in football heaven, but it turned out to be football hell for us.

After earning a 0–0 draw at Roker thanks to keeper John 'Budgie' Burridge saving a pen, we were favourites to progress. But I refer the right honourable reader to chapter two in which I wrote, 'But football is a bastard with a red-and-white comedy nose sometimes.' It certainly was in 1956, and it was again in 1990. Eric Gates and Marco Gabbiadini scored the goals at SJP which ensured we'd be playing Second Division football once again the following season. Many fans couldn't take it and staged a pitch invasion, holding up the match for 20 minutes and provoking a Football League inquiry.

I had just moved from Granada to become a producer at the BBC, joining the team at *On the Line* who'd made the *Newcastle Dis-United* documentary. For my first programme, we had to react to the previous night's incidents at St James' – a painful day's work, that one.

Even though we'd finished six points and three places above Sunderland, we had to watch as the Mackems played Swindon in the final at Wembley (well, we didn't *have* to watch, and most of us didn't, but you get my drift). Those of us who sniggered when Sunderland lost 1–0 soon had our faces slapped when it emerged, ten days later, that Swindon were to be relegated to Division Three for making illegal payments to their players. Sunderland would be promoted in their place. Thanks a bunch, God.

* * *

While our gallows humour was being tested to the limit by the football fates, peace had broken out in the Newcastle boardroom. Well, almost. Both sides realised the stalemate wasn't doing anyone any good, so John Hall accepted the offer of a seat on the board. Both sides also agreed that a public share issue was the best way forward. Revolution had become evolution.

Unfortunately, the share issue was an embarrassing disaster. While saddos like me and Sime stumped up our £200, there simply wasn't enough interest from fans or big business, and the plan was scrapped. It was a major humiliation for the club, and Gordon McKeag did the honourable thing and stepped down as chairman, his place being taken by George Forbes. Another significant move saw John Hall leave the board and install his son Douglas in his place. But he didn't stay either, and a feeling of paralysis surrounded the place. All that fighting for this?

It was so frustrating. Thousands of us had thought this was the moment when everything was finally going to change. Sime's feelings at the time just about summed up the way we all felt: 'I was angry with the existing board – the decades of abject failure, how they never addressed the core issues, the way they treated the fans. When Hall and Dix tried to get rid of them, I was old enough to be suspicious but revolutionary enough to want change. When the share flotation happened, we put our £200 in. We wanted to put our money where our mouths were. We wanted to be part of changing the club. It was typical that it all came to nothing, and, once again, we were left wondering why the hell we bother.'

After the near miss of 1989–90, we went into the new season reasonably optimistic, but by New Year, we were as flat as Christmas beer. Smith started blooding the kids – and gave debuts to Lee Clark and Steve Watson, among others. Watson became the youngest Newcastle player in the club's history, aged 16 years and 223 days, and by the end of the season, he was our first-choice right-back. There was also one particularly good signing – Gavin Peacock came from

Bournemouth and found instant popularity with the fans, mainly because he was neat and tidy, gave his all, and knew where the back of the net was.

However, we were knocked out of the Rumbelows Cup (the latest name for the League Cup) by Middlesbrough, and after beating Arthur Cox's Derby County at SJP in the FA Cup, we lost to Nottingham Forest after a replay in the fourth round.

With the team thrashing around in lower midtable and the line-up constantly changing (we used thirty-six players – one more than in the relegation seasons), we were getting a horribly familiar feeling. Jim Smith was too. He quit in March, saying, 'I just felt I'd had enough. If you make a mistake here, it's not just a mistake – it's a disaster.'

I got in touch with Jim to find out if he still felt the same way now. It was obvious that time had dulled his anger, and he looks back with some affection at his days at SJP: 'It's a great club, but I just went at the wrong time. You get jobs because a team is at the bottom of the league, and when I joined, they were a very ordinary side. But I probably did a bit too much surgery, and we just failed to survive.

'After that, there was always an undercurrent with the John Hall takeover, and that made it nigh-on impossible to do the job. I felt sorry for Mr McKeag – he was trying to do his best. But when Sir John said he wouldn't put money into the academy scheme as long as I was manager, I'd had enough. We were in the middle of a long unbeaten run, and we'd just won 1–0 at Portsmouth. It's a long journey back, but it gave me plenty of time to think about things, and that's when I decided to go.'

New chairman George Forbes acted quickly to avoid the fiasco which had preceded Smith's appointment and brought in the Argentinian World Cup legend Osvaldo Ardiles as the new manager. Ossie had been a major success as a player with Spurs and was doing superbly managing Swindon. It was a bold and enterprising move, and most of us were happy to give it a whirl. It seemed like we'd tried everything else, so why not a foreign manager?

We'd also appointed yet another World Cup winner. But that's where the similarities between Ossie and Jack Charlton ended. They were opposites in just about every possible way, from appearance to football philosophy. And while Ossie would preside over a virtual disaster at Newcastle, no one seemed to dislike him.

His appointment was certainly popular with the players, as Gavin Peacock explained to me: 'We liked him from the minute he came. He was like a mate with the players. We played great football, and he brought in lots of good local youngsters. Most of them had no experience – I was only 23, but I was one of the senior players in that team. Despite the problems we had, the fans never turned on him.'

Ossie had 11 games in charge at the end of the season. He only won two, but he put the emphasis on attack and filled the team with home-grown youngsters. At West Ham in April, our full-backs were Steve Watson and Robbie Elliot, both of whom had just turned 17 and both looked the part. Things like this gave us a feeling of optimism for the new season. That's Geordies for you – suckers for a new broom and the promise of some sunshine football. We really ought to learn.

What followed was a disaster, but it was the strangest disaster of the many I've witnessed at Newcastle. No one could hate Ossie with his constant smile and his disarming South American charm. We'd rattled on for years about how we wanted more Geordies in our team, and here they were: Lee Clark, Steve Watson, Robbie Elliot, Kevin Scott, David Roche, Lee Makel, Matty Appleby, Steve Howey. There seemed to be a new kid every week, and most of them looked pretty good. But while it was refreshing, it was also naive in the extreme – especially the defending. The average age of the side had plunged from 28 to 22 in a few short months, and most of the kids were playing in defence in front of Pavel Srníček, our new, eccentric young Czech keeper.

Results were desperate, and by the start of October, we still hadn't won a league game at St James' Park and were bottom of Division Two for only the fourth time in our history. The rawness of our play was scary at times. I remember travelling to Crewe Alexandra to watch us in the League Cup (sorry, Rumbelows Cup) and being in a state of shock after 25 minutes. We were 3–0 down to a Fourth Division side and being completely outplayed. It hit me at that moment that this was the lowest point I'd witnessed, and, worse still, there didn't seem to be any light at the end of the tunnel.

Incredibly, we got two goals before half-time, and Gavin Peacock completed a hat-trick in the second half to get us an unlikely 4–3 win. We beat them 1–0 in the home leg, only to lose to Peterborough of Division Three in the next round. And there was another classic example of the playground nature of our football in the Zenith Data Systems Cup (another bizarre confection designed to give everyone a chance to win a bit of silverware – apart from us, of course). We drew 6–6 with Tranmere Rovers after extra time and then lost on penalties. But the fragile nature of the kids' team was never better illustrated than in a home league game with Middlesbrough on Boxing Day 1991.

Alan Oliver of the *Chronicle* has witnessed all of Newcastle's recent low points, but even he was gobsmacked by what happened: 'Having all the kids in was great, and we christened them "Ossie's Babes". But we soon discovered they couldn't defend. Against Middlesbrough, everyone had gone up for a corner – and I mean everyone. When the ball broke to Middlesbrough's Paul Wilkinson, he was literally on his own on the halfway line. He ran towards the Leazes goal and actually stopped to look back because he couldn't believe there was no one anywhere near him. Eventually, he just ran on and stuck it in the net. It was farcical.'

My old schoolmate Chris Baines and I have sat together in the John Hall Stand since it was built. Like Mick, he'd given up on Newcastle during the Jim Smith era, but even he was drawn back by this new-found boyish enthusiasm: 'There had been no heart in the team when Jim Smith was in charge, and I remember vowing that I wouldn't come back till he'd left. I can take most things, but I couldn't take them playing with no heart. I went back when Ossie took over, and there was certainly no shortage of heart, but it was like watching school kids on the playground! The likes of Stevie Watson, Alan Neilson, Alan Thompson and Robbie Elliott would tear around gang-tackling everyone! It was great to watch, but it was suicide stuff.'

At around this time, the BBC decided to update the *Newcastle Dis-United* documentary for my programme *On the Line*. I convinced editor/reporter David Taylor that there was only one man who could produce this tricky assignment, and I duly got yet another front-row seat at the crazy Newcastle United circus.

The situation behind the scenes had moved on. When the board paid out £300,000 to Leicester City for David Kelly in December 1991, they were in breach of an undertaking they'd given to the bank not to buy players. The bank demanded its money back, and given that United were in debt to the tune of £5 million, it meant that the club was about to go under. John Hall (now Sir John Hall) was on a world cruise when his son Douglas rang him saying they had two hours to save Newcastle United.

Hall coughed up, but he was furious that the board had acted so irresponsibly and vowed to take complete control of the club from then on. He brought in football business consultant Freddie Fletcher, as well as his key ally in the takeover battle, long-standing shareholder Freddy Shepherd. These two, along with Hall's son Douglas, ran the club from that day forward. The old guard were completely blown away. Gordon McKeag was given an honorary title in order to allow him to continue as president of the Football League, but he wasn't allowed back into the Newcastle boardroom. This was the beginning of the new age of Newcastle United. The dithering, cautious board of old, which had lacked any ambition, had been supplanted by a dynamic, vigorous – and ruthless – new regime.

I met up with Sir John Hall and asked him about the club he inherited back in the early '90s. He told me, 'The club was going nowhere at the time – it was always the bridesmaid, never the bride. It was badly managed. Newcastle United to me reflected British industry, which was ruled by the old families. The great entrepreneurs of Newcastle in the Victorian times put the club together, they had money and enterprise, and the team was successful, but over 100 years, the family money was dissipated. The power was split among a lot of people, so nobody really had control here, and they certainly didn't have the cash to put into the club. There was so much that needed to be done.'

When our *On the Line* documentary crew arrived at St James' Park in January 1992, he put it even more emphatically: 'Had this been a normal business, I would have closed it down, got rid of it, lost the money and moved on to the next job. But it's Newcastle United.'

Ossie Ardiles was putting on a brave face. He told our camera, 'It looks very gloomy, the situation here right now, but it's not . . . We have wonderful young players developing very nicely indeed. They've been thrown into the first team and have had to grow up very quickly. In the medium term, we will have a very good team indeed, but in the short term, of course, we have a problem.'

Hall then expounded on the dangers of sacking managers, saying it was far better to give them your full support. 'You've got to keep your nerve,' he told us. A week later, Ossie got the bullet.

To be fair to Sir John, it was actually his son Douglas who'd insisted that the manager had to go. And to be fair to Douglas, the team was in freefall. We'd lost 4–0 at Southend on New Year's Day, and then more cartoon defending saw a 3–0 lead at home to Charlton turn into a 4–3 defeat. On top of that, we'd been knocked out of the FA Cup at home by Third Division Bournemouth on penalties.

Gavin Peacock told me that the squad were sad to lose Ardiles: 'All those kids went on to have great careers, and you have to admire Ossie for that. The kids were learning all the time, and the players loved him. Lee Clark was really upset when he came to say his goodbyes. He was great fun on the training ground, he was a World Cup winner, and he was Maradona's idol. Enough said.'

Freddie Fletcher drove to Ossie's house at 7.30 a.m. to sack him, and a few hours later, to audible gasps from the assembled media, Newcastle United unveiled their new manager. Kevin Keegan had been playing golf in Marbella since his helicopter exit from SJP eight years earlier. But now he was back.

Gavin Peacock almost crashed his car when he heard the news: 'I was driving over the Tyne on my way in to training when I heard it was Kevin Keegan. It was unbelievable – I used to have a poster of him on my wall!'

As for me, I remember being absolutely shell shocked. It looked like a massive gamble by the Newcastle board. The last desperate throw of the dice by a desperate club. But it seems I was in a minority of one. All my mates swear they were delighted at the news. Mick reckons he was 'shaking with excitement', while Sime says he thought it was 'the second coming'. However, he did add, 'But being Newcastle, I knew it could still go tits up'.

Since that helicopter day in 1984, Keegan had shown no inclination to get involved in the game whatsoever, and he certainly hadn't been away on coaching courses planning his assault on the English game. It seemed to me that Sir John and Co. were praying that the magic dust that Keegan brought in 1982 would work again in 1992. If it didn't, Newcastle United, founded 1892, were going down to the Third Division for the first time in their centenary year.

As far as our BBC documentary was concerned, it was all change. We'd only just filmed Sir John telling us, 'You've got to keep your nerve.' Now we were applying for access to Keegan's first match, at home to Bristol City.

For a fans' perspective, I pulled in Chris and Mick, and we filmed them pre-match in the upstairs room at the Trent House pub just behind the East Stand. Chris spoke for many when he told David Taylor, 'Bringing in Keegan is a short-term measure to get quick money into the club. There'll be 30,000 there today to watch a team that's second bottom and hasn't won at home this year.' He was right.

REVOLUTION

Gavin Peacock remembers being amazed at the reaction of the Geordie public: 'For his first game, the place was full – they'd all come to see Kevin Keegan, and he wasn't even playing!'

But he was equally impressed by the new boss: 'He went round the dressing-room talking to individuals. He told me that Bill Shankly used to tell him to "drop hand-grenades" around the penalty area, and he wanted me to do the same. I thought, "Flipping heck! Bill Shankly said it to Kevin Keegan and now he's saying it to me!" I felt ten feet tall.'

Talk about getting close to the action. I was actually *on* the pitch as the players did their warm-up, David Taylor declaring in his 'piece to camera', 'What's supposed to happen next is a modern-day miracle: the transformation of a bunch of losers into a winning football team – all because they're being managed by the totally inexperienced but charismatic Kevin Keegan. Well, we'll see.'

As the Geordie messiah walked onto the pitch, we were there next to him. The roar was deafening, and I struggled to keep the fan in me in check. I just wanted to shake his hand and say, 'Go on, Kev – you can do it!', but you're not supposed to walk into the shot when you're a TV producer.

Suffice to say, Keegan *had* brought the magic dust with him, and we won 3–0, our best result of the season. Keegan had said when he arrived that if he could get Newcastle going it would be like a giant snowball rolling down a hill – unstoppable. After the match, someone asked him if the ball had started rolling. Quick as a flash, Keegan said, 'No. It's just started snowing.' No wonder the media loved him.

To continue the metaphor, the snow didn't actually settle at first. In fact, it very quickly turned to slush. A month later, we'd arranged to interview Sir John once more about the changing circumstances at the club when disaster struck. Seven games into his reign and on the back of two straight wins, Kevin Keegan walked out. He said he'd been promised cash for players and walked when it wasn't forthcoming, famously declaring, 'It's not like it said in the brochure.' Sir John got on the phone and equally famously said, 'There's only two people who can save Newcastle United, and they're talking to each other right now.' Happily, by the time we got to Wynyard Hall, Sir John's fabulous country estate, the situation had been resolved.

Sir John and his wife Lady Mae had written a personal cheque from their joint account so the club could buy a new centre-half. With a twinkle in his eye, David Taylor asked Sir John, 'How does Lady Hall feel about owning Brian "Killer" Kilcline?'

After a 1–0 win over Sunderland (in which Sime and I completely disgraced ourselves with our goal celebrations in the St James' Park press box), we lost five games in a row, and relegation seemed certain. It got to the situation where we had to win our last home game against Portsmouth or else it was all over. Talk about ringside – I was sat on the edge of the pitch with cameraman Tom Ritchie as we filmed for our documentary. When David Kelly hit the only goal near the end, he ran right in front of us to celebrate. Every bit the TV professional, I somehow resisted the urge to jump on his back and sing 'Staying up, staying up, staying up!' We could still have gone down the following week if results had gone against us, but when we won 2–1 at Leicester, in another cliffhanger, we were safe.

That week, I put together my Newcastle film, which went out on Thursday's *On the Line*. It concluded with Sir John insisting that he wasn't going to get tied up with Newcastle long-term, and with Keegan saying he planned to walk away, now that he'd kept Newcastle in the Second Division. But on the day of transmission, we had to rewrite the ending. Keegan, contrary to all predictions, signed a three-year contract, while Sir John, contrary to his own statement, bought a controlling interest in the club. Like Keegan, he'd learned that once Newcastle United gets under your skin, it's very hard to walk away.

12

KEVIN 2 (1992–96)

'Walking along, singing a song, walking in a Keegan wonderland.'

Song heard at every match for five years

The genius of Kevin Keegan knew no bounds. Not only had he saved us from dropping from Division Two into the Third Division, he'd also got us into Division One, all in one amazing manoeuvre. Well, actually, it wasn't down to Kevin at all, but, at this point, we would happily have given him the credit.

What had happened was that the clubs in Division One had announced a breakaway Premier League which gave them the power to negotiate their own TV, sponsorship and advertising deals. Basically, it was the start of the process that was to make the rich clubs richer and the poor clubs poorer. Therefore, Division Two now became Division One and the old divisions three and four were now 'upgraded' to two and three. What's in a name, eh?

The new regime at St James' Park was only too aware that there was only one place to be, and it wasn't where we were just now. The gravy train had just left the station, but if we could get the Keegan express moving quickly, we might just hook up with it at the next junction. Now that Sir John and his merry men had full control of the business, and now that the crowds were rolling back to watch Kevin Keegan sit in a dugout, they had the confidence to give him some spending money.

Apart from Kilcline, Keegan also bought Kevin Sheedy from Everton to help with the relegation fight. Then Barry Venison from Liverpool, Paul Bracewell from Sunderland and John Beresford from Portsmouth all signed up, and the new-look team started like a train, winning its first ten games and storming to the top of the table.

Gavin Peacock had a close-up view of the Keegan magic at work: 'He was a great man-motivator, but he had ideas as well. After all, he'd played at the highest level in England and on the Continent. He never criticised you in training. He had a go if we lost or we did badly, but then it was forgotten. He was very clever. He'd praise a different player in the *Chronicle* every week, usually the unsung heroes. He was very positive and probably the manager I enjoyed playing for the most.'

As the team started to lift off, both Sime and I took – with hindsight – the very sensible decision to buy season tickets for the Gallowgate End. The 'house full' signs had been going up regularly – with thousands being turned away at times. So we stumped up for tickets which we knew we'd only be able to use from time to time, but we had very little difficulty getting rid of them when we weren't able to get up from Liverpool. That was the Keegan factor for you. When we *were* able to make it, it was like an old school reunion: Chris, Mick, Sime and I were together again – in front of the scoreboard.

I was now working for a brilliant BBC football 'fanzine' programme called *Standing Room Only*. One week, we decided to do a feature on training methods, so I argued that the obvious place to visit was the only team with a 100 per cent record in the country. I was duly despatched to Durham to film the Toon training and to interview the key people, Kevin Keegan and all. It turned out that the conditioning coach was another old school-pal, Steve Black. It was good to see that St Cuthbert's was playing a leading role in the resurgence of my team!

The ten-game winning run, added to the two wins at the end of the previous season, meant that we needed one more victory to break the club record, and, as luck would have it, our next match was at Roker Park – against Sunderland. It was one of those days that have passed into Toon folklore. The streets of Roker were awash with black and white, the sun shone and horns were honked as flags and scarves trailed from cars. As usual, we were crammed into the uncovered Roker End. This was a ground I'd been going to (only when I had to, mind) since 1968, and I'd never seen us win there. In fact, not many could say they had – our last league win at Roker was in 1956 when Jackie Milburn was among the scorers. But we were feeling pretty invincible after our flying start.

When Kevin Brock forced an own goal out of Gary Owers up at the Fulwell End, we all went mental. This was it. We were going to hammer them. But the goal rush didn't come. Instead, the Mackems battled their way back into it and equalised midway through the second half. Damn (and other words which can't be reproduced here). However, a saviour was at hand. Step forward Liam O'Brien, signed by caretaker boss Colin Suggett in November '88, survivor of the Smith and Ardiles eras and a scorer on this very same ground in the previous season's 1–1 draw. Some men are born for Geordie greatness. It didn't matter that he was never one of our greatest players, he scored against the Mackems – twice!

No goal was sweeter than this one. We won a free-kick on the edge of their box with about ten minutes to go, and Liam floated a perfect shot into the left corner. There's a great photo of the moment the ball hits the net, taken by Stuart Clarke, which he used on the cover of his book *The Homes of Football*. The picture, taken from above the TV gantry on top of the stand, shows eighteen players but only one knows it's a goal: Liam O'Brien, arms aloft. What's fantastic about the picture (apart from the fact that it's a Toon goal against Sunderland) is that it's a true time-stood-still moment. A split second later, there was complete pandemonium as we all went crackers, and O'Brien's teammates chased him halfway round Roker Park.

The club record was achieved and another bogey was laid. It couldn't last, of course, and the next week, we lost 1–0 at home to Grimsby. But we had the feel of champions, and despite a slight wobble in January and February, we were soon back on track. Keegan had added Rob Lee and Scott Sellars to the team, and then he splashed out £1.7 million on a young striker from Bristol City called Andy Cole. We were reinforcing while we were strong, something which was to become a Keegan trait.

Before that, we did our traditional thing of not getting to a Wembley final – however, we did have a mini-run in both competitions. Because of our nightmare the previous season, we had to enter the League Cup (now the Coca-Cola Cup!) at the first-round stage for the first and only time in our history. After wins over Mansfield and Middlesbrough, we lost 2–1 at Chelsea. In the FA Cup, after beating Port Vale and Rotherham, we made the trip to Blackburn for the fifth round. Sime and I were at Ewood Park, unlike Kevin Keegan, who was listening at home on the radio. He was sick. A couple of hours later, so were we. We lost 1–0.

But we were all very well indeed in April when another victory over the Mackems, 1–0 at home, saw us move tantalisingly close to promotion. In our next match, we did it, and, once again, I got lucky thanks to my job with *Standing Room Only*. A few weeks earlier, we'd been filming an interview with the Grimsby chairman Peter Furneaux. I joked with him that we'd probably beat them to win promotion, and he immediately offered me a pair of tickets for the game at Blundell Park.

Sime and I drove over from Manchester and had a brilliant night. Cole and Kelly got the goals which not only guaranteed promotion but also won the title. We had passes for the sponsors' lounge where, appropriately, we drank the last bottles of Newcastle Brown Ale. As we passed the boardroom, I asked the commissionaire to thank the chairman on our behalf. Instead, he brought him out, and Mr Furneaux insisted we join him and his guests for a glass of promotion champagne. So there we were, supping bubbly with Sir John and Lady Hall, when it got even better. Lady Mae said, 'You must come into *our* boardroom at the weekend.'

On Sunday, 9 May, we were in dreamland. Newcastle proceeded to score *six* goals in the first half against Leicester – a team that was in the play-offs! Wave after wave of that great song 'He gets the ball, he scores a goal, Andy, Andy Cole' rippled across the terraces. We eventually ran out 7–1 winners with both Cole and David Kelly scoring hat-tricks. After the final whistle, Newcastle were presented with a piece of glinting silverware before our very eyes – the old Football League Division One trophy which Newcastle hadn't won since 1927. Of course, it was somewhat devalued as it was now the Second Division trophy, but we weren't going to let that little fact spoil a perfect day.

Lady Hall was as good as her word, and we were soon in the St James' Park boardroom enjoying promotion cake and more champagne. Kevin Keegan also dropped in and poured us both a beer. 'The highest-paid barman in Newcastle!' joked Sir John. Kevin then made Sime's day even more perfect when he looked up at my 6 ft 3 in. mate and said, 'Crikey! Do you want to come and play centre-half?' To this day, Sime tells everyone that Kevin Keegan once asked him if he'd like to play for Newcastle.

I drifted off into town to meet up with Steve O'Brien and a few of the lads from Wallsend. I found them in the Monkey Bar on Pilgrim Street, and we sang Toon songs long and hard into the night. I remember a young fan coming up and saying, 'This day is for the likes of you lads, who've had to suffer all these years.' It made me feel old, but it also made me feel good – because he was bloody right.

* * *

While being served beer by the 'greatest manager in the world', I'd come over all professional and asked him if he'd give us an interview for 'Standpoint' – the star interview which was a central feature of *Standing Room Only*. Kevin asked me to drop him a line after the holidays and said he'd be happy to fix a date. A month or two later, we filmed Jack Charlton up at his home in Northumberland, so I decided I'd drop Kevin's letter off in person at St James' Park. As luck would have it, the great man was walking across the car park on his way in to the ground, and I seized the moment.

What happened next was pure Keegan. He could have come over all business-like, saying he'd be in touch, but, remembering that I was a fan, he got Dee the receptionist to open the doors to the stadium and walked me down the tunnel.

'Come and look at this,' he said as he strode out onto the pitch and pointed to the new stand which had been quickly taking shape behind the Leazes goal towards the end of last season and was now (miraculously for Newcastle) just about complete. My jaw dropped. For the past 15 years, the Leazes End had been a shell of its former self, an apology for a terrace. Now it was a state-of-the-art superstand. 'Wow! It's amazing,' I said (or words to that effect) and told him we'd upgraded our season tickets and would be sitting up there from now on. He then gushed about what it would be like when it was full of screaming Geordies, how the club was finally taking off and how at last we were going where we really belonged. He was genuinely excited, and because he was, so was I. He was right. *This* was what we'd been waiting for. But more than that, and I don't think he realised this, *he* was what we'd been waiting for.

Arthur Cox's comment about Keegan being the catalyst in 1982 was spot-on, but ten years later, the catalyst was proving even more potent. The man had no managerial experience, but he'd come back to a club which was heading in completely the wrong direction and not only turned it round but managed to get it racing back to where it came from. And he'd made it all look so breathtakingly simple.

KEVIN 2

By the time the interview came around, Keegan had signed a few new players, including, to everyone's absolute delight, Peter Beardsley. After leaving us for Liverpool, Peter had won two league titles and the FA Cup. He'd then moved across Stanley Park to Everton for a couple of seasons. But now, six years after I'd given him a lift in my car to the Granada TV studios, Beardo was back!

He told me that the transfer had been as much of a surprise to him as it had been to us: 'I was absolutely shocked to be asked back. I'd watched it gradually grow and grow from afar, and I was in the Tyne Tees TV studio for the Leicester game, which was unbelievable. I remember thinking, "That's going to get massive now." But I didn't have a clue what Kevin was thinking and that he'd already been on to Howard Kendall asking about me. I genuinely didn't know that.'

Did he notice the difference when he returned? 'Yes, of course. The club was definitely on the move. It was probably more ambitious, and I think Sir John gave it that. In my first spell, the club always did things the right way, but if anything, they were too genuine in everything they did. Everything was done by the book. But with Kevin and Sir John, and Freddy Shepherd and Douglas Hall, the ambition was unbelievable, and Kevin had buying power that other managers hadn't had before.'

The new season dawned, and 14 August 1993 had the makings of a brilliant day. We met in Rosie's, as usual, to lubricate our tonsils then made our way to our brand spanking new seats in our brand spanking new stand. It was fabulous. Our capacity was now back up from 30,000 to 36,000, adding to the noise level. The sun was shining as the lads ran out to a heroes' welcome. We were in the Premiership – back with the proper teams. Unfortunately, Tottenham were a bit too proper that day and won 1–0 thanks to Teddy Sheringham. Bizarrely, Spurs never really looked like conceding a goal that day. I say 'bizarrely' because their manager was Ossie Ardiles.

We may have started slowly in the league, but there was renewed optimism that we'd finally crack the cup jinx when we beat Notts

County 11–2 on aggregate in the Coca-Cola Cup, Andy Cole (who else?) getting a hat-trick in each game. This was easily our best-ever win in the League Cup, and we began to harbour ambitions that this could be the year we'd finally win the elusive trophy. But by the time the third round came along, the first signs emerged that there was trouble in paradise.

Lee Clark had been dropped for the tie at Wimbledon, for showing a bit of petulance after being substituted at Southampton. His big mate Andy Cole was also absent – but for very different reasons. It emerged that Coley had 'done a runner' after a row with Keegan and was simply AWOL when the side went to south London. Not surprisingly, with all this going on, we slumped to a hugely disappointing 2–1 defeat and were out of the cup. The situation was quickly resolved and both players were restored to the starting line-up for Saturday's home league game against – Wimbledon. Result? 4–0.

The season took off from then on, and we hit a real purple patch. We had a great Monday night trip to Oldham when we won 3–1 with Coley and Beardsley sharing some blinding goals. I remember talking to some of the locals who said we were the best team they'd seen that season. We realised then (if we hadn't already) that we were definitely on to something. A couple of weeks later, we stuffed Liverpool 3–0 at SJP with another Cole hat-trick, all the goals coming in the first half. The team were now known on Sky TV as 'The Entertainers', and the fans were officially in dreamland.

Despite this, the cup jinx just wouldn't go away. After beating Coventry, we were knocked out of the FA Cup in the fourth round by Luton. It seemed churlish to be upset by the odd defeat, but we were aching to win something, and one of the two domestic cups certainly seemed well within the capabilities of The Entertainers, as well as being much more likely than the Premiership title.

We kicked on again in the league and won ten of our last fourteen, including a 2–0 win at Anfield – the penultimate game before they pulled down the legendary Kop. The match marked the fifth anniversary of the Hillsborough disaster, and there was a lump in my throat when the Newcastle fans laid their own floral tribute in the goalmouth – to thunderous applause from the home support. The result meant we'd done the double over Liverpool, and with Steve and his wife Janice also down for a visit, it was a perfect weekend. For once, I could hold my head up after the Toon had played on Merseyside.

That strong close to the season meant that we finished in third place – our highest final league position since we'd last won the title, way back in the mists of prehistoric football time. Yes, 1927, a year which hangs even heavier round the necks of Newcastle fans than 1955. In 1927, we won the league title by five points from Huddersfield Town with Sunderland in third place. We won 19 out of 21 home matches – a feat only Liverpool have achieved since. The legendary Hughie Gallagher was top scorer with 39 goals, but now, here in the 1993–94 season, he had finally been eclipsed. Andy Cole scored a staggering 41 goals in league and cup that season, and was just unbelievable to watch. Everything he touched seemed to fly into the net, thanks largely to the brilliant service provided by Beardsley, Lee, Sellars and Clark. Coley couldn't put a foot wrong, and we knew that with him in the side, the following season we might even have a chance of winning the big one – the Premiership title.

It seemed like we were really going for it when we won our first six games of the 1994–95 season on the bounce, clocking up a goals tally of 22–7 in the process. Keegan hadn't gone mad in the transfer market but had brought in Phillipe Albert, the classy ball-playing Belgian centre-half, as well as a Swiss full-back called Marc Hottiger. The Continental additions were no coincidence, because we were also back in Europe for the first time since the dark days of Richard Dinnis, way back in 1977. The difference this time was that we were blazing a trail.

I remember listening to the radio and pinching myself as we thrashed Royal Antwerp 5–0 on their own patch. Even in Joe Harvey's glory days with Bob Moncur, Pop Robson and the mighty Wyn, such a result would have been completely unthinkable. We cruised the home leg 5–2 to rack up a club record European win, and then prepared for the visit of Athletic Club Bilbao.

I was now a freelance TV producer, and, once again, I ended up doing a documentary about Newcastle United. (All my mates insisted that I engineered these situations, and, I had to admit, the evidence was fairly overwhelming, but, in my defence, you couldn't get away from the fact that the club was compelling viewing.) The latest programme, for regional BBC, was an examination of Sir John Hall's claim that when Newcastle United did well, so did the regional economy. When we interviewed him, he told us that, to coincide with the UEFA Cup match, a business delegation from the region was flying out to Bilbao to extend trade links between the North East and the Basque region. We should come and film it. This sounded like an eminently sensible idea, especially as everyone on the trip was getting a ticket for the second leg.

And so it was that we toured Basque business parks by day and watched Newcastle get knocked out of Europe by night. Andy Cole had helped us to a 3–2 win in the home leg but was missing in Spain through injury, and we lost 1–0. He came back at the end of November, but by the turn of the year, he was gone again – this time for good.

The story of how Keegan sold our star player to our biggest rivals, Man United, for £7 million and then stood on the steps of St James' Park to justify his decision to a mob of angry fans has been told many times. In his autobiography, Keegan said:

> It was when we began to stumble that I began not to tamper
> with the system itself but to rethink our strategy. I didn't want
> the team to become one iota more defensive, but rather to
> attack in a different direction. That is when the Andy Cole
> deal came about.

But, of course, we didn't understand this at the time. We'd been brought up following a club that sold its best players. We'd seen Waddle, Beardsley and Gascoigne sold for fat profits and not replaced. We'd been waiting almost 40 years for a domestic trophy. We'd begun to think that everything had finally changed and that now we really were a professional club about to win something at last. But it seemed that, once again, we'd been kicked right in the bollocks.

Keegan's appearance on the steps was extraordinary. As journalist Colin Malam put it, he looked 'like one of those sheriffs in a Hollywood Western who have to pacify townspeople infuriated by some outrage or other'. The fact that he was successful speaks volumes for the hold he had over the Geordies. Of course, he spoke in memorable, eternally quotable sound bites: 'If I've got it wrong, there's a bullet with my name on it.' Pure Keegan. And, of course, he hadn't got it wrong. There was a plan – it was just that we didn't know it yet. (Something else I didn't know at the time: in the week we lost our goal-scoring hero, I also met my future wife. Good old Jules – she could obviously tell my world was falling apart!)

The league season, which had started so promisingly, inevitably tailed off, and we finished sixth. In the cups, we again flattered to deceive. After beating Barnsley over two legs, we knocked Man United out of the Coca-Cola. They usually treated the League Cup as a minor competition, and, not surprisingly, Fergie filled his team with kids. It was our first glimpse of youngsters who'd come back to haunt us in years to come, but on that particular night, we were more than happy to beat them 2–0. Man City were next, and they beat us 2–0 at SJP after a replay.

In the FA Cup, we went as far as we ever did under Keegan. We drew at home with Blackburn in the third round and sold Andy Cole two days later. By the time we went to Ewood Park for the replay, we were all still in turmoil. I'd cadged a couple of tickets from the Blackburn defender Graeme Le Saux, who I'd worked with on *Standing Room Only* when we went to America to film a

World Cup preview special (it's a tough job but someone's got to do it).

The match was a brilliant tonic for the Geordies still suffering from post-Cole trauma, Hottiger and Clark's goals earning us a 2–1 win. Graeme 'Le Sox', as we knew him, had also thrown in a couple of tickets for the players' lounge, so Sime and I found ourselves celebrating with the lads (well, a few yards away from them). And then drama: all the players made a dash for the exit door. Coley had turned up! The transfer had happened so quickly that none of them had had a chance to say goodbye to him. I'm afraid I can't throw any light on what was said as the exchanges all took place on the other side of a glass door – suffice to say they all looked pleased to see him, with lots of backslapping and handshaking going on. Funny game, football.

Our run continued with wins against Swansea City and Man City, which put us into the quarter-finals for the first time since 1976. Sadly, we were bundled out 1–0 at Everton – more misery for our small band of Mersey-based Mags. Our sixth-place finish meant that we hadn't even qualified for Europe, but as Keegan later put it, 'Now we could make the league title our focal point. It was almost the making of us.'

13

THE NEARLY MEN (1995–96)

'We are top the league, said we are top the league.'
Terrace chant, August '95 to March '96

We'd waited patiently for the 'post-Cole plan' – about six months, actually. While most of us believed that Keegan wouldn't have sold our star striker without having something up his sleeve, there was still a part of us (cultivated through years of simply following this zany football club) that bristled with suspicion.

But when Les Ferdinand, Warren Barton, David Ginola and Shaka Hislop all arrived for a cool £14 million in the summer, it seemed that Sheriff Keegan was now keeping the promises he'd made to the angry townsfolk at the top of the St James' Park steps.

As the new season kicked off, Paul Robertson, *The Journal*'s sports editor, wrote a comment piece which said that what had happened in the past four years was 'nothing short of a miracle'. Raving about the ground, the atmosphere, the team, the manager and the board's commercial acumen, Robertson concluded by saying, 'The fans believe this is finally the year when Newcastle United will end up with at least one piece of silverware in the trophy cabinet.'

That captured the excitement and anticipation exactly. We'd all finally begun to believe. We kicked off at home against Coventry and won 3–0, but it was the next game away to Bolton when everything fell into place.

There was a good turnout from the lads. Sime and I drove up from Liverpool and met up with Steve, cousin Richie, Chris Baines and some other Toon stalwarts. We weren't disappointed: Ginola was spellbinding and Ferdinand was awesome.

Sir Les is another hero I was thrilled to talk to about his time at Newcastle. He admitted that he'd succumbed to the Keegan charm: 'I'd spoken to a few clubs, but after five or ten minutes with Kevin Keegan, my mind was made up. I wanted to better myself as a player, and who better to learn from?'

He told me that Keegan had made it clear to the rest of the team just what he needed: 'Kevin Keegan was phenomenal. He told David Ginola and Keith Gillespie, "Supply him with crosses because he's the best header of the ball in the country." He made you feel ten feet tall when you walked out of the tunnel.'

That last remark might explain why Chris Baines is fond of saying, 'Les was about thirty feet in the air for the first goal at Bolton,' but when your new centre-forward actually is as good as the pre-season hype, you're allowed a little bit of hyperbole. Sir Les scored two that night, but Ginola was something else – the 'Frog on the Tyne' had arrived.

We won nine of our first ten games (we always lose at Southampton, so nobody was too shocked by that one) to give us twenty-seven points out of thirty. We were top of the table and the talk of the land. Sir Les equalled a club record by scoring in eight consecutive matches (he actually scored twelve in eight!). He was the focal point of a team playing football from another planet.

Like everyone else, he was blown away by the quality of football we were playing: 'Winning is a great habit. But we also played some great football, and everyone in our team was comfortable on the ball.

People were always telling me that they never missed us when we were on TV.'

His goal supply was coming from Keith Gillespie and David Ginola on the wings, Peter Beardsley in the box, and Lee Clark and Rob Lee in the middle of the park. Even the defenders were given licence to attack, and it wasn't uncommon to see Warren Barton and John Beresford ahead of the wingers or Darren Peacock and Phillipe Albert turning up in the penalty area. Shaka Hislop in goal must have been a pretty lonely bloke!

I also spoke to Warren Barton, who described it as the best football he'd ever been part of: 'The game I remember very clearly was against Man City. Ginola was brilliant – some of the stuff he was doing with the ball was unbelievable. I remember saying to Les, "I've never seen things like that before!"

'The whole city was on a high, and everything about that time was great, even going in to training. The players were part of the fans, and the fans were part of the team – we'd all mix together in town. I remember when I first arrived Peter Beardsley and Lee Clark told me, "Have time for the fans, and they'll have time for you." And that was exactly how it was.'

We were ten points clear of Man United when we went to Old Trafford for the final game of 1995. Sime and I got ourselves into the press box and suffered in silence as we lost 2–0. Andy Cole, inevitably, got the first, even though he'd been having a bit of a mare since his move, and Roy Keane scored the second. To add to our misery, Keith Gillespie got a bad injury and was ruled out for a couple of months. His absence would disturb the balance of the side, but, to be honest, I'd felt our away form had gone off the boil several weeks before we went to Old Trafford.

Despite these nagging doubts, we were in the unusual position of going into the New Year still in the running for all three domestic trophies. We're usually out of the title race by September and out of the League Cup by October. But we were flying in the Coca-Cola

Cup, having beaten Bristol City 8–1 over two legs, Stoke City 4–0 away and then, most memorably, Liverpool 1–0 at Anfield. For me, this was manna from heaven. I'd already seen us beat Everton and Liverpool in the Premiership, and here we were beating the Scousers again. This was becoming addictive!

Keegan – always one to set the bar as high as possible – declared he wanted to win the lot. However, January 1996 turned out to be the month when all our cup dreams turned sour. We lost 2–0 at Arsenal in the Coca-Cola quarter-finals with the game being dominated not by Ferdinand or Beardsley, Wright or Bergkamp, but by an annoying little man in black called Gerald Ashby, who had a stinker and sent off Ginola. Then, a week later, we were out of the FA Cup as well. We drew our third-round game 1–1 at Chelsea but lost the replay on penalties. A certain Ruud Gullit scored a last-minute equaliser for the cockneys to force the penalty shoot-out. Did I mention that we *never* win penalty shoot-outs?

Whenever we go out of the cup, we usually say, 'Now we can concentrate on the league,' and it's always said with great irony because we're never in with a shout of the title. This time it was *exactly* what everyone was thinking. We played three league games in January and won them all. By 20 January, the league table looked like this:

	P	Pts
Newcastle	23	54
Liverpool	23	42
Man United	23	42
Spurs	23	41

This was the day of the legendary 12-point lead. But we didn't have another game for two weeks, and by the time we beat Sheff Wed 2–0, the gap had been cut to nine points and seemed to shrink gradually each week. Arguments still rage as to why that happened, but what Kevin did next usually comes top of most people's list. He gave

£6.7 million to the Italian club Parma for the Colombian striker Faustino Asprilla, a signing which some say completely destroyed the balance of the team. I actually believe that the loss of Gillespie was more damaging on that front but also tend to think that the money might have been better spent strengthening the defence. But that would have been boring, and this was Kevin Keegan spending the cash.

'Tino' had skill to burn and a personal life to match. He arrived in a snow storm and lived through a permanent blizzard of publicity. As Alan Oliver once wrote, 'Guns, drugs, bar brawls, porn queens. And that was on a quiet day.' The first time we saw him on the pitch was when he came on as a sub against Boro when we were trailing 1–0. In a flash of red boots, black gloves and rubber legs, he conjured an equaliser for Steve Watson and then started the move which led to Sir Les knocking in the winner. We were in awe once again. The man could do things with a football that even Ginola couldn't!

Les Ferdinand has his own view on the arrival of Tino: 'After we lost to Arsenal in the League Cup, Kevin Keegan said to me, "We're too reliant on you." He thought I needed help, and then he signed Asprilla. I can see why he brought him in, but to accommodate him, the system had to change, and, suddenly, we had square pegs in round holes.'

The changes began to have an impact. We lost our next away game 2–0 at West Ham, and the lead was cut to just six points, though we did have a game in hand. Then we had our third away game on the trot – against Man City at Maine Road – and my first chance to see the legendary Colombian in the flesh. It was another extraordinary game in which we were behind three times but kept coming back, Tino making one and scoring one. However, it was his forearm smash and head-butt on Keith Curle that made all the headlines, even if the City defender writhed for England after spending most of the afternoon kicking Tino up the arse. Worse still, Man U won yet again, and our lead was now down to just four points.

Nine days later, we finally had a home game, and this time our opponents were Man United themselves. The date was Monday, 4 March, and it was a night game live on Sky. Sime and I were gibbering wrecks as we drove up to Newcastle. I cross-examined him from Burtonwood Services to Washington Services – could we do it? *Would* we do it? Neither of us were that confident. We were preparing ourselves for disaster. Sime's got this theory that we've had a built-in defence mechanism ever since the 1974 FA Cup final: the bit that warns you, 'Don't get too excited. This is where we blow up.' It sounds negative, but when you've been following Newcastle as long as we have, it's an essential part of the armoury.

There was another new face on the team sheet that night. Keegan had paid £3.75 million to Blackburn for David Batty, whom he saw as the ideal man to sit in front of our defence, which most people thought was our Achilles heel. Batty was to provide a bit more steel to go with the rapier thrust of Ginola, Ferdinand and Beardsley.

The noise when the teams took to the field made the hairs on the back of your neck stand on end. This was our moment. A win against Man U would not only restore our seven-point cushion, it would also fill the side with the confidence which would surely sweep us to our first title since 1927 and our first domestic trophy in forty-one years.

The first half was one of the most one-sided we'd seen all season, as we threw everything at them. If only we'd had a kitchen sink. Peter Schmeichel was unbelievable, making a string of world-class saves, notably from Sir Les. The closest we got to breaking them down was when Phillipe Albert's free-kick crashed against the bar and Les fired the loose ball over. I think we knew deep down that we had to score in this period, so when the whistle went at half-time, the ovation for the team was loud but almost consolatory. Sure enough, they hit us with the sucker punch in the second half.

For the previous six weeks, as Man United clawed back the twelve-point lead, it seemed that every time you checked out their score it read '1–0, Cantona'. That night, the sequence was maintained, 'Eric the Red' popping up on the right to fire an angled shot past Pavel

Srníček. The Geordies cranked up the volume once again, but you could see the confidence draining from our lads. We battled for the rest of the half, but the goal wouldn't come, and we lost 1–0.

I suggested to Warren Barton that even a draw might have been enough against Man United. He agreed but didn't think it would have been in our nature: 'We never ever sat down and said, "Let's work out what we need to do over the next 15 games." It wasn't like that. If we'd drawn, we'd still have been four points ahead with a game in hand, so, with hindsight, we should have said, "Let's not lose," but we never thought like that. We wanted to show them that we were going to win the league, and we wanted to show them *how* we were going to win it.'

But the reality was that Man United's win meant they were now just one point behind with the wind in their sails. Alex Ferguson, quoted in the *Evening Chronicle*, was in generous mood:

> You work all your life in football to come across an experience like the one on Monday. I don't want to sound patronising, but I thought the Newcastle supporters were not only a credit to their club but a credit to the game. There was none of the usual 'We hate Manchester United' stuff or the bile that we often get. All the Newcastle fans wanted to do was to support their team, and I've got to say that it was marvellous stuff. I can genuinely say that if we do not win the championship, then I hope Newcastle United do.

There was a touch of 'He would say that, wouldn't he?' about his final remark, given that the only other team in the race was Liverpool. A few weeks later, the old Fergie would resurface with comments that would really blow the lid off the pot.

An emphatic 3–0 win against West Ham (twenty-seven shots on target, thirteen off target and seventeen corners) put us back in the groove, but two away defeats brought us crashing back to earth. First, we lost 2–0 at Arsenal when some slack defending cost us the game. Warren Barton remembers it vividly. His mistake cost us the second goal and him his first-team place for the rest of the season. My own abiding memory is watching it on a Norwegian TV channel in a Liverpool pub with Jules and, later that night, her agreeing to become the future Mrs Clarke.

Ten days later came the 'match of the century' on Merseyside. No, we didn't organise a quickie wedding, Newcastle came to play at Anfield, and Liverpool won an astonishing game 4–3. It's a match which has gone down in football folklore with the lead changing hands three times before being decided by Stan Collymore's injury-time winner. The iconic images shown on TV were of Keegan slumped over the advertising hoardings and the United fans staring in disbelief, no one quite able to take in what they'd just witnessed.

Sime and I had somehow got tickets in the front row of the main stand at Anfield, right next to the pitch. As the final whistle blew, we headed for the exit, and I swear Sime couldn't speak for about an hour afterwards – the pessimistic 'defence mechanism' hadn't quite worked that night. When I reminded him about it recently, he said, 'I even find it hard to speak about it now. It was a microcosm of everything to do with Newcastle United and the great clash of our two cultures. On the one side was "We can do this, and we will play great football", and it was smashing against the hard rock of "We're doomed to fail." For me, that was the point when the one had just slaughtered the other. I was traumatised then, just like I'd been after the 1974 cup final.'

The game symbolised everything about our title charge – brilliant, but cavalier, attacking football which left the back door open for those teams clever enough to exploit it. How many sides score three at Anfield and get nothing? In the *Chronicle*, Alan Oliver wrote, 'Have Newcastle United ever been more magnificent in defeat?' But he also asked, 'Was this the night when Manchester United were handed the FA Carling Premiership title on a plate?'

Les Ferdinand certainly thought so. He told me, 'Liverpool was the most poignant game for me. If we'd have won or drawn that one, I think we'd have been OK. It would have sent out a pretty strong message that we were back, if we'd got a result at Anfield. After the way we played, Kevin said, "How can I bollock any of you after that?" but, with hindsight, I think he should have. We should have bollocked each other for losing it.'

Keegan later wrote in his autobiography:

> I worked on the principle that if we scored three then the opposition had to score four to beat us, and that, of course, is exactly what Liverpool did in that massive game . . . which probably cost us the championship.

He was right. We'd won just one game in six, and no matter how brilliantly we'd played against Liverpool, we still lost. We still had our game in hand, but we were now three points behind and needed Man U to slip up. Fat chance: the '1–0, Cantona' mantra was still being chanted on a weekly basis. We beat QPR, but then committed hara-kiri live on TV once more. Batty marked his return to Blackburn by putting us 1–0 up, but with just four minutes to go, one of Rovers' subs, a virtually unknown striker called Graham Fenton, scored two goals to put another nail in our title coffin. The irony dripped from the back pages – Fenton was a Geordie who supported Newcastle. At least Alan Shearer had the decency to have a quiet match.

Sky TV were now regularly screening post-match shots of Newcastle fans sitting with their heads in their hands, some even blubbing. 'Cry on the telly' entered football's pop charts and seemed to stick around for years. Opposing fans love going for the jugular.

We won our next three games, and hopes flickered when Man U lost at Southampton, but as we began the final week of the season, we knew we had loads to do. United hammered Nottingham Forest on the Sunday, giving themselves a six-point cushion and a superior goal difference with just one more game to play. We, on the other hand, had three to play, starting at Leeds the following night.

We battled well for a 1–0 win, but no one remembers that. What the night of 29 April 1996 is remembered for is Kevin Keegan's amazing outburst on live TV. Angry and emotional, he tore into Alex Ferguson, who'd been up to his seasonal trick of psyching out the opposition on the run-in to the title. Fergie allegedly suggested that Leeds and Nottingham Forest, our next opponents, might 'take it easy' against Newcastle.

Keegan's 'I'd love it, love it, if we beat them' remarks are now as famous as the 4–3 defeat at Liverpool. At the time, I remember being absolutely gobsmacked at the sensational piece of TV I was watching. But I also remember standing up and applauding, because, from a Newcastle point of view, he was telling it exactly like it was.

Warren Barton had a similar reaction: 'We were pleased, actually. We were thinking, "Go on, gaffer, give it to him," because we all agreed with what he was saying. We were getting annoyed and frustrated ourselves, it meant so much to all of us.'

Les Ferdinand told me, 'Kevin Keegan wears his heart on his sleeve, and he was desperate to win the title, but I was surprised by his outburst. Most of us had a bit of a giggle about it, actually, but in the cold light of day, we thought, "Good on yer, gaffer." It showed that it really meant something to him.'

But if we couldn't rely on Keegan to stay cool, who could we rely on? Keegan, McDermott and Beardsley were the only people at the club who'd won the league title before. The rest were in uncharted territory.

Three nights later, a 1–1 draw at Forest made it virtually impossible for us. Again, we'd got ourselves ahead only for an Ian Woan 30-yarder to give them a point. We were now two points behind with just one game left.

On Sunday, 5 May, Man United were away to Middlesbrough while we were at home to Spurs. The maths was simple enough: they had to lose, and we had to win. As we gathered in Rosie's for the last time that season, Mick Ramsey admitted he'd been to church that morning to pray for a miracle. I allowed myself a little nostalgic wallow, recalling that it was almost exactly 30 years to the day since my first-ever Newcastle match. 'Wouldn't it be fantastic if Man United slipped up at Boro and we won to make it the perfect anniversary?' I thought. Chris Baines, however, has never been a romantic. In fact, he subscribed to the conspiracy theory: 'It's Bryan Robson's first season as Boro manager. They're bound to lie down for Man U. We've got no chance of winning now.' Bryan Robson might dispute the manner in which it was done, but Chris was right. They think it's all over? It is now.

The 1995–96 season was the ultimate Newcastle United roller-coaster ride. Our only other near misses in the previous forty years had been two cup finals in which all the hopes and dreams of the faithful rested on ninety minutes of football, each time ending in a day of massive disappointment. But this was different. This time we clearly were one of the best two teams in the country – and for a long time, the best. But, in the end, all the usual clichés attached to league football had applied:

- It's much harder to win the league than the cups;
- The best team is always the one at the top at the end of the season; and . . .
- It's a marathon not a sprint (Brian).

Of the 50 seasons that have passed since Newcastle United last lifted one of the major domestic prizes, this was the one which hurt the most. It hurt in a different way to those dreadful years of relegation and those dismal seasons of Second Division darkness where players hardly worthy of the black-and-white shirt somehow got to wear one. We got through those dark days with liberal helpings of gallows humour and a fatalistic worldview: this was our lot, forever doomed to be one of the game's also-rans.

But in the 1995–96 season, not only had we finally gatecrashed the party normally reserved for the likes of Man United, Liverpool and Arsenal, and not only had we assembled a team that was actually quite capable of winning the league, but we'd also put together a team which was capable of winning it in a way which had never been done before: with a style and panache that made people gasp, and which made football lovers all over the country adopt us as their second-favourite team. We'd truly aspired in the grand manner. We were going to do it better than anyone else. We were Newcastle United. We were different.

In his autobiography, Keegan admitted:

> I still have nightmares about the way we gave it away as half a dozen of the players who had performed so well became so nervous that they couldn't put their game together. The virus spread through the team, and that is what gave Manchester United the chance to close that massive gap.

Because this was the high water mark of Newcastle's last 50 years – the closest we've come to winning English football's biggest prize – it's worth hearing from all those I managed to speak to. Peter Beardsley believes a Newcastle title could have had historic consequences: 'If we'd won the league, I genuinely believe it would have changed football for ever. Everyone would have become attack-minded. They would have said, "Look how Newcastle have won the title – this is the way to go forward." Instead, football has become more negative with teams happy to get one-nils, and that's what turns fans off.'

Beardsley was also aware of what it all meant to Keegan: 'It hit us all hard, but it hit Kevin hardest. He felt he had let the people down, but he hadn't – we had. We made individual errors, odd mistakes, but we had a 12-point lead. Of course we should have won it.'

Sir John Hall revealed that they almost tempted fate: 'We were actually planning the victory parade at one point – maybe we shouldn't have done that. When we didn't win the league, it was a tremendous blow, but Keegan's time here was the most exciting time in soccer. Not just for Newcastle but for the whole league. It was tremendous. We played soccer which was out of this world, and we were everybody's second-favourite team.'

Sir John pointed to Keegan's obsession with attacking football as one of the main reasons he thought the title slipped away: 'We knew the defence had problems, but he said, "No, I'm going to win it my way." We were 12-points clear, and we should have consolidated the defence, and we would have won it. We gave the league away by what we did. But he'd got us that far, and he wanted to do it his way, and at the end of the season, it didn't work. The pressure on the club at the time was tremendous. If we *had* won it, then that would have turned the club around.'

Warren Barton thinks credit is due to the eventual champions: 'We changed our system a bit and that distorted the pattern. But all respect to Man United – they had an unbelievable run in the back half of the season. It became psychological, and we were inexperienced. We needed to calm it down, but that wasn't our mentality. It was devastating, and it took a long time to get over it.'

Arthur Cox, who'd returned to SJP as Keegan's trusted coach, stressed that psychology is vitally important in football: 'Once you start losing, that worm gets in. You think you're still leading comfortably, even after defeats like the ones at Liverpool and Blackburn, but those points have gone. It just wasn't to be. It was the most glorious failure ever, but that's football. Kevin wanted so badly to bring the Premiership to Newcastle, so he really felt it. He'd given it his best shot, and we came up short, but only just.'

Les Ferdinand thought we should have been more ruthless: 'Once we'd got 12-points clear, there was a feeling creeping in that it was already won, and I hated that. Someone said – and I won't say who – "At this rate, we'll have it won by March!" And another time I turned up at training and there was a fan wearing a "Champions 1996" T-shirt. Because of this attitude, when we lost a game the response was not what it should have been. Losing is a slippery slope to get off.'

The day after the dream died, John Gibson wrote in the *Chronicle*:

> I've waited half a century to see Newcastle go into the last day
> of a season capable of winning the championship. And that
> for me doesn't make this a season of failure but one of dazzling
> attacking football, entertainment and, above all, promise of a
> club's destiny.

That's the trouble with Newcastle fans: beneath the thick layers of pessimism lies a fine seam of eternal optimism which gurgles to the surface at the slightest invitation.

Euro 96 came and went – a pleasant distraction from the high-octane stuff that really mattered to Newcastle fans. Although we now knew that our club was undoubtedly, and finally, a fully paid-up member of the Premiership elite, we also had this nagging doubt that we'd missed the best chance we'd ever have to win the title. We waited to see if Keegan would rebuild the defence or tighten the midfield, but we really should have known better.

I was in Africa when I got the news that Newcastle United had broken the world transfer record by buying the most prolific goal scorer in the Premiership. I'd landed a job directing a new adventure travel series for Sky TV called *Walker's World*, which was fronted by Anna Walker. We were going to climb Mount Kilimanjaro, and the producer Nick Pisani and I had flown out ahead of everyone else to carry out a 'recce'. I was in my hotel room in Nairobi when I got a call from Jules telling me the news. We'd spent £15 million on Alan Shearer! I leaped about the room, screaming like a mad thing. 'He's coming home, he's coming home, Shearer's coming home!'

THE NEARLY MEN

It was the most expensive return ticket ever bought. The best Geordie goal-machine England had seen since Wor Jackie was heading back to his homeland. Bloody hell! £15 million! Was this really us? Newcastle United, the selling club, was now the 'spend, spend, spend' club.

Warren Barton had been in Toon long enough to realise what this meant for the locals: 'Signing Alan Shearer was the biggest transfer in the world at the time, and they couldn't have bettered it. They could have signed Ronaldo, and it wouldn't have been as big for the Geordies.'

Of course, there was a back story. As a kid, Shearer had attended a Newcastle United open day for promising young players. The story goes that a coach asked him, 'What position do you play, son?'

The young Shearer replied, 'Centre-forward.' However, there was a surfeit of wannabe centre-forwards, so Alan Shearer spent his Newcastle United trial playing ... in goal. Only Newcastle.

On top of all this, Shearer had turned down Man United to come to us! It was inevitable then that his first game for Newcastle would be against ... Man United. The FA Charity Shield match, which kicks off each new season, is traditionally played at Wembley between league champions and FA Cup winners. As Man United had won both, we were invited to take on the all-conquering Old Trafford lot. I flew in from Nairobi (God, it sounds romantic, doesn't it?) early on the morning of the match, suffering from the sorts of afflictions you'd expect to get when climbing an almost 20,000-ft mountain in Tanzania. I met up with Jules and Sime, and we headed for Wembley via selected hostelries (the best medicine, I've always found).

Of course, this was a glorified friendly, but it meant everything to the Geordies who were down in force and made up the lion's share of the 73,000 crowd. It was great to be back at Wembley for the first time in 20 years, and we even allowed ourselves to daydream that this might become a regular thing from now on. Of course, we were brought rudely back to earth by what happened on the pitch.

Newcastle were shocking, and we were hammered 4–0. We'd found another domestic trophy we couldn't win.

When the league season got under way, things still weren't right. In contrast to the previous season when we'd started like a train, this time we started like a milk float with battery trouble. Warren Barton told me, 'It really took us a long time to get over what happened at the end of the previous season. The hangover lasted a good while, and we didn't get it out of our systems for a few months.'

Sir Les thought the pre-season preparation was wrong: 'I blamed our poor start on the pre-season tour. We'd been to Thailand, Singapore, Japan and Hong Kong, and we felt knackered going into the season. It took us a couple of weeks to recover.'

Eventually, we clicked into gear. After beating Sunderland 2–1 at Roker (hurrah!), we recorded seven straight wins, and it was the seventh of these which had the football world talking about Newcastle United once again. The Double holders came to town, and we took them to the cleaners. Newcastle 5, Manchester United 0. All the frustration of last season's collapse was banished as players and fans revelled in a complete annihilation of our nemesis. It was a similar performance to the crucial 1–0 defeat back in March, except this time we converted our superiority into goals.

The press went to town. Martin Samuel in *The Sun* summed up everything about that performance, and Newcastle under Keegan, when he wrote:

> He wins no leagues for it, no trophies, no medals. But even if the title does not sit on Tyneside at the end of the season, this 90 minutes will stand as the epitome of everything Keegan stands for and strives to achieve. It stands as the reason he believes he is right, as the evidence you can build a championship-winning team from the front, that you do not have to compromise your principles.

Sir Les told me it was 90 minutes of football he'd never forget: 'That game was one of the best performances I've ever been involved in, but it was a day for the supporters. They'd been shattered the previous season and humiliated at the Charity Shield, so it was like giving them something back.'

Bizarrely, I was back in Africa again when all this was going on. The new job meant I was seeing lots of the world but missing lots of football, and no miss was greater than this. We had been filming on the Zambezi and had actually survived a hippo attack on the day that Man United *didn't* survive a Magpie attack. At least I can always answer the question 'Where were you when the Toon stuffed Man U 5–0?' with a degree of certainty. (Anna Walker later appeared on *TV Nightmares* recounting the hippo story but completely failed to mention the score – a major oversight on her part, I thought.)

One of the recurring themes of Newcastle United's history is our complete inability to build on platforms of potential. When we get ourselves into a position to go on to greater things, we inevitably fall flat on our arses. This was a classic example. With the Man United monkey off our backs, we should now have mounted our title challenge, safe in the knowledge that we feared no one. But, instead, we went on our worst run for years – winning just two of our next ten games. We also got knocked out of the Coca-Cola Cup by Middlesbrough.

When we lost at Blackburn on Boxing Day, Les Ferdinand suspected all was not well: 'Kevin said a few things at half-time and at the end. Then he said, "I'll know when it's the right time to leave this place." We looked at each other and said, "Something's up." There was something not quite right.'

Keegan was going through a bit of a crisis, convinced he couldn't motivate the players any longer. He offered his resignation to Freddie Fletcher, who realised that not only was Keegan deadly serious, he might also be right. Fletcher called a board meeting.

No one wanted Keegan to go, especially as the club was about to float on the Stock Exchange. But the board realised that if Kevin felt it was for the best, then there was little alternative. They struck a compromise: Keegan would leave at the end of the season.

We won our next two games, 7–1 against Spurs and 3–0 against Leeds. But four days later, Keegan went ballistic when the story of his plan to quit appeared in the *Sunday Mirror*. He wrote in his autobiography, 'Someone at that very confidential meeting simply couldn't keep the details to himself . . . I was livid.'

On the same day as the article appeared, we drew 1–1 in the FA Cup at Charlton, but after the match, all the hacks wanted to talk about was the *Sunday Mirror* report. Keegan simply walked out of the press conference.

He walked out of the job two days later when the board called him to a meeting at Sir John's stately pile at Wynyard Hall. They admitted that the deal they'd struck couldn't work because Keegan was a crucial part of the Stock Exchange flotation document. The uncertainty could seriously damage the flotation – Keegan had to sign up for two years or not at all. He realised that this was the end of the line and left.

Les Ferdinand told me how he heard about the news at the training ground: 'Terry McDermott came in and read out a statement from the manager. We just sat there open-mouthed. Afterwards, I went home and thought, "He never recovered from last season." We were so close but so far away the year before, but I think he felt he couldn't lift the boys and do it all over again.

'For me, there were still some unanswered questions – we'd never really sat down and analysed it. We should've sat down as a team and said we can't make these mistakes again – but we didn't. The atmosphere wasn't quite right. We used to go out feeling ten feet tall, but I'm not sure it felt the same the next season.'

Although I'd known instinctively that all wasn't right behind the scenes (you get used to reading between the lines of the press reports and the club statements), none of us knew for sure what was going on until the following day when the club formally announced that Keegan had resigned. The response was typically apocalyptic: it was the end of the world according to some; he'd been pushed according to others; he was a traitor claimed yet more; while dozens gathered outside the ground chanting, 'There's only one Kevin Keegan.' A banner was unfurled saying 'Please don't go'. The Lord Mayor pleaded with him to think again, and even the Prime Minister paid tribute. But the lad was not for turning. Almost five years after he rode to our rescue, he was gone. It truly was the end of another Newcastle era, one which is unlikely ever to be repeated.

The players had seen it coming. Peter Beardsley told me, 'I think Kevin felt that it had all got on top of him, and when the club wanted to become a PLC, that totally killed it for him. His hand was totally changed then. A lot of new people came in whose job was just to make money for the club. They really got on Kevin's nerves, because they didn't understand football, and it got to the situation where they were telling Kevin what he had to do. That was the beginning of the end for him.'

Like Beardsley and Ferdinand, Warren Barton felt things hadn't been the same for some time: 'Most of us thought after the 5–0 win over Man United, "Right, we're back," but even then I think Kevin didn't feel it was quite the same as the year before. He wasn't happy even after we beat Spurs 7–1. He just wasn't himself any more. The PLC talk had taken the club off in a different direction, and he clearly didn't want to do it.'

Alan Oliver told me he thought Keegan was on a hiding to nothing: 'Kevin changed. He'd rescued the club from obscurity and still he faced criticism from fans for signing Tino Asprilla and David Batty. Fans have all got opinions, and they all think they're right. It really is a pressure cooker.'

His colleague John Gibson is more critical. He told me, 'It ended in tears because of Kevin Keegan's personality. He was always going to implode, throw the dummy out of the pram and stomp away with his nappy round his ankles. He did it five times at Newcastle United, sometimes when the public didn't realise. That was his Achilles heel. If he'd won the league, it would have been different. There's no doubt that's what knocked the heart out of him, but it also knocked the heart out of Newcastle United. We'd have been a different club. We'd have certainly won things since. It was a great tragedy.'

My mate Steve O'Brien has always had a reputation for saying things simply to be provocative, and when he told me recently that he felt Keegan's biggest mistake was signing Shearer, I thought he was winding me up. But he insisted he really thought this was true, saying, 'What the team needed then was Tony Adams or someone like him, not another striker. But that was Keegan, and I couldn't criticise him. We won the hearts of the nation playing the way he wanted. He was a great man of the people, and I was very sad when he left.'

For me, there was a degree of inevitability about it all. I occasionally wrote articles for *The Mag* fanzine, and right at the start of the Hall–Keegan era, I'd predicted that, because of the nature of the personalities involved, one day it would all end in tears. I'm not the world's greatest forecaster, but I took absolutely no pleasure in getting that one right.

14

WEMBLEY NIGHTMARE, PART 2 (1997–98)

'When the Toon, go up, to lift the FA Cup, we'll be there.'

Pre-Wembley song, 1998

How do you replace the irreplaceable? That was the task facing the men who ran Newcastle United at the start of 1997. But such was the transformation in the club's fortunes in the five years since Kevin Keegan had taken over that the names in the frame were some of the biggest and the best in football.

First up was former England manager Bobby Robson. Bobby was probably the only manager in the world who would have been tempted to leave Barcelona for Newcastle, but, in the end, he honoured his contract at the Nou Camp. Sir John Hall confessed to me that he rues the day he couldn't land his first choice: 'Had we got Robson when we first approached him, that would have turned the club. But he said he was coming, and then he changed his mind.'

Whoever we went for, the players would be consulted and would be the first to know. Or so they'd been led to believe. Les Ferdinand told me, 'The board got together a committee of five players: Peter Beardsley, Rob Lee, Alan Shearer, John Beresford and me. They said they were keen to get us involved in the process and said they'd contact us if anything happened. A few days later, we were told that Kenny Dalglish had got the job. Our "committee" never ever had a meeting!'

Dalglish's name emerged courtesy of a tip on the BBC's *Match of the Day* from TV pundit and former Liverpool legend Alan Hansen. Hansen's a big mate of Kenny's, and he said the job would be ideal for him. That was the only hint Sir John and his board needed.

I renewed my old acquaintance with Dalglish via the telephone recently, to ask him about his Newcastle 'experience'. Looking back to the day he got the job, he said, 'It's not too often you get the opportunity to manage a new team in good form, and Newcastle were fourth when I took over. Kevin Keegan had done a fantastic job there. At Newcastle, he was a messiah.

'Most people in football know all about the passion of Newcastle, and I certainly wasn't disappointed with the place. Liverpool, Glasgow and Newcastle are very similar places with a very similar culture as well as a great love of football. The only difference is Newcastle only has one team in the city, and that makes it a bit special.'

Kenny's big problem was always going to be his PR. *Anyone* following Keegan faced an impossible task. The bloke had charmed the birds out of the trees. He'd been the black-and-white Pied Piper, and we'd happily danced to his tune as he led us to the promised land of the Premiership. Kenny, on the other hand, was renowned for his non-cooperation with the media, something I'd witnessed on many occasions during my time at Mercury Press and Granada. This became his public persona, and your average football fan thought he was a miserable Scottish git. However, I knew that he was immensely charismatic, popular with his players and could be great to work with – when the fancy took him. I was once stunned as I hurried up to Ewood Park for a Newcastle match to hear someone bellowing my name from the other side of the road – it was Kenny, then manager at

Liverpool, also on his way to the game to do some spying. He had a big smile on his face and waved cheerily. Bloody hell, I thought, why are none of your mates with you when something like this happens!

My gut instinct was that Kenny could be ideal for Newcastle. Nobody in the world could repeat the attacking flair that Keegan had encouraged, but a bloke who'd won four league titles would know exactly what had to be done to get last year's runners-up over the line in first place this time. Or so I hoped.

Kenny had left Liverpool in the wake of the Hillsborough tragedy, something which had affected him deeply. At Blackburn, he 'did a Keegan' with the notable difference that he actually won the title, making him only the third manager to win the league with two different clubs. He'd be out on his own if he did it with Newcastle.

I did have one awkward moment with Kenny during his Blackburn days when I was working for *Standing Room Only*. Like Keegan, he'd done the 'Standpoint' interview for me and was perfectly good-humoured as well as being engaging company. The BBC sent out a press release plugging our programme and included sizeable quotes from the interview. The day the programme was due to go out, we got a two-page spread in the *Mirror* – but they'd picked up on one thing he'd said about being nostalgic for the days of the standing terraces, and that became the story. 'Stand By Me' was the headline above an article which said that the man who was so affected by Hillsborough was calling for the return of the terraces. Anyone who watched the TV that night would see he clearly wasn't, but the damage had been done.

Kenny rang me as soon as he'd seen the paper and chewed my ear about it, telling me he'd had grief from the Hillsborough families organisation who couldn't believe he'd been so insensitive. I was devastated. He'd given me an interview in good faith, and it had blown up in my face. I don't think he blamed me personally – he was media savvy enough to know how these things worked – but next time I saw him he blanked me, something he'd never done before.

Kenny's first job was to get us through our FA Cup replay with Charlton, which he duly did, winning 2–1. I remember a classic moment near the end when, 2–1 up, we got a corner. Out of habit, our defenders trotted forward into the Charlton box, only for Dalglish to come racing out of the dugout to wave them back to the halfway line. 'What we've got, we keep' seemed to be the motto, and those of us still bearing the fresh scars of last-minute defeats at Liverpool and Blackburn smiled at the sight. This was what we needed to go the extra mile.

Les Ferdinand confirmed to me what I'd always heard – footballers love working with Dalglish: 'We enjoyed having Kenny about. It felt right, and he made a few changes, because he realised we'd have to compromise somewhere. It wasn't the same old Newcastle, but you'd take that in exchange for winning things.'

We certainly would have, but, sadly, we went out of the FA Cup in the next round, beaten 2–1 at home by Nottingham Forest. League form was variable, and there soon followed a match which would dramatically illustrate the differences between Keegan's Newcastle and Dalglish's. We lost 4–3 at Anfield again, but compared to the feast of football we'd been served up 12 months earlier, this was a boil-in-the-bag affair. In the first half, we were as bad as we'd been in years and went behind 3–0 to a fairly average Liverpool side. It was so bad that one Newcastle fan broke through security and threw his shirt at Dalglish in protest. But in the second half, we staged an improbable fight back to draw level at 3–3. We leapt about, of course, but we were actually laughing because we'd been so poor in the first half, and the Liverpool supporters just couldn't believe it. The chances of us getting a draw had seemed so unlikely – and undeserved – at half-time. Of course, being Newcastle, it couldn't last, and Robbie Fowler popped up with the winner in front of the Kop in the dying seconds. Bollocks.

Either side of that game we'd crashed out of the UEFA Cup, losing home and away to Monaco, and the natives were now getting restless. However, Dalglish rallied the troops, and we then went on an unbeaten ten-match run to the end of the season which saw us finish in second place again, this time seven points behind Man United. A storming 5–0 win over Nottingham Forest on the last day of the season meant that we finished above Arsenal and Liverpool on goal difference (hey, maybe there is a God) and made it into the Champions League qualifiers. From 1997, teams finishing second in the 'stronger' (wealthier?) European leagues were admitted to the 'Champions' League competition. This was yet another rule change designed to make rich clubs even richer and poor clubs yet poorer. The madness of it was that here we were, a club that hadn't won the domestic title for 70 years, being admitted into a competition for champions. Bonkers. But we were about to make about £10 million from the arrangement, so there weren't too many grumbles from Gallowgate and surrounding areas.

Kenny was now just about accepted. The fans even started singing his name, but I could never take it seriously, because 'King Kenny's black-and-white army' always sounded like 'Kinky knees, black-and-white army' to me. Oh, and there was one more significant match that season – Jules and I managed to fit in our wedding, the day before we lost 1–0 at home to Southampton.

Many fans were unhappy at this point. They hadn't expected the level of excitement and flair to drop off so dramatically. But most of us were prepared to wait and see what would happen once Kenny had a chance to do his own fine-tuning of the squad. After all, we'd finished second and we were in the Champions League for the first time. He obviously had the knack.

The 'fine tuning' turned out to be a bit of an overhaul, something I felt a bit uncomfortable with. After all, the team wasn't broke, so why fix it? But in came Alessandro Pistone, Shay Given, Temuri Ketsbaia and Jon Dahl Tomasson. But more worrying was the recruitment of three 'veterans'. Stuart Pearce, John Barnes and Ian Rush were among the best players British football had seen in the recent past. Unfortunately, the key word was 'past'.

If we were concerned by some of the arrivals, we were horrified by the departures. David Ginola, a Keegan icon, was sold to Spurs for a cut-price £2 million, while local hero Peter Beardsley was sold to Bolton at the age of 36. Beardsley is philosophical about it now, but I suspect it still hurts. He told me, 'Kenny came in and decided, for whatever reason, that I wasn't good enough, so I had to move on, but I still think – and this may be big-headed for me to say when you look at some of the players that Kenny brought in – I still think I was good enough to be in that team.'

Because both Ginola and Beardsley had played so rarely under Dalglish, we'd all braced ourselves for their inevitable departure. Local lads Lee Clark and Robbie Elliott also moved on, but one other transfer shocked and upset every United fan. Sir Les Ferdinand, one of the true heroes of the Toon Army and one half of a sensational strike partnership with Alan Shearer, was sold to Spurs for £6 million when he was at the height of his powers.

Sir Les gave me his version of his departure: 'There were rumours that the club had to raise £6 million and that I might be sold to raise it. Kenny and I had a chat, and he said he didn't want me to go and was going to talk to the board to ask if I could stay. But I felt he didn't really mean it.

'Later, I went into his office and told him I was thinking about buying a house and needed to know what was happening. He said, "We've had a bid from Spurs, and the club has accepted. You are free to go and talk to them." But as we shook hands, he said, "I don't want you to leave. I hope it falls through."'

Then fate took a hand. The day Les travelled to London, we played Everton in a pre-season tournament, and Alan Shearer picked up a freak injury. Les, of course, didn't have a clue about this. He said, 'I met Alan Sugar on the Saturday, and we shook on a deal. That night, I was in a restaurant with my girlfriend, and there was a phone call from my agent telling me, "Alan Shearer has broken his ankle – Newcastle want to offer you a new deal." I couldn't believe it – they'd wanted to sell me five minutes earlier! But I'd given Spurs my word, and I wasn't going to go back on it. I hadn't wanted to leave Newcastle, but they made it so that I had to leave. Later on, I spoke to Alan Shearer to commiserate with him over his injury, and he told me, "I don't blame you for not re-signing. It was crap the way it was done."'

Warren Barton and those who survived the cull were a little disconcerted by the changes: 'Kenny came because he was the number-one candidate. He'd done it all, and we thought he was the final bit of the puzzle. Lots of players left, but of all of them, I never understood why Les left. Losing Les should've been a no-go – he was a real personality, such a major figure in the dressing-room.'

The transfer dealings seemed a bit excessive. Lots of departures, lots of arrivals and, overall, a clear profit for Newcastle United. The suspicion was aroused that the board were clawing back some of the money spent by Keegan in his quest for the elusive title. There had long been stories that one of the reasons Kevin left was that he'd been told to raise £6 million to keep the bank happy, something he was loathe to do. The fact that Ferdinand was sold for precisely that amount was just too much of a coincidence for many fans.

We're a cynical breed. It doesn't take much to get us wondering if there's a hidden agenda or whether we're being taken for a ride. When we bought Shearer, we were convinced we were one of the big players on the European stage. OK, we had now reached the Champions League, but none of the other Euro giants were selling their star strikers. One thing was certain – we were now a public limited company, and the days when John Hall could take a wild, speculative but ultimately inspired gamble were a thing of the past. And our suspicion that our big chance to win the title had passed us by in 1996 was about to be proved correct.

Thanks to transfers and Shearer's horrendous injury, we began the new season with a strike force of Tino Asprilla and Jon Dahl

Tomasson. Ask anyone who saw it about the 'Jon Dahl Tomasson' moment, and they'll immediately tell you that inside the first minute of his debut against Sheffield Wednesday the young striker was put clean through on goal and missed. It set the tone for his unhappy stay on Tyneside, and Geordies everywhere would shake their heads in later years as JDT became the scourge of European defences while scoring freely for AC Milan and Denmark.

Premiership season 1997–98 is best forgotten. The swashbuckling and exciting football was gone, although that wasn't really a surprise. But also gone were regular wins, which we'd kind of hoped were now par for the course. Even the return of Alan Shearer at the end of January didn't change things. At one stage, we won just two league games in nineteen, prompting Kenny to go into the transfer market again. Gary Speed, Nikos Dabizas and another young Scandinavian striker called Andreas Andersson arrived to shore up a squad which was looking a pale imitation of the one which had thrilled the entire country two years earlier. Most fans expected Kenny to make us less attractive but more consistent. What we got was dull, sometimes turgid football, and 11 wins, 11 draws and 16 defeats left us in 13th place. Some comedown.

Kenny defends his record at Newcastle, and, on paper at least, it's hard to argue with him. He told me, 'You can only do your best, and we qualified for the Champions League because of the goals we scored. We won the last game of the season 5–0, and there were a few threes and fours as well. When I was at Blackburn, we were top goal scorers, and my Liverpool teams always scored goals. I've never changed my philosophy.'

But to make matters worse, the club found itself in the glare of the media spotlight when chairman Freddy Shepherd and majority shareholder Douglas Hall became the victims of a tabloid-newspaper sting. The pair were photographed in a Marbella brothel and were recorded boasting about how they ripped off fans by charging £50 for cheap, imported replica shirts. They also labelled Geordie women 'dogs' and called Alan Shearer 'Mary Poppins', presumably because he wouldn't dream of going into a Marbella brothel, let alone accept free booze and hookers when a mystery 'millionaire' offered them on a plate. The mystery man was the *News of the World*'s 'fake sheikh' Mazher Mahmood, who'd established a dubious reputation for his ability to sting the rich and famous, usually through their weakness for sex, drugs, booze, money or a combination of two or more of the aforementioned.

Dalglish defends the pair to this day: 'I stood by them at the time, and I still stand right beside them over that incident in Marbella. When someone approaches you with a business proposition, you go and talk to them in good faith. But it's very difficult when people use entrapment. When you talk to someone in a pub, you have a completely different conversation to the one you'd have with a press man.

'Of course, it's something you don't need at a football club. But I don't blame Freddy Shepherd and Douglas Hall. They were pursuing something which they thought was in the best interest of the club. There was a lot of exaggeration around at the time – for example, Alan Shearer wasn't upset at all by the Mary Poppins thing.'

Despite Kenny's loyalty to his former employers, this was just about the most embarrassing thing that had happened to Newcastle United during the 40-odd years I'd been following them. On-the-pitch humiliations are one thing, but this was in a different league. The club's name was dragged through the papers and across radio and TV for days afterwards. The two (married) men stood down in shame and Douglas's father, Sir John Hall, flew back from his Marbella retirement to steady the ship. But to many of us, the scandal was the final evidence that the club had lost its way both on and off the pitch. Those weeks had the feel of the last days of a once great empire or government which had been in power too long and had become rotten to the core. The freshness and excitement of the past few years was well and truly gone.

If there was a silver lining that season, it came in the form of the cups. Our Champions League adventure took us past Croatia Zagreb and into the group stages, and for one glorious night on Tyneside, we started to get silly Fairs Cup-type dreams again. The first game in Group C saw the arrival on Tyneside of the mighty Barcelona, who, predictably, had not been loyal to Bobby Robson and were now managed by Louis van Gaal. The game was a belter, and we played the kind of football we'd become accustomed to some years earlier with Keith Gillespie running riot down the wing and Tino Asprilla scoring a memorable hat-trick in a 3–2 win. However, it turned out Barcelona weren't so 'mighty' after all, and while we finished in third place behind Dynamo Kiev and PSV Eindhoven, the Catalan giants sat humbly in fourth.

We also had a bit of a run in the Coca-Cola, reaching the quarter-finals. Because of our Champions League status, we were exempted from round two, and after beating Hull City and Derby County, we then faced Kenny's old mates from Liverpool at home in the quarter-finals. We lost 2–0.

However, against all the odds, we went back to Wembley in 1998 to play in the FA Cup final. Don't ask me how we did it – we were firing on two cylinders most of the season – but get there we did, taking us within 90 minutes of finally ending the domestic-trophy jinx which had dogged us since 1955. Sadly, we had to play league champions Arsenal in the final.

It all began, fittingly enough, on Merseyside. Kenny took Barnes and Rush back to the ground where they'd always been successful – Goodison Park. Since his arrival at Newcastle, the most prolific goal scorer Liverpool had ever seen had clearly forgotten how to do what used to come naturally to him, and by the time 1998 arrived, Ian Rush had failed to score a Premiership goal in a black-and-white shirt. But this was the FA Cup, and this was Everton, and Rushie had always had the hex on Liverpool's neighbours. Happily for us, old habits die hard. Result? 1–0, Rush. It was a scruffy goal as well, which hacked off the Evertonians even more.

Next came a miserable exercise in how not to conduct a football match between a big club and a little club. When we were drawn away to non-league Stevenage Borough, my first reaction, and that of many Newcastle fans of a certain age, was, 'Oh, no, not another Hereford.' The first reaction of the people who ran the two clubs was, 'Let's switch the tie to Newcastle.' For Stevenage, it meant more money; for Newcastle, it meant a better chance of progressing. But the thing then became a political mess with Stevenage changing tack to insist the game be played at their ground and Newcastle demanding rigorous safety checks before agreeing to play. Everyone thought we were scared. The most surreal point came when our manager turned up on *Newsnight* and was asked by Jeremy Paxman, 'Is Kenny Dalglish a big girl's blouse?'

When I asked him about the Stevenage debacle, Dalglish insisted the media made a mountain of a molehill: 'It was another thing instigated by the press. All we ever said was, "If it's safe and secure, we'll play them at Hackney Marshes." We didn't have a problem.'

The exchanges between the clubs, conducted in the press, were an unseemly and undignified PR disaster for all concerned, and, of course, when it came to play the match, the whole country wanted the little team to beat the big team. And they nearly did. The game at Stevenage was Shearer's first after his long injury, and he headed us into a 1–0 lead, but they equalised before half-time, leaving us to survive some sticky moments before escaping with a replay. We saw them off 2–1 at SJP thanks to two more goals from Big Al. It was just a relief to get it out of the way.

Ever since we beat West Brom on the way to the cup final in 1974, I've always regarded the fifth round as the crucial one. Win that and you're in the quarter-finals and everyone starts thinking, 'This is our year.' The football gods, who, let's face it, have not always smiled kindly on Newcastle United, were in generous mood in 1998, giving us an eminently winnable home tie with Tranmere Rovers of Division One. The performance was not an eminent one, but we did win it 1–0 with that Shearer bloke scoring again. We also got a home draw in the quarter-finals, this time against Barnsley, with Ketsbaia, Speed and Batty scoring in a 3–1 win.

That result put us in the semi-finals for the first time in 24 years, where we joined Arsenal and two First Division sides, Wolves and Sheffield United. Luck really was on our side now, pairing us with Sheffield United and giving us a hell of a chance of a trip to Wembley.

The big day arrived. Sime and I made the short trek from Liverpool to Manchester and met up with Chris, Mick and the lads in the Sawyer's Arms on Deansgate, where we watched on the big screen as Arsenal eased past Wolves and into the final. Soon it was our turn.

Old Trafford is a fantastic venue for a semi-final, and on 5 April 1998, it reverberated like never before. With over 53,000 people split 50–50, it was a riot of noise and a sea of red, black and white. To drift into cliché for a second, this was Sheffield United's cup final. They were the lower-division side who nobody expected to win and who were thrilled just to have got this far. But there was an added twist in that they knew with a fair wind they quite easily *could* win against an out-of-sorts, struggling Premiership side – which is what we'd become.

In the end, one man was the difference – England's centre-forward Alan Shearer. Big Al was the first to rise to a John Barnes cross, and when his header was stopped at point-blank range by the Sheffield keeper Alan Kelly, Shearer was the first to react, thrashing the loose ball into the net from a couple of yards. The place went berserk – well, at least half of it did.

Kenny Dalglish realised at that moment what the promise of success means to the Geordies and exactly how 43 years of waiting for a trophy had affected us. He told me, 'When we scored in the semi-final, the passion and the thrill on the faces of the Newcastle punters is something I will never ever forget. It was unbelievable.'

Once the final whistle blew, all the disappointment of the league season evaporated with the thought that at last we were in the cup final. To a whole new generation of the Toon Army, this was a first.

To us veterans of 1974, there was the security of knowing it couldn't
be any worse than last time – could it?

The road to Wembley lacked the drama and excitement which
characterised the 1974 run, but we were there – even if we'd sneaked
in under the radar. We'd got lucky with home draws and inferior
opposition, but we felt that we were long overdue a break.

As 16 May approached, there was another significant date on my
horizon. I was about to become a dad. Jules's due date wasn't until the
end of the month, but I was still having surreal dreams in which I was
the bloke whose name got read out over the Wembley Tannoy at half-
time: 'A message for Ged Clarke in the Newcastle end – your wife has
given birth to a 7 lb 7 oz silver trophy.' I needn't have worried. Rachel
wasn't born until 31 May, and there was never any danger that the 11
midwives in black and white would deliver us a bit of silverware.

Sime and I caught the very early train from Liverpool and read all
the papers (well, the bits about the football anyway). The *Mirror*'s
Brian Reade, a Scouser, wrote a nostalgic piece about his memories of
the Newcastle fans at the 1974 final:

> It was quite unbelievable. In the 32 years I've been going to
> football matches, I've never experienced this scale of generosity
> in the face of slaughter. Much is spoken, mainly by managers
> in trouble, about fans deserving success, and much of it is
> patronising drivel. But in Newcastle's case, it is possible to
> make an exception. After 43 years without a major domestic
> trophy, after the insulting season they have had to endure on
> and off the pitch, and after their single-handed contribution
> to keep our shirt-making industry afloat, they deserve the cup
> today.

He also compared the two Liverpool greats who'd both tried to finally
end our trophy drought:

Keegan and Dalglish were both winners as players. But no matter how you look at it, as managers, only one of them is a natural winner. Keegan broke their hearts when they were last at Wembley. If Dalglish mends them today, he will erase the memory of 1974. And of Keegan. He will be Newcastle's new messiah. And that is one hell of an incentive to stop Arsenal doing the Double.

After meeting the lads at an unfeasibly early hour in a Notting Hill pub (which, by happy coincidence, was run by Mick's brother), we got to the stadium in boisterous mood. But despite several pints of courage – that's 'courage' with a small 'c' – we were not brimming with optimism. After all, Arsenal had just won the Premiership and were going for the Double. (We don't pick our fights very well when we get to Wembley.)

As you'd expect, Wembley was awash with thousands of Geordies dressed as footballers, their black-and-white replica shirts a timely reminder of the two men who'd run the club until their tabloid humiliation at the hands of the fake sheikh. Messrs Shepherd and Hall had decided to stay away from the final in case their presence upset Newcastle fans. Wise move.

When all's said and done, it wasn't as bad as 1974. We hit the bar and the post in our (very short) purple patch at the start of the second half, but by then, we were chasing the game. Dalglish, obviously concerned about the pace of Arsenal's left-winger, Dutchman Marc Overmars, sent out a strange-looking, lop-sided team. Pistone, who was usually a left-back, played at right-back in order to keep track of Overmars. Barton, normally a right-back, played on the right of midfield in order to protect Pistone, while Shearer was playing up front on his own against one of the best defences in Europe.

The Pistone experiment failed miserably, and he was outpaced by the flying Dutchman, who scored Arsenal's first goal midway through the first half. Warren Barton told me that he wasn't totally happy with the line-up: 'I was in midfield in front of Pistone, and, to be honest, I'd rather have had Stevie Watson. It was a cup final – you just wanted to have a go; you wanted to go down fighting. We were so flat at half-time in the dressing-room, and we tried to rally, but they were too good.'

The 'rally' consisted of Dabizas's header onto the top of the bar and then Shearer, pouncing after a slip by Martin Keown, slapping a shot against the inside of Seaman's left-hand post. If only that had gone in . . . although you suspect that Arsenal would simply have stepped up a gear and put us out of our agony, as they did 20 minutes from time when Nicolas Anelka ran on to Ray Parlour's through ball and stroked it past Given. Two-nil. All over. Again.

Another ex-player I tracked down was Gary Speed. I asked him for his memories of the big day, and he put it bluntly: 'Confidence was low going into the final, whereas Arsenal were just the opposite, and that showed in the game. We were never in the match, although we could have equalised when Al hit the post. If that had gone in, you never know what might have happened.'

I asked Dalglish if, with hindsight, he would have done anything differently. He said, 'I don't think we had too many options. We were not overconfident, but neither were we going there thinking we were going to lose. They were a good side, but we weren't too bad either. We wanted to win the thing, and I think we did as best we could.

'We would have liked to have played better, but when you hit the woodwork twice, you wonder if it's going your way. We were starting to dominate, and Arsène Wenger admitted afterwards that if we'd scored then, they would have been in trouble.'

As usual, our star performers were on the terraces, the Toon Army staying behind en masse to applaud Tony Adams and his Double-winners. *The Sun*'s headline was 'Newcastle fans show their class as they stomach yet another sour show'. And below it, John Sadler wrote, 'My abiding memory of the 1998 FA Cup final will be of all those people who converged on Wembley with their dreams. And left as losers.'

He was taken by the image of Alan Shearer, who cut a lonely figure at the final whistle: 'The England captain just stood in the centre-circle and stared . . . looking on in apparent disbelief at the human black-and-white wall of people clapping, dancing and roaring out their undiminished message, "Oh Newcastle, we love you."'

Warren Barton's pals were equally impressed: 'My mates are all Arsenal fans. They'd just won the Double, but all they kept saying to me was, "Your fans are incredible!" And they were right.'

Both Dalglish and Wenger were quick to praise our proud, defiant but sporting display towards the celebrating Arsenal players. But, actually, most of us just wanted to see what the FA Cup looked like in real life.

The next day, the team did the traditional thing of touring round Newcastle on an open-top bus without a trophy. Not a pleasant experience, as Gary Speed remembered: 'All we'd seen on the way in to Wembley was the Newcastle fans, and they were fantastic all day. On the open-top bus in Newcastle, they were fantastic again. We knew we'd been poor, and it was difficult to go through with it. We knew we'd let the fans down, and we were being paraded as heroes when we felt anything but.'

It's a strange phenomenon, the losers' homecoming party, but one we've perfected in Newcastle. To be honest, lots of the people who turn out aren't diehard fans. There's always a good sprinkling of mums and dads with kids, as well as the usual high percentage of Geordies who'd go anywhere if there's a hint of a piss-up. But, having said that, Newcastle fans have shown remarkable forgiveness to the teams who've let them down, or even embarrassed them, on the big occasions. I think this is an in-built, Geordie thing which we do spontaneously and with effortless charm. To be honest, I don't think we'd have a clue how to react if they actually turned up with a silver pot one day.

On the night of the cup final, I travelled back to Liverpool alone. As I returned from the buffet car on the train with a consolation can of beer in hand, I got a knowing smile from a bloke in an Arsenal shirt.

I stopped for a chat, and he made this observation: 'Arsène Wenger came in and realised our defence was good, so he left it alone and rebuilt our attack. Now we've won the Double. Dalglish took over a team with a brilliant attack and a dodgy defence. What does he do? He leaves the defence alone and rebuilds your attack!' The man had a point.

The next day, on another train home, two Newcastle directors were pinned in their seats by a large group of Toon fans who 'offered their views' on the manager and what he was doing to their team. Drink had been taken on board but so were the views. And in the summer, they'd be discussed in the boardroom.

When he wasn't watching the World Cup in France, Kenny Dalglish spent the summer of '98 doing more radical alteration work. He spent £13 million bringing in French defender Laurent Charvet, German midfielder Dietmar Hamann, the Peruvian winger Nolberto Solano and the French striker Stéphane Guivarc'h, amongst others. Guivarc'h was a member of France's World Cup-winning team but most commentators were distinctly unimpressed by him – he hadn't managed a goal in the entire tournament.

The revolving door at St James' Park had been busy all year – Asprilla, Beresford, Rush, Tomasson, Peacock, Srníček and Hislop were all gone as Kenny shuffled the pack like a card sharp. But, unbeknownst to him, he was playing his final hand. The game was almost up, and two games into the season, it was.

The decision to change the manager was almost certainly made after our opening fixture of the new season ended 0–0. The players were booed off St James' Park after the game against newly promoted Charlton Athletic (who played much of the match with ten men). A week later, we drew 1–1 at Chelsea, but the spectacle was grim. Two days later, a boardroom delegation flew to Amsterdam for talks with their next potential manager. 'Sexy football' was high on the agenda.

15

WEMBLEY NIGHTMARE, PART 3 (1998–99)

'When the Toon, go up, to lift the FA Cup, we'll be dead.'

Post-Wembley song, 1999

Shortly after Kenny Dalglish took on the job at St James' Park, Kevin Keegan offered a prediction which is worth looking at, sentence by sentence. He said, 'If he brings a trophy to St James' Park, he will experience a public reaction and celebration the likes of which he didn't see even at Liverpool or Blackburn. Newcastle United is a roller-coaster – one you want to ride. He is going to have the time of his life.' These three sentences speak volumes about Newcastle United and Dalglish's time there. Sentence number one was prefaced with the biggest little word of all: 'if'. And because sentence one didn't come true, sentence three couldn't have been further from the truth. Kenny would point to sentence two as the reason.

No Newcastle manager had won a trophy in almost thirty years, and Joe Harvey was in the job seven years before he achieved it. Kenny had been in the job just over a year and a half. In that time, he finished second in the Premiership then second in the FA Cup, so, on paper at least, he got pretty close. But perhaps Kenny's big problem was that he didn't truly understand the NUFC roller-coaster. It is the ultimate ride, and anyone who installs seat belts is missing the point.

When I asked Warren Barton the differences he'd noticed under Dalglish, he said, 'We were a lot more defensive-minded, always trying to nick a goal. But Newcastle fans would rather lose 3–2 than get a 0–0. They need to be entertained. Some players came in, but they didn't have the same mentality as the players did under Kevin. We knew the football wasn't as good, and it was frustrating for us as well. But to be fair to Kenny, he always protected his players. There were times when he should have said we were crap, but he stood up for us.'

Kenny himself is philosophical about his experience: 'I have no feelings of animosity towards anyone at Newcastle. It was a huge disappointment, of course, but people have to make decisions, and to this day, Freddy Shepherd is someone who is still a friend.

'The step up from second to first is the hardest step you will ever make in your life. We finished second, qualified for the Champions League and the following season we reached the FA Cup final. If I was asked to do it all over again, I'd give the same answer, because it's a fantastic football club with great supporters. If anyone was being offered the job and asked me for my opinion, I'd say, "Don't hesitate. Don't think twice about it. Just go and do it."

'The day it ended was very sad, but it meant a great deal to me up there. It's a club and a place that our whole family hold in deep affection. I just wish I had been the guy who had walked away with a trophy – not for me and for my CV, but for the supporters.'

Whatever your views on the way we played football under Kenny Dalglish, what can't be argued is that the timing of his dismissal was perverse in the extreme. He's probably the only Premiership manager ever to have been sacked without losing a match in a new campaign. But more to the point, he was sacked weeks after having being allowed to spend £13 million on completely revamping the squad.

The men behind this curiously timed decision were the same men who had supposedly stepped down a few months earlier, following their embarrassment in the pages of the *News of the World*. Whether Freddy Shepherd and Douglas Hall ever actually vacated their seats in the boardroom isn't clear, but by the time the new season kicked off, they'd slowly eased their way back into place and were behind the move to sack Dalglish and replace him with Ruud Gullit.

No one on the terraces had forgiven them, but, then again, no one on the terraces had any influence. Now that Newcastle United was a PLC, most of us felt that any bond we'd had with our club had been pretty much dissolved. They seemed to be a law unto themselves; they could do what they wanted to, and that's just what they were doing. I, for one, felt that Newcastle United had become the finest example of all that was going wrong with the game I loved. The problem was, and is, that it's not like anything else. You can't just walk away when you're pissed off. It's your club, and it always will be. And, of course, there's always that nagging little feeling: what if this is a master stroke? What if Ruud Gullit *is* the answer? You know you have to be there – just in case. And, of course, they know that. They also know that a new big-name boss will excite us, because we are football fans – mugs of the highest order who live in continual hope, clutching at the flimsiest straws.

Not that there was anything flimsy about Ruud Gullit. He was one of the most famous faces in world football. A former European and World Footballer of the Year, his flowing dreadlocks and fabulous skills made sure he stood out, whether he was winning the European Championship with Holland or Italian titles and European Cups with AC Milan. The club which once settled for Gordon Lee, Richard Dinnis and Bill McGarry had certainly bagged a big one. As a TV pundit, Gullit had coined the phrase 'sexy football', and it became his trademark – Shepherd and Hall were quite happy to pay for a bit of sexiness at Newcastle.

The deal was done quickly. Dalglish was in charge on the Saturday at Chelsea, the directors flew to Amsterdam on the Monday and Kenny was out on the Wednesday. The first the fans knew was when we saw the *Daily Mirror* on the Thursday morning.

Gary Speed got his first inkling as he drove to the club's Durham training ground: 'I passed a Tyne Tees TV van heading down the A1, and it followed me into Durham. That's when I knew that something was up.

'It was a great shock. We were disappointed, because Kenny was very popular with the players – and, of course, he was the manager who brought me to the club. That always means something to a player.'

When Ruud arrived at St James' Park, there was quite a reception committee, many fans wearing dreadlock wigs in his honour. Someone had even plonked one on Jackie Milburn's statue. Only 19 months earlier, there had been a similarly enthusiastic welcome party for Kenny.

Gullit signed a two-year deal and said all the right things on arrival: 'I'm very proud I've been given this job – it is a great opportunity. My only target is to make Newcastle the greatest and overtake Arsenal and Manchester United. I want to win; I must win. I have won things all my life, and I am coming to Newcastle to be successful.'

The next game was at home to Liverpool, and Gullit said he'd watch from the stand and take formal charge of the first training session the following week. But by half-time, he was in the dressing-room in front of the blackboard, trying to salvage a degree of respectability. Liverpool had taken us to the cleaners, with a young Michael Owen running riot and scoring a hat-trick. Gullit's rearranged team stemmed the tide, and we ended up losing 4–1, Stéphane Guivarc'h scoring on his debut. He'd start one more game and would never score again for United. Early in November, Gullit sold him to Glasgow Rangers for £3.5 million, the same amount Dalglish had paid for him.

Gullit got off to an impressive start and Gary Speed certainly liked what he saw: 'I thought it was great. I'd loved him as a player, and I was excited because he'd done a great job at Chelsea. He had an aura and was hard to ignore. He was very confident in himself. He actually left me out for a few games. I'd never been through a period like that before, so it probably did me good because I won him over in the end.'

The good start didn't last, and Gullit soon started moving players out, including David Batty, Keith Gillespie and, to the upset of all Geordies, local boy Steve Watson. From the off, there were stories that Alan Shearer would be the biggest casualty of all. Shearer was seen as a Dalglish man and was clearly the biggest personality at the club. But now the ego had landed, in the shape of Gullit, who, during his Chelsea days, once described Shearer as 'a waste of money' at £15 million. The press seemed to circle the club, waiting for the inevitable confrontation. But it didn't happen – not in public anyway. Instead, Gullit brought in a new strike partner for the England No. 9, splashing out £8 million for Everton's cult hero, the big, brawny, injury-prone, former jailbird Duncan Ferguson. 'Big Dunc', as he was universally known to fans and players alike, lasted just five games before he got injured in the last game of 1998 and we didn't see him again until May.

We were also out of two cups before the end of the year. The only good thing to come out of our dismal FA Cup final appearance in May had been a place in the European Cup-Winners' Cup for the first time in our history. Yet again we were in Europe under false pretences. The previous season we'd been in the Champions League when we hadn't been champions since 1927, and now, because Arsenal had won the Double, we were in the Cup-Winners' Cup when we hadn't been cup winners since 1955. The mad, bad world of modern, cash-driven football.

Still, it didn't last long. We beat Partizan Belgrade 2–1 at home, but a 1–0 defeat in Yugoslavia meant we were out on the away goals rule. The League Cup was now the Worthington Cup (sixth different name, if you're counting), and we had an interesting night at Tranmere in the third round. Sitting in the main stand, not far along to our left, was one Kenny Dalglish, who'd come to see his son Paul playing for Newcastle. Dalglish had signed his son on a free from Liverpool a year earlier, but it was Gullit who gave Dalglish junior his debut. Paul made three substitute appearances before forcing his way into the side, ahead of his dad's expensive World Cup signing Guivarc'h. (Pick the ironies out of that lot yourself!) Anyway, suffice to say we won 1–0 at Tranmere with the only goal being scored by . . . Paul Dalglish. No one jumped higher than the Scottish bloke in the camel coat to our left.

In the next round, we played Blackburn Rovers at home but lost on penalties with young Aaron Hughes and Didi Hamann missing for us. My mate Chris is always first with a witty one-liner, even in times of desperation. This night was no exception. As soon as Hamann missed from the spot, Chris weighed in with, 'Typical. We buy the only bloody German who can't take a penalty.'

We were miles off being a settled side and even further away from being a good one.

Hamann, in and out of the team like most players, launched an angry outburst which just about summed up what most fans were thinking: 'We are selling and buying players week in, week out. It creates a negative atmosphere. We have 15 internationals at this club. They should give us time to become a team.'

More disturbingly, he spoke of a divided dressing-room with English and foreign players in separate camps. (Hamann was reportedly given a copy of Hitler's *Mein Kampf* as a 'present' at the players' Christmas party, while injury-prone Italian Alessandro Pistone received a sheep's heart! Not surprisingly, Hamann also accused the English players of having the wrong attitude.) Next, the press got hold of a Shearer–Gullit 'bust-up' story, and it was open season at Newcastle once again.

* * *

Shearer's training-ground row with Gullit had been a long time coming. At that stage, they were barely speaking to each other, but the bust-up was more than just a clash of styles or personalities. Shearer was convinced that the manager was treating some players unfairly and was determined to speak up for his mates, especially Rob Lee, who'd been dropped from the team.

Gary Speed gave me a bit of insight into what was going on behind the scenes. He said, 'All wasn't well. It certainly wasn't a healthy environment, but there was definitely no split in the camp among the players. It was just between Ruud Gullit and Alan Shearer. On top of that, Ruud had alienated Rob Lee and Stuart Pearce. You could see it coming. He knew what his team was, and he just disregarded the others.'

Warren Barton endorsed Speed's view: 'I'm convinced that Ruud only got at Rob Lee because he couldn't get at Alan Shearer. There was always a tense atmosphere between the two of them – Alan just got on with his job, but Ruud let it get personal . . . You can't let that sort of stuff get in the way.

'Don't get me wrong – I got on fine with Ruud. We all respected him when he first came. He was a great player and a good coach with some interesting ideas. He'd proved that with his success at Chelsea. But we didn't find out about his man-management until a lot later. He brought in some good players, but I don't think he showed a lot of respect to the ones who were already there – senior pros like John Barnes, Stuart Pearce and Nikos Dabizas. Naturally you start to wonder, "When will it be my turn?"'

With dissent in the ranks and league form patchy at best, Gullit's first season was saved by another unlikely run to the FA Cup final. It was after the third-round match with Crystal Palace that our eccentric boss first hinted that he thought dark forces might be at work. We'd won the game 2–1 but had to play most of it with ten men after Shay Given had been sent off for supposedly handling the ball outside the box. This, combined with a number of injuries – especially Duncan

Ferguson's – had pushed Ruud into thinking the club could be jinxed. He said, 'If there's a curse, then we must try to do something about it. We can't be in this situation all the time with strange incidents occurring.'

It later emerged that he contacted the city's Roman Catholic cathedral and asked for some help. Monsignor Kevin Nicholls told *The Journal,* 'I spoke briefly with Mr Gullit after he came to the cathedral . . . He asked if he could have the ground blessed in an attempt to improve the fortunes of the club, and we were more than happy to oblige. I did not carry out the ceremony myself, but I believe it involved the spreading of holy water around the ground and the saying of prayers for the club.'

It's amazing how quickly Newcastle United can get to you. Alan Oliver tells a story about Gullit having the away dressing-room at Southampton sprinkled with salt to help rectify our appalling record on the south coast. We lost 4–2. Despite these various interventions, it seems we still remain 'cursed' never to win a trophy.

Ruud could have been forgiven a degree of paranoia when the Newcastle managerial circus came to town, disguised as Peter Beardsley's testimonial. The Toon's favourite son had organised an all-star line-up to play for United against Celtic, including Kevin Keegan, Kenny Dalglish and his now out-of-favour son Paul. The fans loved it, especially the late appearance of Keegan, who hadn't been seen since his dramatic departure over two years earlier, while the ovation given to Rob Lee made it clear what the fans thought of Gullit's treatment of their No. 7.

Then, after several transfer deals fell through and his ex-wife had a few unflattering things to say in one of the tabloids, his agent organised a charm offensive. Soon Gullit was dismissing stories that his players didn't like him or that he was an absentee manager. He also claimed he got along fine with Alan Shearer, who wasn't going to be transferred.

In a clear reference to the supposed training-ground bust-up with his star player, he said, 'The whole context of things seems to get out of proportion at this club. Somebody sees me in discussions with a player, then it is described as a row and then someone else says there's been a fight. There's always a lot of chit-chat around this club, that's the problem at Newcastle.'

I have to say, Ruud was spot-on with that assessment. Speaking as a journalist, I am constantly amazed at the amount of information which has emerged from the confines of St James' Park down the years. Often it's down to good journalism from the likes of John Gibson and Alan Oliver, but there are times when you wonder who on earth is spilling the beans and whether they really think they're doing the club any favours. In recent years, there's been a standing joke among fans about a mysterious character known as 'club insider' who seems to know everything that goes on at Newcastle. That person really ought to learn that, occasionally, silence is golden. Or who knows? Maybe even silver.

Despite the 'chatter' and the 'curse', Ruud's boys marched relentlessly towards Wembley in 1999. Bradford came and went in the fourth round, followed by Blackburn in the fifth – thanks to a replay goal from a young, on-loan French striker called Louis Saha. Suddenly an old song was given new lyrics: 'Que Saha, Saha, whatever will be will be, we're going to Wem-ber-lee, que Saha, Saha.'

We could sniff the final once again, and Everton felt the force as we thrashed them 4–1. It was possibly the highlight of Gullit's reign, and St James' Park rang to the sound of his name for the first time. We were through to the semis once again, and when the draw was made by Peter Beardsley, the laddo did us a big favour by avoiding Man United and Arsenal, instead pairing us with Spurs. There was another bonus – it looked like we were in Europe just for reaching the semis! Man United and Arsenal were almost certainly in the Champions League, while Spurs had already won the Worthington Cup, which meant that we would get the UEFA Cup place reserved for the FA Cup winners (the Cup-Winners' Cup no longer existed). We'd done it again – qualifying without winning anything. Mind you, if European competitions were only for winners, Newcastle fans wouldn't need passports.

Once again, Sime and I met up with the lads in Manchester for the semi, but this time I'd organised a special treat. A pub called the White Lion ran match-day barge trips along the canal to Old Trafford, so I booked a dozen seats. There were several advantages to this. First, it dropped you right outside the huge North Stand where we were due to sit; second, you avoided car park queues and long walks after the match; and third, there was a bar on board.

We were genuinely confident – Newcastle may have lost a few finals in my lifetime but never a semi. We got on the barge and sailed triumphantly up to Old Trafford. People were hanging over bridges and waving as we made our noisy approach: 'Toon Navy! Toon Navy!' and 'We're on the barge with Ruudi's army!'

Inside the ground, we spotted Jimmy Nail in the row in front of us, and some of the lads reported seeing Peter Beardsley and his son in the queue at the burger bar at half-time. Apparently, the crowd opened like the Red Sea, and Peter was ushered to the front. The perks of being a Geordie legend, eh?

The game was still 0–0 after 90 minutes, but in extra time, we won a penalty when Sol Campbell blatantly handled sub Duncan Ferguson's flick-on. Once again, Shearer stepped up to fire us in front. Bedlam at Old Trafford became delirious, unbridled joy when the world's greatest goal scorer thrashed a 20-yarder into the top corner in the final minute. We were going back to Wembley!

The scenes at the final whistle were tumultuous. While one half of the ground quickly emptied, the other half was in carnival mood. Players celebrated with fans, and there was even a hug for the centre-forward from the manager! Nobody could have predicted that.

The barge ride back to the White Lion was pure bliss, especially when the pilot handed everyone a bottle of lager as we climbed aboard. And while everyone else was sat in the gridlocked car parks, we were back in the pub, dreaming of Wembley once more.

WEMBLEY NIGHTMARE, PART 3

Time for a confession now. At this point in time, I was working for MUTV – Man United's own TV channel, which had launched in the autumn. My excuse was, being the father of a small child, I needed a job with some stability, one which allowed me to go home every night instead of being chased around Africa by hippos. I was given the title Head of Programmes on a one-year contract to help get the channel on the air. I was expecting grief from the lads, but there were no calls of 'traitor'. In fact, they were genuinely fascinated. Brendan Egan said, 'That's a good move because you'll be in pole position when Newcastle start their channel.' He was deadly serious – I could start with a little club and wait till the big one came along!

It was inevitable then that our opponents in the final would be Man United – Ryan Giggs's wonder goal in the replay saw to that. I was now officially working for the enemy! Sime was too, as I'd persuaded him to take on a news editor's job. I managed to secure two media overflow tickets for Wembley, which I delegated to two deserving, hard-working channel employees – me and Sime.

Those looking for cup-final omens would have been disturbed by what they found. We'd just finished the season in 13th place and were about to play the league champions for the FA Cup – precisely what had happened the year before. Worse still, we'd ended the season with a seven-game winless streak, exactly the same as we'd done back in 1974. We should have known what was coming next – there is often symmetry in our misery.

Ruud's big game plan included dropping Warren Barton and Shay Given, without telling them to their faces, and introducing a new kit with white socks. 'Teams look better and play better in white socks,' he bizarrely said.

As usual, the Geordies had bought tons of the new shirts, forming a giant human bar code at the tunnel end, despite the chairman and vice chairman's boasts about overpriced merchandise a year earlier. Messrs Shepherd and Hall were in attendance this time, and Freddy even got to sit next to the most powerful Newcastle supporter in the country: Mr T. Blair of 10 Downing Street.

Despite the absence of our best defender Steve Howey, who'd been injured in the semi, and despite the fact we were playing a team going for the Treble, not just the Double, there was more optimism around than there'd been the year before. And not just among the fans, as Gary Speed confirmed: 'The '99 final was totally different. I certainly wanted Man United rather than Arsenal to win the semi-final replay. United had had some hard games, and they also had the European Cup final to come on the Wednesday. I thought we were going to win – I just had a feeling.'

After just 15 minutes, every Newcastle fan thought that perhaps the fates had finally conspired in our favour when Roy Keane hobbled off following a hefty challenge by Gary Speed. 'When Roy Keane limped off,' said Speed, quickly adding, 'and it was a good tackle, not a foul, no free-kick was given, and he had a dodgy ankle – when he limped off, I wondered if this was our chance.'

Despite more years of hurt than even I have racked up, my pal Mick still clutches at every little straw of hope that blows our way. Along with 40,000 other Geordies, Mick's spirits were suddenly lifted: 'As soon as Keane went off, I thought "Maybe this is our year at last", but within a split second, I thought "What the hell am I doing? Why am I letting myself think like this?"' There speaks a man with decades of bitter experience.

He was right to bite his tongue. Fergie sent on Teddy Sheringham, who immediately swung the game their way with his first touch, taking a return pass and slotting the ball past Harper. One-nil. For those watching in black and white, the goal scorer is wearing red – again.

We took the fight to them and were even criticised in some quarters for being too physical. (Newcastle? Too physical?) When I asked Warren Barton for his views on the way we played, he said, 'We thought we had to face them up. We couldn't let them get into their flow or else they'd murder us. As Alan Shearer once said, "Man

United don't like it up 'em." We were also very aware of the previous year, and we wanted to give it a proper go.'

Gullit changed things a bit at half-time, sending on Ferguson, who wasn't fully fit, in place of Didi Hamann, who'd been our best player in the first half. There were reports later of a dressing-room row, Hamann insisting he wasn't injured.

Meanwhile, we had to wade through rivers of piss just to use the facilities at the decrepit old stadium, which may have looked an absolute picture on TV but behind the façade was just a crumbling old wreck. This was the 'home' of English football, as rotten as the industry it represented. Somehow it felt an appropriate place to watch our cup-final exploits of '98 and '99.

The game was all over as a contest shortly after the break when Paul Scholes drilled home the second. That was it, and we knew it. A late and lame attempt by substitute Silvio Maric summed up our enterprise. Ketsbaia scuffed another shot against the outside of the post, but, again, it was far too little, far too late. The Man U fans loved it, rubbing it in till the end – especially to Shearer, who'd twice rejected Fergie's overtures, to first join Blackburn and then us. 'David May, superstar, got more medals than Shear-ah' they sang in honour of their reserve centre-back.

Once again, the Lion of Gosforth looked thoroughly fed up by it all, although Gullit was less than happy with the centre-forward's contribution, according to Harry Harris's book *Newcastle Out of Toon*: 'Gullit felt that Shearer was a disgrace. He believed that a player of his stature and earning his level of salary ought to be an example to the younger players and the rest of the team.'

For the first time, Sime and I left Wembley without watching the lap of honour. We couldn't face the prospect of yet more gloating reds – we'd get enough of that back at work on Monday. We also felt that, at that moment, this was one defeat too far. In '74, '76 and '98, the games felt like enough of a special occasion for us to take defeat on the chin, whether thoroughly deserved as in the two FA Cup finals or unfortunate as in the League Cup final. But this felt different – we were getting a bit sick of going through the same old routine again and again.

My cousin Richie, who'd stood with me when I embarked on this whole supporting lark back in 1966, had been optimistic too: 'I didn't expect us to win the year before under Dalglish, but under Ruud Gullit I thought we might. I had a feeling that our name was on the cup, but, of course, it was another shambles. You just feel that they're always waiting to let you down.'

Chris Baines looked back on this and all our defeats and lamented, 'I don't think it would be so bad if we didn't get within touching distance so often. We get into a position to kick on so many times, but we don't bloody do it. But that's Newcastle for you.'

Sure enough, there were lots of tributes to the Toon Army in the papers, but more disconcerting were some of the quotes supposedly emanating from our camp. George Caulkin of *The Times* wrote, 'When Didier Domi, a Gullit signing, declares, "Manchester United were always going to win the Cup. Tactically, they were much better than us", it does not say much for his manager or his teammates.' Caulkin described Gullit as 'casual and arrogant', quoting him as saying, 'It took Manchester United seven years to reach this point. It took me one at Chelsea, but I had better players.'

Peter Beardsley was there as a fan, and felt as let down as the rest of us: 'We were too negative in the two FA Cup finals. The team did brilliantly to get there, but Kenny was really negative in the first one, and Ruud was in the next one. We were almost trying to draw two cup finals, and I thought that was pointless.'

History had repeated itself within the space of just 12 months, and it would do so yet again in August.

Gullit spent £11 million on three defenders in the summer, which seemed like a good idea at the time, although when you look back and trot out the names Marcelino, Franck Dumas and Alain Goma, it doesn't seem so clever. We also paid £6 million for England Under-21 star Kieron Dyer from Ipswich. We could easily afford him – Didi Hamann had finally got his way when he landed an £8 million move to Liverpool. George Georgiadis, Phillipe Albert and Stuart Pearce finally said their farewells, while Rob Lee was being frozen out – he wasn't even given a squad number.

Despite his strained relationship with the manager, Alan Shearer signed a new five-year contract designed to keep him at the club till the end of his career. We certainly needed that sort of stability. In the previous season, we'd used thirty-four different players, just one fewer than the thirty-five who'd got us relegated in '78 and '89. Not that relegation was on anyone's mind when the new season kicked off. In fact, there was no hint of the tensions that would explode from the Gallowgate volcano in the coming weeks.

Three straight defeats gave us our worst start to a season in forty years, and the knives were soon out for the manager. Speculation filled the back page of every newspaper, but the board backed him. Stacks of injuries didn't help, and when a patched-up side could only manage a 3–3 home draw with Wimbledon, we realised that the next game, four days later, would be absolutely critical for the manager and the club. It was against Sunderland.

It's now enshrined in Newcastle United legend that on 25 August 1999 Ruud Gullit wrote his own suicide note, heavily disguised as a team sheet. On the morning of the match, *Mirror* journalist Harry Harris ran the story that Alan Shearer would be on the bench for the must-win local derby. Alan Oliver of the *Chronicle* refused to take the bait: 'Harry Harris was close to Ruud, and he wrote that Alan Shearer would be dropped. We didn't report it because we just couldn't believe he'd do it. I didn't think the story could be right. But he dropped Alan Shearer, and we all know what happened after that.'

Warren Barton told me that the bib-wearing routine on the training ground gave it away: 'Things were pretty bad at that stage. The manager and the captain weren't talking to each other, but when

I saw Alan wearing a bib – the reserves were always given the bibs to wear – I thought he was messing about. I asked him why he had it on, and he said "Because I'm not playing." I honestly couldn't believe it. It was obviously Ruud's way of trying to make a point, but it backfired on him badly.'

Gary Speed was equally incredulous: 'I was shocked when Ruud left both Al and Duncan Ferguson out against Sunderland. It looked like we were going to play in a local derby with no strikers! I wondered what the hell was going on.'

Up until that week, most of the fans were still backing Ruud. Much as it hurt me to side against Alan Shearer, I felt that for the club's sake the manager always had to be right, otherwise there's anarchy. But there was a tectonic shift against Gullit when he made pre-match remarks about the Sunderland game. He said it 'wasn't a proper derby' because it didn't involve two teams from the same city. It was 'just another game' and 'just another three points'. This was a massive error of judgement from a man trying to curry favour with the supporters in this huge battle of egos and wills. Nobody tells a Geordie (or a Mackem, for that matter) that the Newcastle v. Sunderland game is not significant. Not if they want to hang around.

The scene was set for an epic encounter. A biblical storm raged, and the pitch was soon under water. Work had begun on the new third tier around two sides of the ground so the roof had been taken off. We stood there getting rained on for 90 minutes without interruption. Unlike the old days of terracing, when you could huddle together for protection, we all had our allotted square metre, and we all got thoroughly drowned. There are memorable images from the TV coverage of a Newcastle fan wringing out his saturated shirt and of others standing bare-chested because it was actually more comfortable. A match-day magazine floated down the terracing from step to step, like a raft on the ocean. The TV montage was cut to a newly released song called 'Why Does It Always Rain On Me?' It could have been for the fans, but it was aimed at the manager.

Gullit watched intently as Kieron Dyer fired us into the lead. The iconic TV shot is of Gullit in front of the dugout, 'lucky' crucifix in his mouth, while Alan Shearer and Duncan Ferguson stand stony-faced and defiant behind him, arms crossed. Gullit finally made a substitution, but it was Ferguson not Shearer. Another point made. When Sunderland drew level, he finally sent on Shearer, but it didn't work. Sunderland won 2–1.

After the game, Gullit was cross-examined by the press about his team selection, but he simply pointed out that Newcastle were winning until the two strikers came on, as if this had nothing at all to do with him. Sime and I heard this on the radio as we drove back to Liverpool. We were soaked through, but, being typical Geordie suckers, we'd actually spent money in the club shop before the game, so we were able to put on our new, dry polo shirts. We were miserable in relative comfort.

The Shearer–Gullit confrontation that everyone had predicted for the past year had finally come to a head and the shock waves swept across Tyneside. The bad news for Ruud Gullit was that the case for the defence was played five, lost four, points one.

Alan Oliver knew something had to give: 'In Friday night's *Chronicle*, I wrote a piece under the headline "Sort it out or go". It was sorted on the Saturday, and he was gone.'

16

OLD FATHER TYNE (1999–2004)

'I will be here as long as my brain, my heart and my legs work together.'

Bobby Robson arrives, clearly
forgetting about chairmen

Ruud's biographer Harry Harris said that when Gullit joined Newcastle he 'went to the wrong club at the wrong time in the wrong place for the wrong reasons'. Let's simplify that, eh? How about Newcastle picked the wrong manager. For all his superstar status and his charisma, Gullit just didn't get Newcastle. He had no history with the club and no understanding of its idiosyncrasies. You can read about it or listen to people telling you about it, but unless you've lived it, you'll never understand it.

One thing you had to give Ruud was that he realised this in the end and went with dignity, saying, 'The moment I came to Newcastle, the journalists asked me if I understood how big the job was, and I thought I knew – now I know what they really meant by that.' He made a courteous farewell speech in which he seemed to thank half of

Newcastle, and then walked away without asking for a pay-off, a bit of a rarity in modern football.

There's usually a sense of relief when a manager goes, and Gullit's departure was no exception. Everyone knew that there had long been something rotten in the state of Gallowgate, and, apart from that, we were deep in the relegation clarts. 'Sexy' football hadn't materialised – the nearest we got was a brief flash on the way to Wembley, hardly enough for the red-blooded Geordie fans.

But there was also a feeling of controlled anger at the people in charge who'd now moved on three very high-profile managers in just over two-and-a-half years. The next 'Sort it out or go' headline would be aimed in their direction if they didn't pull their collective fingers out – fast.

We all thought we knew the ideal characteristics required for Ruud's replacement: the new man had to be a proven manager with a strong track record at the highest level; he had to be a good man manager who believed in attractive, attacking football; he had to be charismatic but not flash; he had to understand the passion of the Geordies; ideally, he had to *be* a Geordie. In fact . . . he had to be Bobby Robson.

It had pained Robson to turn down Newcastle when Sir John had called on him in Barcelona three years earlier. Now he couldn't get here quick enough, signing up till the end of the season with a simple brief – to keep us in the Premiership. Once again, crowds gathered at St James' Park for the anointing of yet another saviour – this was getting to be a bit of an annual event.

Robson seemed to have been around for ever. In 1955, when Newcastle were winning their last FA Cup, Bobby was at Wembley cheering for them. In 1966, when I went to my first-ever Newcastle match at St James' Park, he scored for our opponents during his second spell at Fulham. In 1969, when we were winning the Fairs Cup, Bobby was just starting out on his fabulous reign at Ipswich.

In 1974, when we lost so horrifically against Liverpool at Wembley, Robson was there again as a fan. My mate Steve saw him as he left the ground and approached him (as Steve tends to do). 'What did you think of the game, Mr Robson?' he asked. 'You got there, son. You got there,' came the sympathetic reply.

In 1978, when we were being relegated with Bill McGarry (Robson's predecessor at Portman Road), Bobby was winning the FA Cup with Ipswich. When Kevin Keegan arrived at Newcastle in 1982, Robson was starting out as England manager – and dropping Kevin. Just after we lost our promotion play-off to Sunderland in 1990, Bobby's England team lost on penalties to the Germans in the World Cup semi-final. When Keegan and Sir John Hall were breathing new life into Newcastle a few years later, Bobby was doing the same to PSV Eindhoven in Holland. When we begged him to be our manager in 1997, Robson was being loyal to Barcelona. Fat lot of good it did him.

But now the opportunity he thought was gone for ever had miraculously arrived. His life had come full circle, and he was back in the North East where he was born in 1933 – six years *after* Newcastle's last league championship. That's how long it is.

In his time in management, Robson had looked after some of the biggest names in world football: Bryan Robson, Paul Gascoigne and Gary Lineker with England, and Luís Figo, Ronaldo and Ruud van Nistelrooy at club level. Warren Barton tells a story which contradicts Bobby's reputation for being forgetful when it comes to names. He said, 'At our first training session, he walked up to me and said, "Hello, Warren, how are you?" Just the fact that he knew my name was a great compliment when you consider the players he's had.' And, more importantly, Bobby quickly changed the atmosphere: 'From the moment he arrived, the awkwardness and uncertainty was gone. He was full of energy, desire, charisma and passion, and it immediately rubbed off on everyone.'

Robson took his bow at Chelsea, his first-ever game in the Premiership, and his first in English club football for 17 years. We lost 1–0. But it was Robson's homecoming that made us all believe in fairy tales. The team that couldn't score and hadn't won one of its last fourteen league matches thrashed Sheffield Wednesday 8–0 with Alan Shearer, the centre-forward who couldn't score, getting five. It was nothing short of incredible and marked the beginning of the revival.

There was a new lease of life for Big Al's old mate Rob Lee too. Gullit hadn't even given Lee a squad number, but Robson put him back in the team, along with Nikos Dabizas, another of Ruud's rejects.

With league form improving, Bobby turned his hand to the really impossible task: getting Newcastle to enjoy a run in the Worthington Cup. Unfortunately, some miracles take a little longer than others, and we were knocked out at the first hurdle, 2–0 by Birmingham City.

However, Robson used all his Euro know-how to steer us through a few rounds of the UEFA Cup. CSKA Sofia and FC Zürich were seen off before Roma did a traditional Italian job on us – beating us 1–0 at their place and holding out for a 0–0 at SJP.

But our new knack of winning FA Cup ties (apart from at Wembley, of course) hadn't deserted us, and for the third year running, we had a serious tilt at winning the famous cup.

In season 1999–2000, everyone had to start their FA Cup campaigns *before* New Year (more red-tape guff from the FA). But it didn't seem to worry us – we hammered Spurs 6–1 after a draw at White Hart Lane, then, in our first cup tie of the new millennium, we beat Sheffield United 4–1 at home. Next up was a rare away win, 2–1 at Blackburn, Shearer getting both goals on his return to Ewood Park. He completely shocked everyone after the winner when he didn't do his traditional one-arm-raised salute. Instead, the normally unfussy Mr Shearer slid along the grass on his belly, something he's never done before or since. Surreal.

We were away again in the quarter-final, but it was a 'home' game for me – at Tranmere Rovers. It was a cracking match, played just after Bobby Robson's birthday. The travelling contingent regaled him with lusty choruses of 'Happy Birthday', and the players gave him the ideal present: a 3–2 win. We were in the semis for the third time in three years – our opponents would be Chelsea.

Unfortunately, there was no return trip to Old Trafford and therefore no ride on the barge with the Toon Navy. In their wisdom, the FA had decided that both semis would be played at Wembley that year despite the fact that our fans had an all-day round trip of about 600 miles while Chelsea's fans had the hardship of a 20-minute tube ride across London. (Neutral ground? My arse.)

I was safe in the knowledge that we'd never lost a semi-final in my lifetime. Unfortunately, this was tempered by the knowledge that we'd never won at Wembley in my lifetime. Something had to give, and there are no prizes for guessing what did . . .

When Gus Poyet gave Chelsea the lead, we got a sickeningly familiar feeling. So thank God for Rob Lee. The man who Ruud Gullit wanted out of Newcastle gave us our happiest moment in years when he got on the end of Alan Shearer's right-wing cross to plant a header into the Chelsea net. The tunnel end went absolutely mental. Previous Wembleys flashed before me until the rewind stopped at 1976 and Alan Gowling's League Cup final effort at the other end. Rob Lee had scored our first goal at the national stadium in 24 years. Hallelujah!

Of course, our joy lasted for all of five minutes. Poyet scored again, and we lost 2–1 despite having played well. But that was scant consolation: we were trophyless for yet another season.

Gary Speed was nearly as sick as me. He told me, 'That semi-final was a right kick in the balls. We played well and knew we were the better team, and when you saw who was in the final . . .'

This bit is like that moment on the old TV game show *Take Your Pick* when Michael Miles says to the gallant loser, 'Now let's see what you *could* have won.' Yes, for once we would not have been playing a team going for a Double or a Treble or one universally acknowledged as the best team in living memory. We would have been playing Aston Villa, a sort of pale imitation of us: great history, crap present. We would have hammered them. 'Oh, dear. You would have won tonight's star prize!' In the great game show of life, Newcastle United seem destined to always go home with a *Blankety Blank* chequebook and pen. And a cuddly toy – if we're lucky.

On the train journey home, I worked out that in the 34 years since I enlisted in the Toon Army, my record at Wembley watching Newcastle was:

P 6　　W 0　　D 0　　L 6　　F 2　　A 15

A fan who started watching Newcastle when Wembley was first opened (in 1923) and followed them for the same length of time as I had would have had a Wembley record of:

P 5　　W 5　　D 0　　L 0　　F 10　　A 2

And all of his would have been FA Cup finals – no Charity Shields or dodgy semis for him. Talk about being born at the wrong time!

Having steadied the ship and taken us to a very respectable 11th place in his first season, Bobby had been rewarded with a one-year rolling contract and set about rebuilding the team. In came Carl Cort; out went Duncan Ferguson. Other departures included Alessandro Pistone, Steve Howey, Laurent Charvet, Didier Domi and Alain Goma, but the new arrivals didn't really inspire: Andy O'Brien, Wayne Quinn and a host of sub-standard South Americans, including Daniel Cordone, Clarence Acuna, Christian Bassedas and Diego Gavilan.

Robson's plans were severely hampered by injuries, although Alan Shearer soldiered on with his usual grit. At the beginning of March, Bobby revealed our centre-forward had been having pain-killing injections before every match. But now his season was over – he was going to America to get the operation he needed. In that brilliant way Bobby always has of putting things, he said, 'Alan Shearer has been looking after Newcastle United for a long time. Now it's time for Newcastle United to look after Alan Shearer.'

Kieron Dyer was injured around the same time and also missed the last few months. All season the forward line tended to be made up of anyone who was fit, often including stop-gap signing Kevin Gallagher, a spindly young foal called Shola Ameobi or a Congolese acrobat with a bagful of tricks and no sense of direction called Lomano Tresor Lua Lua. We finished 11th – the same as the previous season.

The Worthington Cup produced wins over Leyton Orient and Bradford City, but in the next round, we were knocked out at Birmingham City – again. Our FA Cup dreams also died in the Midlands as we lost 1–0 at Aston Villa after a replay.

The only silver lining that season was the opening of the magnificent new top tier of St James' Park, with both the Milburn and Sir John Hall stands increasing their capacity. Instead of 36,000, the ground now held 52,000 – the second highest in England, and for most league games it was just about full. It also *looked* fantastic and helped to cement our status as a genuinely 'big club'. Now all we needed was a team to match and some silverware to go with it. Sixteen thousand more Geordies every fortnight also meant lots more money was coming into the club, and Bobby spent a big wodge of it on a couple of pacy forwards: Craig Bellamy and French winger Laurent Robert.

Because we weren't in Europe, the club had entered the much-derided Intertoto Cup – which was better than pre-season friendlies, even if it didn't quite serve its purpose of getting us into the UEFA Cup. Alan Shearer was finally back to full fitness, and Bellamy was looking like the perfect foil. We realised he was a bit quick during a home match with Man United. He ran their back-four ragged, and we won a pulsating match 4–3. Robert also scored with a blinding free-kick from the edge of the box, something which was to become a bit of a trademark. To round off a fabulous afternoon, Roy Keane got sent off for throwing the ball at Alan Shearer. Big Al had wound him up with something he said, and when Keano exploded, Shearer just eyeballed him and didn't flinch. What a man. As if all that wasn't enough, Fergie said after the game that Newcastle had to be considered as genuine title challengers again. Get in.

And what a good judge he was. In December, we went on a blistering run of five straight wins, including a 3–1 win midweek at Highbury, which was our first win in London for about 500 years. By Boxing Day, we were on top of the Premiership for the first time since the heady days of Keegan. Our assault on the league title eventually ran out of steam, but the football was exciting, and we finished 2001–02 in fourth, our highest final placing for five years. We also got to the quarter-finals of both domestic cups before losing to top sides: Chelsea in the Worthington and Arsenal in the FA Cup.

In the summer, Bobby was knighted for services to football, although most Newcastle fans had been calling him 'Sir Bobby' for the previous 12 months. Everyone loved him. Geordies are fiercely tribal, and ever since his arrival, there had been a warmth shown to him that hadn't been extended to his two predecessors. The appointments of Dalglish and Gullit had provoked excitement, and probably a bit of bewilderment, that these two legends of the modern game had come to Newcastle, but Bobby was 'one of us'. Now he was showing that not only was he one of us, he was also a bloody good manager, moulding a squad that had previously been in chaos into a proper team which played for each other. The fact that the football was exciting ticked another very important box in the 'Essential Guide for Newcastle Managers' handbook.

As season 2002–03 dawned, there was a renewed optimism about the place, and there was a genuine feeling that at last we were back on track. It all looked so simple, as football always does when it's played by a good side, working for a great coach. If only we'd got Bobby straight after Keegan, as the club had attempted. How many Geordies have lain awake wondering what Robson would have done with Ferdinand, Ginola, Asprilla and Beardsley? Even without them, we had enough good players to win something, and maybe now was the time. Nothing would be better than to finally win that elusive trophy with a Geordie legend in charge.

At the turn of the year, Bobby spent £5 million on Jermaine Jenas, one of the best prospects in the game. In the close season, he spent big again, on Titus Bramble and Hugo Viana. Viana was the European Young Footballer of the Year and regarded in Portugal as the new Figo. We licked our lips in anticipation.

By finishing fourth, we'd earned a place in the qualifying rounds of the Champions League (nowadays you only had to finish fourth to be regarded as 'champions' – embarrassing, but we were happy to take it). After sorting out NK Zeljeznicar without too much bother, we found ourselves in the group stages. We seemed to be way out of our depth when we lost our first three matches against Dynamo Kiev, Feyenoord and Juventus, but we turned the competition on its head by becoming the first side ever to qualify after losing its opening three games. We beat Juventus and Kiev at home and in a fantastic match in Rotterdam, beat Feyenoord 3–2 with Bellamy getting a dramatic last-gasp winner.

We'd made it through to the second phase, and everyone celebrated as if we'd won the bloody European Cup. It was only after coming down from the drama of that victory that I realised we were actually celebrating the fact that Newcastle had won a stack of money, which was what the second phase represented. OK, we were celebrating a memorable victory in Rotterdam, but if we'd drawn, we would have dropped into the UEFA Cup – and, unlike the Champions League, that was a trophy I felt we had a realistic chance of winning. It seemed that, in an age where a top-four finish in the Premiership is regarded as paramount, everyone was beginning to forget why we actually played football: to win cups and medals, to finish first in something – anything!

'European Adventure Part 2' was almost as exciting. We got turned over at home 4–1 by Inter Milan, with Craig Bellamy and Alan Shearer both banned after a rough old game. Then we lost 3–1 in Barcelona, and we thought that was that. But home and away wins over Bayer Leverkusen kept hope alive, and 10,000 Geordies thronged the San Siro for the away game with Inter, one of the great nights in modern Toon Army history. Despite two goals from Shearer in a 2–2 draw, it wasn't to be, and our last flicker of hope was snuffed out when Barcelona came to Newcastle and did a thoroughly professional job, beating us 2–0.

Perhaps the European adventure meant we'd taken our eye off the ball at home – we were knocked out of the League Cup at the first stage (i.e. the third round for those teams playing in Europe) after we'd played a 3–3 draw at St James' Park with Everton, who included their new wunderkind Wayne Rooney. The kid looked very tasty. He even helped them win the penalty shoot-out. All together now, 'Newcastle never win penalty shoot-outs!'

This first-hurdle exit was repeated in the FA Cup when we lost 3–2 in the third round to Wolves, who were in the division below us. Our form in the league was good, but as soon as we were knocked out of Europe, we seemed to fall to bits. Although we won fewer points and scored fewer goals this time round, we still finished in third place, one higher than the season before.

Our quest to end the trophy famine was in good order under Robson. We'd been finishing higher each season and were gradually building a stronger side. In the January transfer window, Bobby had signed possibly the best defender most of us had ever seen at Newcastle. With Leeds United going into financial meltdown, Freddy Shepherd got Jonathan Woodgate for £8 million. Woodgate was a class act, but he'd made headlines for the wrong reasons during his time at Elland Road. Along with his teammate Lee Bowyer, he'd been accused of attacking an Asian student. After a lengthy court case, Woodgate was cleared of causing bodily harm and convicted of affray, but the papers had a field day, and the case followed him wherever he went.

His arrival also coincided with the departure of Marcelino, who finally had his contract cancelled after almost four years of receiving a fat salary for zero return. His scandalous record featured just fifteen Premiership starts in two seasons, followed by a season and a half picking up his money and refusing to budge when he knew he wasn't wanted. Given that we paid £5.8 million for him to start with, that works out at just under £400,000 per start. Add to that his salary of £1 million a year, and it is no wonder football's going down the pan.

The fate of both these players shows how important luck and good judgement are to the team that wants to win trophies. The signing of Marcelino and his subsequent behaviour illustrate how little research went into the player's character as well as his suitability for the Premiership. With Woodgate, we were unlucky as he was continuously dogged by injury. However, our wily chairman Freddy Shepherd sold him for a sizeable profit to Real Madrid, for whom he has played even fewer matches. But ask any Newcastle fan and they'd rather take a fully fit Johnny Woodgate than all the Euros in Madrid.

As we went into the new season, there were just two further reinforcements. We brought in a young Ipswich midfielder called Darren Ambrose and then – and only Newcastle United could have done this – signed up Lee Bowyer, Woodgate's old pal from Elland Road and Hull Crown Court. There was outrage in some quarters, but the club argued that Bowyer, like Woodgate, had learned his lesson and would be no trouble. But, unlike Woodgate, Bowyer had also made headlines for transgressions *on* the pitch, and these would surface more than once during his time at Newcastle.

With consecutive Premiership finishes of fourth and third, Sir Bobby had got us back into the elite group where we felt, and Freddy Shepherd insisted, we belonged. The next step was to stay there and to win something, and under Bobby that felt distinctly possible. Unfortunately, we were about to play a match which, although we didn't know it at the time, would ultimately start the decline of Robson's Newcastle.

The Champions League is absolutely crucial to the modern-day 'superclub'. To stay at the very top level, you have to be in it. Without it, the money dries up and you quickly find you're one of the also-rans. Newcastle were no exception, so when we lost our Champions League qualifier with Partizan Belgrade at the start of 2003–04, alarm bells must have been ringing like crazy in the Newcastle boardroom. We'd actually won 1–0 in Serbia and were settling for a 0–0 at home when Partizan scored a late equaliser to force extra time and eventually penalties. So, obviously, we were out, especially when Shearer, Dyer and Woodgate *all* missed from the spot. The defeat meant we'd miss out on six guaranteed Champions League matches, as well as all the other payments the competition brings.

To make matters worse, we also went six Premiership matches without a win, leaving us at the wrong end of the table and missing Woodgate and Bellamy, who'd picked up serious injuries. Remarkably, Robson's boys fought back, and by Christmas, we were fifth, having lost just one more game, thanks largely to the assists of Robert and the goals of Shearer, who banged in ten in nine games at one stage.

After the defeat by Partizan, the message from the boardroom was clear: finish in the top four and then get into the Champions League, source of all riches. But we were now 35 years on from the Fairs Cup and 49 removed from the last FA Cup, and, frankly, I just wanted us to win something.

I have always felt that, as a club, we fail to appreciate what winning the League Cup could do for the whole well-being of Newcastle United. The first trophy would surely open the floodgates – so let's win the easiest one first! With the players we've had since 1993, it is nothing short of pathetic that we haven't got further than the quarter-finals, especially when Man United, Arsenal, Liverpool and Chelsea routinely put out virtual reserve teams in the competition.

In 2003, having embarrassed ourselves in the Champions League, we then shot ourselves in the foot in the League Cup. For our home tie with West Bromwich Albion from the division below, Bobby decided to 'rest' Alan Shearer, even though we were already without Craig Bellamy because of injury. We lost 2–1 after extra time (Albion spared us the indignity of yet another penalty shoot-out), closing off yet another avenue to ending the trophy blight.

In the FA Cup, we were drawn away to Southampton. The Dell was always our 'bogey' ground (in football speak) but, fortunately, the Saints had moved and now played at the St Mary's Stadium. Kieron Dyer took the opportunity to do a very passable impression of the absent Craig Bellamy minus the sweary bits. He played up front, he was fast, he scored two goals and we won 3–1. Unfortunately, we were then drawn away to Liverpool, and even a blinding Laurent Robert goal couldn't stop us losing 2–1.

All that was left for us to win was the UEFA Cup. Our Champions League failure meant that we'd 'dropped' into the secondary competition, another bizarre ruling by UEFA. Anyway, yet again we were grateful just to have something to play for. This was a trophy we genuinely *could* win, and to be fair to Bobby and the boys, they put up a helluva fight.

We marched relentlessly through the competition, beating NAC Breda of Holland, FC Basel of Switzerland, Vålerenga of Norway, Real Mallorca of Spain and, in the quarter-finals, Bobby's old club, PSV Eindhoven. We'd cruised through to the semis, and there was no reason to think that 35 years after we'd won the same competition we couldn't go all the way again. Then disaster struck. Four days before the first leg with Marseille, three key players got injured in our Premiership game at Aston Villa. Craig Bellamy, Kieron Dyer and Jermaine Jenas all missed the home leg, which ended 0–0. The following week, we lost Jonathan Woodgate, so we went to Marseille for the second leg with four of our best players missing. It was a bridge too far, and we lost 2–0, Didier Drogba scoring both goals.

Back in the Premiership, we were stumbling towards the line, and the fans were getting increasingly frustrated. But the club had been experiencing a lot of problems all season, both on and off the pitch. They just kept coming, one after another, until the pressure became almost unbearable.

In the January transfer clear-out, Nobby Solano went to Villa for around £2 million. The fans loved Nobby and were angry when he left. Bobby also sold Carl Cort to Wolves for a similar fee, and he went ballistic when the notorious 'club insider' was quoted as saying Cort had been a waste of money. But Robson's generous remarks in support of the player irritated the fans, who, for once, agreed with 'club insider'. Robson's rapport with the supporters was disintegrating, some accusing him of losing the plot.

Then, Lua Lua was allowed to go on loan to Portsmouth, and an unholy row developed after he scored a last-minute equaliser against us when we played at Fratton Park. When a player goes on loan, it's always part of the deal that he doesn't play against you for the simple reason that he could screw your season. Well done, Newcastle.

Earlier, there had been front-page tabloid headlines about Premiership footballers involved in an alleged rape incident in a London hotel following our match at Arsenal. Rumour and counter-rumour spread like wildfire, but there was no doubt that Newcastle United had been implicated. In the end, nothing came of it, but the investigations dragged on for months, and lots of United staff were questioned. No one believed they would ever see the headline 'Rape Cops Quiz Bobby Robson', but appear it did.

Several members of our now infamous 'brat pack' made further headlines for their exploits off the pitch. Gary Speed was one of the wiser heads at the club, and he told me that he felt a mixture of sympathy and disappointment towards his younger colleagues: 'Some of those things should have been avoided, but that's the nature of Newcastle. If they'd been in London, what they did probably wouldn't have been noticed, but in Newcastle, it's different. Everything you do is scrutinised. Perhaps they were too young, but I think they know they could have handled themselves better.'

On top of all that, there were rumours that Robson and Shearer had fallen out. The captain reacted badly to being rested for a UEFA Cup tie, and there was a story doing the rounds that Bobby had tried to sell him to Liverpool, something he later refuted. The UEFA Cup run was all that was keeping the fans onside, and when we lost in Marseille, the emotional dam burst. Our last home game of the season was against struggling Wolves. We needed to win to have any chance of finishing in a Champions League spot, but we were poor and drew 1–1 against a team which finished bottom of the division. Shearer even missed a penalty in the last few minutes. Hugo Viana, who'd had a nightmare in Marseille, was actually booed when he came on as sub. And when the team came back out to do their annual 'lap of honour', they emerged to find that just about everyone had left the stadium.

The resentment grew when Bobby was quoted comparing our fans unfavourably to those of Leeds, who'd given their relegated team a heroes' send off. We drew our last two games, finished fifth and only qualified for the UEFA Cup.

To the outsider, it was probably hard to understand why our fans were so hacked off. We'd had some filthy luck with injuries at crucial times in the season. We'd got into the last four of the UEFA Cup and had qualified for Europe once again. However, I genuinely believe that after all we'd been through, especially since Keegan's side so very nearly won the Premiership title in 1996, the hardcore support had finally reached breaking point.

We'd picked ourselves up off the floor after Keegan walked away, bitten our tongues as Dalglish's team bored us rigid, turned the other cheek when Gullit indulged his surreal notions and sat patiently while Bobby sorted out the mess. But now it all seemed to be falling away from us again. Bobby and Freddy Shepherd didn't seem to be singing from the same hymn sheet, Robson and Alan Shearer appeared to be at loggerheads, some of the younger players appeared to be out of control and the manager was apparently criticising us fans. But there was only one fan's opinion that Bobby really had to worry about. The bad news for Robson was that Freddy Shepherd was growing restless.

17

FIFTY YEARS OF HURT
(2004–2005)

'Rest in peace – another Newcastle United season of mediocrity, shame, controversy and, of course, abject failure.'

The *Daily Mail*'s Colin Young assesses another glorious Geordie year

Bobby Robson had been in the game long enough to know that all was not right. From the night we lost to Partizan Belgrade to the failure to finish in the top four of the Premiership (via the rape inquiry, the rows about Solano, Cort and Lua Lua, the frosty relationship with Shearer, the injuries, the failure to reach the UEFA Cup final, the comment about the fans at the end of the season and two early domestic cup exits), everything that went on must have jeopardised Robson's position in the boardroom. As he himself would later observe, 'The sands were shifting beneath my feet.'

Many fans thought the time was now right to thank Sir Bobby and look for some younger blood. But five days after the end of the season, Freddy Shepherd backed the manager. However, subsequent transfer movement suggested that Robson had been stripped of some of his authority. In the close season, four new players were brought in. Versions differ as to which man actually signed them, but we got James Milner from Leeds, Nicky Butt from Man United, Patrick Kluivert from Barcelona and Stephen Carr from Spurs for a combined total of around £8 million. Hugo Viana went back out on loan to Sporting Lisbon, and we sold Gary Speed to Bolton.

Then, on the eve of the new season, came an Exocet from the chairman. Shepherd was quoted in a newspaper interview saying that 2004–05 would be Bobby's last year as Newcastle boss. This was an extraordinary declaration which served only to undermine the manager and therefore the club. To me, and those I talked to, it smacked of an unsure chairman desperately trying to show people he was boss but merely illustrating that he'd been weak not to sack a manager he no longer trusted in the close season. Hardly the right way to build for a successful new campaign.

But, bizarrely, in one of the classic episodes of the surreal footballing soap opera that is Newcastle United, Shepherd then asked Robson if he'd like him to buy the best player in Britain, probably Europe and possibly the world, Everton's Wayne Rooney. Of course, there was a catch. Real Madrid had offered Shepherd £15 million for Jonathan Woodgate, and the chairman was keen to do business, especially with Woodgate's terrible injury record.

Now, logic would tell you that once you'd agreed to sell, you'd rush out and buy another world-class centre-back, especially as the defence had been seen as our main weakness for the past 12 years. (It's actually been our main weakness for the past 30 years, but no one was paying much attention for the first 18.) But Freddy had a weakness for buying big. Extra big. (Remember, we broke the world transfer record when we signed Alan Shearer in 1996 when we really, really needed to strengthen our defence.)

The Rooney bid was doomed to failure, and once Man United came in, the Everton boy wonder did what Shearer didn't – he went to the club best placed to win him a stack of medals. This meant that as the transfer window was about to close, we'd lost a world-class centre-half and spent several days in a fruitless chase for another striker. We'd also made another awful start to the season.

After three games without a win, Robson did a very brave thing. He dropped Alan Shearer for an away game at Aston Villa. Well, it was either incredibly brave or very foolish. Remember Ruud Gullit?

This sent the media into a frenzy. They loved the idea that Shearer was 'bigger than anyone at the club' and decided the fate of all and sundry. To them, Gullit was sacked because he dropped Shearer, and now Bobby had to win or else he'd suffer the same fate. Robson knew all this, of course, but, undeterred, he gave Patrick Kluivert his first start, and the Dutchman duly scored. However, we lost 4–2, a result and performance which once more illustrated our glaring need for a commanding central defender. The result stirred Freddy Shepherd into more drastic action. He decided that, after five years and four games in charge, it was time for Bobby Robson to go.

I must admit the journalist inside me tingled with the excitement of the big emerging story, but the fan inside me was angry and upset. For the third time in succession, we'd sacked our manager in August, weeks after allowing him to spend a fortune and before the new players had had a chance to get to know each other's names.

Why wasn't Robson sacked at the end of the previous season? He could even have been offered the chance to move 'upstairs' with immediate effect, helping with the appointment of his successor. If that was the wrong time, he should have been allowed to stay on a damn sight longer than four matches. For God's sake, a week earlier he was being offered £20 million to spend on Wayne Rooney and was just trying to assimilate four new big-name players into the squad.

There was an outpouring of grief in some parts of Geordieland. 'Uncle Bobby' was gone; Old Father Tyne had been booted out in unceremonious fashion. It's true that, on an emotional level at least, everyone did seem to love him. But the harsh facts were that we'd won just one of our last eleven games and hadn't won away since the previous October. Despite his protestations that everything was under control, some of the squad clearly weren't. And the fabulous, energetic performances of two and three years ago were now a rarity.

Freddy Shepherd fed the papers a line they all gobbled up greedily: 'Sacking Sir Bobby Robson was the hardest thing I have ever done in my life. I didn't want to be known as the man who shot Bambi.' The fact is, Freddy should have done the deed at the end of the previous season. Now we were all paying the price.

The quest for a replacement descended into farce. Steve Bruce, Birmingham's Geordie manager, was clearly being courted, but with little success. The stories went around that we were being knocked back by all and sundry – Bolton's Sam Allardyce, Boro's Steve McLaren and Villa's David O'Leary amongst others. Terry Venables and Gérard Houllier were also mentioned as contenders. As beauty contests go, it was pretty uninspiring. Most fans wanted Celtic's Martin O'Neill or the German legend Ottmar Hitzfeld. We got neither.

Out of the blue, it was announced that the man to take us into the brave new era was Graeme Souness, the manager of Blackburn Rovers, a team who'd won just six games out of twenty-four in 2004 and were currently lying second bottom in the Premiership – they were even below us.

'Sou Must Be Joking' was the headline in the *Mirror*, which just about summed up how we all felt. Had Freddy lost the plot? Just about everyone had agreed with the appointments of Dalglish, Gullit and Robson, but this time I don't think I spoke to one fan who was pleased at the news. But what we thought didn't really matter – it was a done deal. The upside of bringing Souness in was that he wouldn't take any crap from the 'brat pack'. It was suggested that he'd been apppointed to bring discipline back to the dressing-room, but even then there were mutterings that his confrontational style tended to be destructive rather than constructive. Those of us old enough to remember were suddenly getting Bill McGarry flashbacks.

Souness enjoyed a pretty good honeymoon period, firing us right out of the danger zone and up to sixth place. But, unfortunately, the losing habit kicked in again, and soon we were heading back down the table as fast as we'd gone up. In the January transfer window, he splashed out £8 million on Jean-Alain Boumsong, a central defender from Rangers, and also bought Celestine Babayaro from Chelsea and Amdy Faye from Portsmouth. But everything began to unravel for the new manager when he went to war with one of the players he'd inherited.

Craig Bellamy was the ace in our pack. He had speed to burn, and he terrified defenders. Whenever he played, especially away from home, we knew we had a chance. Shearer and Bellamy were complete opposites, both on and off the pitch, but their styles complemented each other perfectly, and together they formed a great strike partnership. Whereas Shearer was the model professional and the master of self-control, Bellamy was, unfortunately, more akin to a naked flame in a firework factory.

After a full-scale training-pitch row with Souness, he was dropped and 'rollocked' by the chairman. When the manager gave his side of the story to the cameras, Bellamy went ballistic, prompting one of the daftest sound bites of the season. He said, 'Not only has he gone behind my back right in front of my face, but he's lying.' This was the final straw for Souness, who vowed Bellamy would never play for Newcastle again. Once more, the club was being dragged through the media sideways, backwards and upside down.

I remember being at the next away game at Man City when a small group of Newcastle fans started chanting for Bellamy. They were quickly shouted down by the majority, who, despite their dislike of Souness, hated the way the striker had behaved.

If Bellamy had a glimmer of a future at the club, it disappeared when Alan Shearer came down on the manager's side. The Welshman was eventually loaned out to Celtic for the rest of the season, and while that may have solved one problem, it created another huge one.

We didn't look the same when he was injured, but now he was gone completely. On top of that, Alan Shearer was due to retire at the end of the season, while the club was certain to be exercising their get-out clause on Patrick Kluivert, who'd looked about as keen as a man who'd just won a disinterested contest. Shola Ameobi was the only striker who looked certain to be at the club the following season – no offence to Shola, but that wasn't an ideal situation.

However, what happened next made the Bellamy situation look like the under-card to the fight of the year, which is not surprising really because what happened next *was,* in fact, the fight of the year. Now, I've seen some strange things on football fields in my time, but nothing beats the incident that put us centre stage once again on 2 April 2005. Kieron Dyer and Lee Bowyer were sent off – for fighting each other.

As scraps go, this was on another level. We were getting tubbed by Aston Villa 3–0 at home, and we were already down to ten men. In the dying minutes, Dyer and Bowyer had an argument, mid-pitch, about one not passing to the other, and suddenly they were doing convincing impressions of Sugar Ray Leonard and Marvin Hagler. It took several players from each side about thirty seconds to separate them – and the ref about three seconds to show both the red card. Frustrated they might have been, but professional they most certainly were not. Once again, the Newcastle United soap opera was all over the papers, radio and telly. Indeed, there was even talk of an omnibus edition every Sunday afternoon.

The timing was, in typical Newcastle fashion, absolutely diabolical. Only the day before, Alan Shearer had publicly announced that he was going to delay his retirement and sign a one-year extension to his contract. What was supposed to be a feel-good weekend had turned into yet another feel-crap one. (Although, to be fair to Dyer and Bowyer, it takes 11 players to be 3–0 down at home to Aston Villa.) Straight after the game, apparently under orders from Shearer, the pair went before the cameras and apologised. In training on Monday, a united front was presented in the form of an unconvincing handshake from our supposedly repentant pugilists.

Souness was under fire. If he had come in to sort out the so-called 'uncontrollable' factions in the dressing-room, he was going about it in a very strange way. We were hovering just below halfway in the table and sputtering from match to match. Fingers were not being pulled out. But we were still in two competitions, and Souness must have known that if he could win a trophy, he'd be a Geordie hero for ever more.

It wasn't going to be the League Cup – after beating Norwich, we'd been drawn against Chelsea, the wealthiest football club in the history of the universe. With their squad of 287 world-class internationals, they were far too good for us, though we did take them to extra time before losing 2–0.

However, things had been going relatively smoothly in the UEFA Cup. A win against the wonderfully named Hapoel Bnei Sakhnin of Israel took us into the group stages. (Yes, they even had them in the UEFA Cup now. Nothing's sacred for UEFA.) Three wins and a draw took us into the knockout phase where, shortly after the Bellamy incident, and in the middle of another poor run, we met Heerenveen of Holland. When we went 1–0 down, the travelling fans started to get a bit twitchy. The first chorus of 'sack the board' had just begun to get an airing when Alan Shearer pounced to put us level. Lee Bowyer then scored a late winner, and the revolt was defused. We completed a 4–2 aggregate victory at SJP a week later, which put us into the fourth round. We then somehow thrashed the Greek side Olympiacos 7–1 on aggregate to go through to the quarter–finals.

At the same time, we'd gone on a pretty good FA Cup run too. With the ghost of Hereford lingering in the wings, we managed to beat non-league Yeading 2–0. Then, after disposing of Coventry, we were drawn at home to 'the wealthiest football club in the history of the universe' in round five. We couldn't believe our luck – we'd been pulled out of the hat with Chelsea for the second time that season.

However, the game proved to be our domestic high water mark. Patrick Kluivert headed us into an early lead, and we fought tooth and nail to hold on for a deserved win. It must have been – even José Mourinho said so! Chelsea lost just two games domestically that season and one of them put us into the FA Cup quarter-finals.

We repeated the performance and result against Spurs, and suddenly we were in the semi-finals. This meant a new experience for us all – a trip to the Millennium Stadium in Cardiff. Things were looking up.

Over the course of four days in the middle of April, we were to play the two games that would define our season and, hopefully, take us a long way to ending our trophy drought at last. On 14 April, we would play the second leg of our UEFA Cup quarter-final, some 36 years after we'd won the forerunner of that very trophy. Three days later, we would take on Man United in the semi-final of the FA Cup, fifty years after we'd won our last domestic trophy, that very same Football Association Challenge Cup.

Five days after the Bowyer–Dyer shindig, we battled to a 1–0 win over Sporting Lisbon in the first leg of the quarter-final. A week later, and with the dust finally settling after the 'Nark at the Park', we set off for the second leg in optimistic mood. So what happens? En route to the biggest game of the season, one of our players decides to tell the press that the side is worse than last year, playing awful football and that the manager doesn't communicate. Step forward and take a bow Laurent Robert, the man who occasionally revealed that he had a sublime left foot – I say occasionally because most of the time it seemed to be stuck firmly in his gob.

The guy just couldn't shut up. His personal website (which Newcastle forced him to shut down) was cult reading, if only for the flights of egotistical fancy that he so often took. Certainly every journalist who covered Newcastle read it because it would guarantee a 'trouble' story every week. Which was a great shame, because when his left foot *wasn't* in his gob, Robert could deliver a killer ball or a dynamite free-kick. The fact that his comments carried more than a grain of truth was irrelevant. Needless to say, Souness was incandescent with anger when the story appeared on the day of the game in Lisbon and immediately dropped the Frenchman.

Despite this, we started the match superbly. Souness actually selected both Dyer *and* Bowyer, although he stopped short of putting stools in opposite corners. Dyer played up front as a 'surrogate Bellamy', his pace destroying the Lisbon back-four, and he actually opened the scoring on the night to give us a 2–0 aggregate lead and a precious away goal. This meant that Lisbon needed three to win, and the way that Dyer was playing, there was always the chance we'd get another.

Sadly, we didn't. Lisbon nicked one back before half-time and then blew us away late in the second half after Bramble and Dyer both limped off with injuries. Lisbon's three goals in the final twenty minutes put us out of the UEFA Cup, the one trophy I genuinely felt we could win that season. Because our manager seemed to feel that Craig Bellamy was unmanageable, we'd relied too heavily on Dyer. And there was one thing you could guarantee about Kieron – if he went to a hamstring bar, he'd pull. Not only were we out of the UEFA Cup, we were heading towards an FA Cup semi-final in total disarray.

Much had been made of the fact that 2005 was the 50th anniversary of Chelsea's last league championship, and they duly marked that anniversary by repeating the title win of 1955. At Newcastle, we're great believers in symmetry. If the league champions of 1955 should do it all again 50 years later, then why shouldn't the FA Cup winners of that year follow suit? Well, for starters, Chelsea had received financial investment equivalent to the gross national product of a small country. Newcastle, on the other hand, were pinning their hopes on a bunch of half-fit, emotionally drained players whose confidence had been shot to bits. And we were playing against infinitely superior opposition. Piece of piss, then.

For us, the trip to Cardiff was a rare opportunity to have a bit of a lads' weekend. Like me, Sime was now also a proud father, and his visits to Tyneside were becoming infrequent, to say the least. Mick and Chris, on the other hand, never missed a home game but had become relative strangers to away travel. So, the day before the game, we descended on Bridgend (there was no room at the inn in Cardiff), and didn't we all go and get completely nostalgic.

The next day, Souness surveyed the wreckage of the past few weeks and realised that finding 11 fit and eligible players was going to prove to be a bit of a challenge. Dyer and Bowyer were suspended following their extra-curricular sparring, Jenas, Hughes and Bramble were injured, several more were 'doubtful', Robert was in the naughty boys corner and Bellamy was exiled in Glasgow.

But the manager rallied the troops. 'We have now got to make sure that we give the fans something to be proud of against Manchester United, because we don't want that taste of defeat again in Cardiff,' he said. 'We have got to roll up our sleeves and show what we are made of.'

Turns out they were made of straw. We were blown away by a far superior team who didn't need to demonstrate more than a modicum of determination, spirit and grit to have the game finished by half-time. Van Nistelrooy hadn't scored since November, but he got two against us. The first one after 19 minutes followed by Paul Scholes's header on half-time meant that it was going to be a matter of 'how many' in the second half.

At half-time, 'sick-note' Babayaro was replaced by Andy O'Brien, whose confidence had been shattered in recent weeks but who always had the decency not to hide. Amdy Faye also went off, replaced by the French teenager Charles N'Zogbia. Suddenly, we started to take the game to United, and the bar-code hordes began to roar. Foolishly, Mick and I started to say really stupid things like, 'If we could just get one back . . .' But on 58 minutes, Nicky Butt forgot that he didn't wear a red shirt any more and started a fantastic Man United counter-attack which led to van Nistelrooy's second and their third. Within a minute,

Shola Ameobi pulled one back, and we started to roar again. Patrick Kluivert then came on for James Milner but looked more interested in comparing dreads with Rio Ferdinand, and soon Ronaldo popped in a fourth to drag us back into the land of football realism. Our season was officially over.

Once again, the Toon Army displayed their seasonal largesse – shouting down the winners with endless chants of 'We'll support you ever more', and many others besides. It was 1974 all over again (and 1976, 1996, 1998, 1999 and any other year which featured a humbling defeat that you'd care to mention).

The bedraggled black and whites stumbled towards the Toon support and lifted their weary arms in embarrassed applause. (All except for one – Nicky Butt was exchanging warm embraces and cheesy smiles with his old pals before sprinting off down the tunnel at a greater speed than he'd mustered all afternoon.)

The Guardian's match report said, 'As always, you had to wonder if the club might not achieve more if those people were less patient and forgiving of a series of underachieving sides.'

Even Fergie, not famed for his generosity of spirit, said afterwards, 'I can understand the passion of Newcastle supporters. It is an unusual club, and that loyalty comes from a deep-rooted passion. Every one of their fans had a black-and-white shirt on, and they will go into work tomorrow sick.'

We wouldn't have to wait until tomorrow, Alex. Most of us felt sick from the moment van Nistelrooy stuck the first one in. As I looked around the Millennium Stadium, I recognised in some of the younger faces that same spirit of defiance that we'd shown in 1974. That spirit which said, 'OK, our team might have been crap but look at us – we're magnificent. Listen to us sing. This is what being fans is all about!' But after a couple of half-hearted choruses, I just couldn't do it. I felt battered into submission. I'd had 40 years of this. Others had had 50 – 50 years of hurt. How many more times would we have to do this? Would the day ever come when it was our turn?

18

HOPE AND EXPECTATION

'Hope is the power of being cheerful in circumstances which we know to be desperate.'

G.K. Chesterton

Sometimes it's been glorious, at other times unlucky. From time to time, it's been dreadful, exhilarating, scary, desperate, outrageous, revolutionary, pitiful, hilarious, sublime and ridiculous. I'm sure it must even have been dull once or twice, though I think I was missing on those days. One thing supporting Newcastle clearly *hasn't* been is successful.

Throughout our 50 years in the trophy wilderness, there have been simple explanations for many of our seasons of failure. At other times, it's left us all completely baffled.

After Jackie Milburn and his pals won three FA Cup finals in quick succession, the club went downhill fast, but there was division and disharmony in the boardroom. Newcastle United was allowed to stagnate, paralysed by mediocrity and shorn of ambition. When Joe Harvey hauled the club back to its rightful place among the elite, there was still apathy, incompetence and a lack of ambition at the top of the club, but despite this, Harvey managed to win the Fairs Cup. So why did his team fail so miserably in the 1974 FA Cup final? OK, we were playing the best side around – as we were in each of our other two losing FA Cup finals – but the '74 team were a bloody good side. That's the one that gets me – 1974 – not so much for the defeat but for the manner of the defeat. We were abject.

I think we were unlucky in the 1976 League Cup final, but there was still a lot wrong at the top. When Kevin Keegan and Arthur Cox dragged us back into the top flight, there was nowhere to go because those problems still remained. Only when John Hall unleashed the genie in the bottle by changing the club's financial structure and by bringing in Kevin Keegan as manager could we dare to dream. The 'dream ticket' fired Newcastle like a rocket to the stars, taking us to a level that was unimaginable just a few years earlier. If we'd broken the spell in '96, when we really should have, who knows where we'd be now? But the fact remains that United crashed and burned. Did we overreach or was Keegan's naturally cavalier spirit the cause of his own undoing? It broke our hearts and, I suspect, his as well.

But why haven't we been able to get as close again? Freddy Shepherd, Hall's successor, brought some of the biggest names in football into the manager's chair, but he seemed prone to the knee-jerk reaction, making a series of appointments each apparently designed to counter the one that went before. After the cavalier Keegan, we enlisted the cautious Dalglish. When that didn't work, we went looking for 'sexy football' from Gullit. When the exotic foreigner failed to understand the essence of Newcastle, in came the father of all Geordies. But when Sir Bobby Robson apparently couldn't control his youthful charges, we went for Souness, the 'hard man'. Ultimately, they all failed, yet the funny thing is, most of us agreed with most of those appointments.

Of course, we all think we could do it better. But has anyone really got the answers?

During the course of researching this book, I asked everyone I spoke to for their thoughts on why one of the game's greatest clubs had failed to win that elusive trophy over such a long period of time. Some were so baffled they couldn't even begin to answer. Others had a go. Here are some of their thoughts:

> I sometimes wonder whether the club makes it too comfortable for the players. If the supporters wanted to put real pressure on, then they should stop going. Then they'd *have* to do something about it. Unfortunately, the supporters are happy to finish above Sunderland.
>
> Malcolm Macdonald

> Everything is in place there for success, but they really need a bit of luck – they're certainly due some. The fans have supported with passion for years – they are unbelievable. They deserve to get something, and the person who gets something for them will be lauded at Newcastle. Up till now it's not happened for them, but I think it's getting nearer and nearer. There's no divine right for anyone to win anything, but most things are in place for Newcastle to achieve it. Is the glass half full or is it half empty? It's all set up, but they need something to go for them.
>
> Kenny Dalglish

> Sometimes you make your own problems. When there's unrest at the club behind the scenes, it goes onto the field. Every time that's happened, there's been a reverse. But it's still a great club.
>
> Willie McFaul

> I can't understand it. They flatter to deceive. I never know what to make of them. It's unfortunate because they have a helluva good crowd, but I suppose they can only take it for so long.
>
> Alf McMichael

275

It's a combination of reasons, but continuity is the thing. The club has to realise it's got to have stability if it wants to get success. They've got to have a steady manager who realises what kind of job it is. It's all about history. As fans, we expect honesty, and the expectation is so high.

Alan Kennedy

You need unity, team spirit. That's the one extra thing you must have, no matter how good your players are. Over the last few years, Newcastle have had a few who like a bit of a good time. When you were on £12 a week, like we were, you didn't know if they'd keep you on, so you did what you were told! But I don't suppose you can tell millionaires what to do. If they don't want to do it, then they won't do it.

Vic Keeble

It's a unique football club. For the manager, one year at Newcastle is three years anywhere else. He needs someone there who will tell him how to be the manager of Newcastle United.

Newcastle players don't always realise their responsibilities. They have got to learn to live with the pressure. The ground is a concrete monstrosity when it's empty, but when the supporters are in there, it is fantastic – pure theatre. If the supporters feel you're not doing what they think you should be doing, they will let you know. But if you do what you're supposed to do, and you do it well, you'll leave the pitch feeling ten feet tall. Nobody deserves it more than those supporters at Newcastle, because they are always there and always will be. The man who brings them success on a regular basis *will be a legend*.

Arthur Cox

HOPE AND EXPECTATION

Fifty years is a long time, but it's about putting a good side out and performing on the day. They've been close once or twice, but you have to beat a better side somewhere along the line. Think about it logically – the longer it goes on, then they've got to win something sometime. I'd be using it as a positive. Fifty years? It's got to be our turn soon. Records are there to be taken away.

Bob Moncur

You make your own luck, and if you're good enough, you will win. Nine times out of ten, the best team wins – certainly in the league. But on the law of averages, you'd think we'd have won something in the past 50 years – even Sunderland and Middlesbrough have won something!

Peter Beardsley

I don't believe in curses; it just hasn't happened. They have been unlucky at times, but the fact is they haven't got it right. The board has to take responsibility because they set the parameters. They've got to cup finals but haven't been good enough on the day, and they've never really been near the title apart from in 1996 when they were unlucky. But the longer it goes on, the harder it gets. I'm desperate for it to happen – I'd love them to win something.

Frank Clark

I get sick of people within Newcastle United hiding behind the fact that it's a unique and unmanageable club. No it's not. The only unique thing about the club is that it's never won a domestic trophy for 50 years but still gets 50,000 Geordies in for every home game. That's what makes it unique – that we tolerate this and come back when nothing's been won. Yes, we are daft, but it's a lovely trait, and I think it's about time it was rewarded.

John Gibson

Someone will get it right eventually. Whoever wins one trophy will be the god of Newcastle. For ever. And I'd be delighted for them – it's the one thing I wish for the club and the supporters. They're fantastic fans, and Newcastle is a fantastic place. *One day it will happen!*

Sir Les Ferdinand

We hope you're right, Les. We hope you're right.

The big problem for Freddy Shepherd and the board is now one of expectation. Where once we used to shake our heads ruefully and mutter 'typical Newcastle', we now demand results. We know that the club is run like a proper business at last (sometimes so ruthlessly, it hurts), and we appreciate it. We also know that 50,000 seats are sold for every home game, and that equates to a lot of money. Our money. And every time we're told that the board has backed a manager with cash, we know it's *our* cash. We're not stupid.

Newcastle United is a weird and wonderful football club. Part of its charm is its complete unpredictability. All we ask for is a 'completely unpredictable' cup win. Just once. We have the support, the infrastructure, the ambition and, some would argue, the players, to be in the very top bracket of English football. People say that the first trophy is the hardest one. Crack that and we'll start winning all the time. But let's not get greedy, eh? Let's just take one cup at a time. History has shown that, with the right amount of luck and determination, just about any half-decent club can do it. So why not us?

Arthur Cox and Sir Les Ferdinand say above that one day it *will* happen. We all share their enthusiasm, but, after all this time, not all of us share their optimism. And if that day does arrive, what will we do next? You can't help but wonder if a little bit of the magic might actually disappear. Let's hope not. One of the reasons we love Newcastle United is because they're barmy. We just want them to win something once in a while.

In the meantime, we will keep going and keep supporting, because, like our club, we too are a little bit special. We will also keep demanding, because after 50 years of hurt, we believe we've earned that right.

TO BE CONTINUED ...

Appendix I

FIFTY YEARS OF GLORIOUS FAILURE

1955

Newcastle United and their legendary centre-forward Jackie Milburn lift the FA Cup at Wembley for the third time in five years. It's the beginning of the longest drought in football.

1961

United are knocked out at the first stage of the inaugural League Cup, beaten 4–1 by Colchester. They are also relegated to Division Two.

1964

United are humiliated in the FA Cup, beaten 2–1 at home by non-league Bedford Town in the third round.

1965

Promotion back to Division One.

1969

United win the European Inter-Cities Fairs Cup, beating Újpesti Dózsa of Hungary 6–2 over two legs.

1972

FA Cup humiliation again – this time on national television – losing 2–1 to non-league Hereford in the third round.

1974

United finally get to the FA Cup final once again – but they're completely outclassed and beaten 3–0 by Liverpool. Kevin Keegan scores twice.

1976

A League Cup final at last, but Newcastle lose 2–1 to Manchester City. The winner is scored by ex-Sunderland hero Dennis Tueart. (This is famously City's last major trophy win – and they think *they've* got problems!)

1977

New manager Gordon Lee seems to be on the verge of success, taking United into the top three. But he quits mid-season to take over at Everton.

1978

Relegated to Division Two.

1980

Beaten 2–0 at home in the FA Cup by Fourth Division Chester. Knocked out of the League Cup by deadly rivals Sunderland – on penalties.

FIFTY YEARS OF GLORIOUS FAILURE

1981

Thrashed 4–0 in the FA Cup by Fourth Division Exeter City.

1984

Inspired by Kevin Keegan in his final playing season, United win promotion back to Division One.

1989

Relegated to Division Two once again.

1990

Finish third but are beaten in the promotion play-offs by deadly rivals Sunderland.

1992

New manager Kevin Keegan saves Newcastle from dropping into Division Three – on the last day of the season.

1993

Keegan leads United to promotion to the Premier League.

1996

United are 12 points clear at the top of the Premiership, only to be caught by Man United in the run-in.

1998

United, managed by Kenny Dalglish, lose 2–0 to Arsenal in the FA Cup final.

1999

United, managed by Ruud Gullit, lose 2–0 to Man United in the FA Cup final.

2000

United, managed by Sir Bobby Robson, lose 2–0 to Chelsea in the semi-final of the FA Cup.

2005

United, managed by Graeme Souness, lose 4–1 to Man United in the semi-final of the FA Cup.

Appendix 2

SEASON-BY-SEASON RECORD SINCE 1955

Season	League	League position	FA Cup	League Cup
1954–55	Div 1	6th	winners	N/A
1955–56	Div 1	11th	sixth round	N/A
1956–57	Div 1	17th	fourth round	N/A
1957–58	Div 1	19th	fourth round	N/A
1958–59	Div 1	11th	third round	N/A
1959–60	Div 1	8th	third round	N/A
1960–61	Div 1	21st [relegated]	sixth round	first round
1961–62	Div 2	11th	third round	second round
1962–63	Div 2	7th	fourth round	second round
1963–64	Div 2	8th	third round	third round
1964–65	Div 2	1st [promoted]	third round	second round
1965–66	Div 1	15th	fourth round	second round
1966–67	Div 1	20th	fourth round	second round
1967–68	Div 1	10th	third round	second round
1968–69	Div 1	9th	fourth round	third round
1969–70	Div 1	7th	third round	second round
1970–71	Div 1	12th	third round	second round

NEWCASTLE UNITED – FIFTY YEARS OF HURT

1971–72	Div 1	11th	third round	third round
1972–73	Div 1	8th	fourth round	third round
1973–74	Div 1	15th	final	third round
1974–75	Div 1	15th	fourth round	fifth round
1975–76	Div 1	15th	sixth round	final
1976–77	Div 1	5th	fourth round	fourth round
1977–78	Div 1	21st [relegated]	fourth round	second round
1978–79	Div 2	8th	fourth round	second round
1979–80	Div 2	9th	third round	second round
1980–81	Div 2	11th	fifth round	second round
1981–82	Div 2	9th	fourth round	second round
1982–83	Div 2	5th	third round	second round
1983–84	Div 2	3rd [promoted]	third round	second round
1984–85	Div 1	14th	third round	third round
1985–86	Div 1	11th	third round	third round
1986–87	Div 1	17th	fifth round	second round
1987–88	Div 1	8th	fifth round	third round
1988–89	Div 1	20th [relegated]	third round	second round
1989–90	Div 2	3rd	fifth round	third round
1990–91	Div 2	11th	fourth round	second round
1991–92	Div 2	20th	third round	third round
1992–93*	Div 1	1st [promoted]	fifth round	third round
1993–94	PREM	3rd	fourth round	third round
1994–95	PREM	6th	sixth round	fourth round
1995–96	PREM	2nd	third round	fifth round
1996–97	PREM	2nd	fourth round	fourth round
1997–98	PREM	13th	final	fifth round
1998–99	PREM	13th	final	fourth round
1999–2000	PREM	11th	semi-final	third round
2000–01	PREM	11th	third round	fourth round
2001–02	PREM	4th	sixth round	fifth round
2002–03	PREM	3rd	third round	third round
2003–04	PREM	5th	fourth round	third round
2004–05	PREM	14th	semi-final	fourth round

* Introduction of Premier League – Division Two becomes Division One.

BIBLIOGRAPHY

Gibson, John *The Newcastle United F.C. Story* (Pelham Books, London, 1969)

Harris, Harry *Newcastle Out of Toon: The Inside Story of Newcastle at War* (Robson Books, London, 1999)

Hutchinson, Roger *The Toon: A Complete History of Newcastle United Football Club* (Mainstream, Edinburgh, 2004)

Joannou, Paul *Newcastle United – A Complete Record, 1882–1986* (Breedon, Derby, 1986)

Joannou, Paul *United: The First 100 Years – Official Centenary History of Newcastle United* (Polar Print Group Ltd, Leicester, 1991)

Keegan, Kevin *Kevin Keegan: My Autobiography* (Time Warner Paperbacks, London, 1998)

Malam, Colin *The Magnificent Obsession: Keegan, Newcastle and Sixty Million Pounds* (Bloomsbury, London, 1997)

Milburn, Jack *Jackie Milburn: A Man of Two Halves* (Mainstream, Edinburgh, 2003)

Powter, David *30 Seasons at St James' Park: 1974-75 to 2003-04* (Soccer Books Ltd, London, 2004)

Robson, Bobby *Farewell But Not Goodbye: My Autobiography* (Hodder & Stoughton, London, 2005)

. . . and the incomparable www.nufc.com